The World Don't Owe Me Nothing

The Life and Times of
Delta Bluesman
Honeyboy Edwards

David Honeyboy Edwards
*as told to Janis Martinson and
Michael Robert Frank*

CHICAGO
REVIEW
PRESS

Library of Congress Cataloging-in-Publication Data

Edwards, Honeyboy.
    The world don't owe me nothing: the life and times of Delta
bluesman Honeyboy Edwards / David Honeyboy Edwards; as told to
Janis Martinson and Michael Robert Frank.
        p.   cm.
    Includes bibliographical references and index.
    ISBN 1-55652-275-4 (cloth)
    1. Edwards, Honeyboy.   2. Blues musicians—United States-
-Biography.   I. Martinson, Janis, 1956–   . II. Frank, Michael
Robert, 1949–   .   III. Title.
ML420.E28A3   1997
781.643'092—dc21
[B]   97-2599
                                                                              CIP
                                                                              MN

©1997 by David Edwards, Janis Martinson, and Michael Robert Frank
All rights reserved
First Edition
Published by Chicago Review Press, Incorporated
814 North Franklin Street
Chicago, Illinois 60610
ISBN 1-55652-275-4
Printed in the United States of America
5 4 3 2 1

To Bessie

Contents

Foreword

All too often, books about and supposedly by folk blues musicians come across as products that are essentially undergraduate social science field trip term papers about people who seem to be regarded as being somewhat pathetic and somewhat provincially exotic and titillating at the same time.

More often than not, such books strike me as having been thought up and executed by some ivy-league type throwback to the likes of the ever so ideological or, in any case, bookish Tom Sawyer rather than some updated extension of a Huck Finn, whose insights and representations of the idiomatic textures of his friend Jim's world are as unspoiled and reliable as those of old Mark Twain himself.

Obviously, if somebody who is not native to the down-home conventions that the blues idiom stylizes into aesthetic statement is going to collaborate with someone who has remained as close to his regional roots as Honeyboy Edwards has, that person must achieve a rapport that is as close to family membership or, in any case, neighborhood membership as possible, so that personal complexities can be seen in proper individual perspective.

My impression of Janis Martinson is such that I feel that Honeyboy Edwards is, if anything, even luckier to have her along with him on this voyage of a book than Jim was to have old Huck on that raft on the river and that encounter with the Royal Nonesuch. After all, besides being more state-of-the-art than old Huck, she's also even more profoundly converted to Honeyboy's conception of his music then Huck was to Jim's conception of himself as a free human being.

In all events, what seems to have counted first and most to her in this undertaking are the nuances of the idiom that have made Honeyboy Edwards the musician he has become.

Albert Murray

Acknowledgments

We'd like to thank the many people who have befriended Honeyboy Edwards, those who have looked out for his welfare over the years and across the continents. You are too many to list, but you are in our hearts.

Our special thanks goes to those who have helped us with Honeyboy's story. Thanks to Phil Givant and Mike Rowe for sharing their taped interviews with Honeyboy. John Brisbin also shared his taped interviews with Honeyboy along with his knowledge of the blues and it was much appreciated. Thanks to George Hansen for his expertise and advice on blues recordings. Jim Feeney's knowledge in this area was also very helpful and much appreciated. Thanks to Steve Stuart for offering his assistance on indexing, to Greenwood County Courthouse mapping department employees Joann Britt and Ginger Gregg, and to the staff members at Chicago's Harold Washington Library and The Newberry Library, who were consistently helpful and knowledgeable. Thanks to Rick Sherry to whom we are greatly indebted for his invaluable assistance and support with the manuscript and for giving so freely of his knowledge, time, and broad shoulders. Thanks to Ian Herbert and Libby

Langworthy for legal counsel. Thanks to photographer Cedric Chatterley, who brought to this work his thoughtful attention, creativity, and endurance for lengthy road trips. Deep gratitude to editor Cynthia Sherry, who provided the advice and insight that gave structure and meaning to this story and kept us sane.

Thanks to Agnes Dodds Kinard for her encouragement, for her support, and for being a historical role model. Thanks to Barbara Spring Frank for her support and encouragement over the years. Deepest gratitude to Ruth Ross (also known as Mom) for her research assistance and belief that her daughter can do anything. Heartfelt thanks to Jeff Herbert, who gave his unflagging support, love, and encouragement throughout the entire project.

Preface

Having heard Honeyboy Edwards's stories over the years, we had a growing feeling that they were just too good to keep to ourselves. Not only has Honeyboy witnessed and participated in the development of the blues but he offers a unique perspective on American history spanning most of this century. He recounted for us with great detail his upbringing as a sharecropper's son. We loved to hear about his years as a hobo during the Depression. We begged for descriptions of the hot towns of Memphis and New Orleans. And so many times we'd wish we had been there—at Muddy Waters's cabin in Rolling Fork, Mississippi; on the streets of Greenwood, Mississippi, watching Robert Johnson play; or with Honeyboy and Little Walter Jacobs as they hopped a train to Chicago. We felt so lucky to know Honeyboy Edwards and to hear his stories, that we decided to work with him to bring his life's story to a wider audience.

Together, over a five-year period, we conducted many interviews at Honeyboy's home. Often, we sat in his spacious Lincoln parked in front of his house drinking beer and talking the afternoons away. One of us would ask a question—"pull the string" as Honeyboy put it—and he'd be off, regaling us with yet another tale. Janis transcribed each interview and pulled Honeyboy Edwards's story together. Eventually a rough book took form and additional rounds of interviews provided more stories and greater detail. Janis continued to transcribe, edit, and arrange the stories until they flowed into one another like the conversations with Honeyboy they came from. She chose the best versions of the best stories and tied them together. These are Honeyboy Edwards's words; Janis's part was to present them in a readable fashion while remaining strictly faithful to his story and his unique speech patterns and rhythms.

The photographer, Cedric Chatterley, retraced Honeyboy's journey using the rough draft of the manuscript as a road map. Between 1990 and 1995, he made several trips to the Delta and then on to Memphis, New Orleans, Houston, and Chicago, just as Honeyboy did throughout his life. Cedric sought out the places that Honeyboy most often spoke of, like the sites of plantations, juke joints, cotton fields, crossroads, and train stations. The photographs presented here juxtapose the Delta of Honeyboy's youth with the South of today. They show how the social, physical, and political landscape of his past has changed and, in many ways, remained the same. Also included are some of Honeyboy Edwards's most cherished personal photographs. Cedric Chatterley's photographs were made possible, in part, by a 1994 Artist's Project Grant from the North Carolina Arts Council, a state agency.

There are three appendices at the back of the book, written and researched by Janis, that offer some interesting background information on the songs, musicians, and sometimes unusual place names and words that Honeyboy mentions. Also included are Michael's recommended recordings of blues musicians. We wanted to avoid interrupting a good story with footnotes, so please check the appendices for further information on a musician or song or an explanation of a term as you read.

We hope that as you read this it will feel a little like sitting down with Honeyboy and hearing him tell his story. Unfortunately you will miss the gleam in his eye, his frequent smile, and the occasional tap on the leg as Honeyboy emphasizes a particular point. He might be a living piece of history, but he is also a vivacious and outgoing man, happy to talk and always laughing. You haven't seen anything until you've seen

Honeyboy Edwards crow like a rooster or imitate a drunk—or a white plantation owner.

We are so grateful to Honeyboy Edwards for the opportunity to work with him. We appreciate his patience, humor, and candor. We treasure the lessons that he has taught us with his open-hearted approach to life. He has been a friend, a father, and an inspiration to all of us.

Janis Martinson and Michael Robert Frank

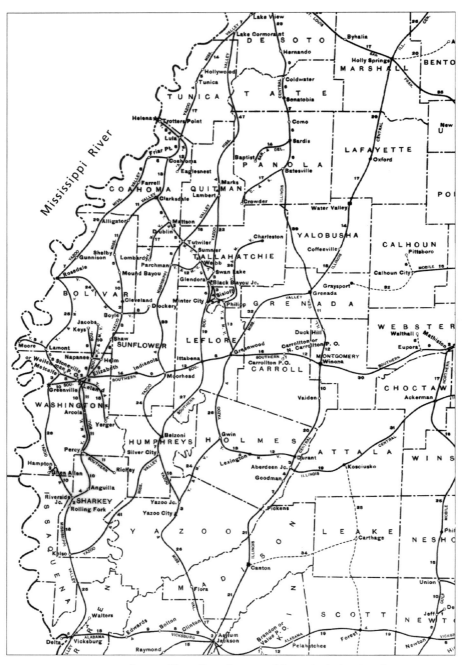

A 1921 Rand McNally railroad map of the Mississippi Delta.
Photo courtesy of The Newberry Library.

Chapter One

All the people flowed to the Mississippi Delta.

The Delta is a wide, flat country, running from the Mississippi River clean up to the hills in the East. When I was young it was full of people, living and working on the plantations. In the Delta we raised so much cotton and corn and pecans and potatoes. People out of the hills used to come in by the truckloads to pick cotton in the Delta, because they couldn't raise no crop in the hilly land. They come to the flat land and stay all the fall—pick cotton by the hundred all the fall. On Saturday nights, they have balls, country dances, and they dance and drink that white whiskey all night long. When all the cotton's picked, they go back to the hills. They made enough money to get them through the winter.

On the farm in the Delta, in the wintertime we don't do nothing—not till about March. In March, around the fifteenth or twentieth or so, we start breaking up the land, burning stalks off the land, turning the ground over. At the time I was, we used both mules and tractors. At the end of April when it done got warm, we'd start planting cotton. Cotton comes out in a sprout, comes up sprouting. There was sometimes a cold draft would catch it in the crook, and if that cold catches it, then it wouldn't come out. We'd have to plant back over again, come right behind and put some more seeds in. And hope it rains.

We plant it, chop it, keep the weeds out of it up until around about the last of August; that's lay-by time. Then you start to vining cotton. You knock the vines so when you get to picking there won't be no vines in the way. When the vines start to growing, you cut them. In the sun they just die. And you can get to the cotton when it opens up. You can start to picking then.

My mother, she told me she was born in Kentucky. Her family moved to Mississippi sometime in the 1800s. My mother was twenty-six years old when I was born and my father was in his forties, so she told me. My father, he was from New Orleans. He worked on the boats down there as a roustabout. He went to school in New Orleans. He had a pretty good education. He could read and write. Back at that time, didn't too many blacks have a good education. I was surprised after I got grown and seen how things used to be, I was surprised that he had that education. And his brother was a schoolteacher, L. D. Edwards. All of them come up from New Orleans. They left the low lands and come up to the Mississippi Delta, looking for work.

My papa, Henry Edwards, drifted up to the Delta. Papa was dark and low, little. He was part Creek Indian. My father was a black Indian and a Mollyglasper. Mollyglasper, that's like a nation of people. Some of them come from New Orleans, from the coast down there, black people. My dad was real black. And his hair was straight just like white folks' down there. That's Mollyglasper. We're all mixed up a little bit.

My daddy come to the Delta and Mama was already there. Her name was Pearl Phillips. She was a young woman then. My father met her in Shaw, Mississippi, where I was born at. My mother had another old man before they got together but she wasn't married to him. She met my daddy, they hooked up together and married and started a family. I was the oldest boy. I was the first one and my sister Hermalie, she was the second one. I was three years older than her.

My father already had two girls from his first wife, Lou. My mother raised them. My mother said when they got together he was a bachelor staying by himself. His wife had died and he had them two girls and he was doing the best he could with them, twisting their hair into braids.

A field outside Shaw, Mississippi, 1993.

They was Blanche, she got killed in Greenwood by her husband. Blanche was born in nineteen ought eight, she was. Blanche had one daughter, Clarine. The other was Lessie, that was the oldest of my dad's children. We called her Kid. Her husband, Sam Gilmore, was from Dubbs. He used to drive a cattle truck. She used to go with him in that truck to Missouri to get cattle, and sleeping on old blankets in the truck she caught pneumonia. She caught her death of cold following that man. She died in 1928.

My father had three sons by his first wife, too, Willie, Bat, and Louis. After I got up kind of big-sized, Willie come around and stayed a while with my daddy in Shaw. After a while he disappeared. Louis and Bat lived around Vicksburg. They was my half brothers.

I was born in 1915 on the twenty-eighth day of June. I was born out in Sunflower County. There was me and Hermalie and Altie and Mack

Henry. I remember in 1920 when the man come around taking up census. That was before Mack was born. The man come around in the wintertime taking up census with a book under his arm, wearing blue pants and a clean white shirt. It had been a flood and my sister was giving me a ride on a float out in the field, pushing me with a hoe. We lived in Bolivar County then, Mama, four girls, and one boy.

My daddy, I didn't know his people. But I knew my mother's mother. Her name was Sarah Phillips. My grandmother was born a slave. My mother told me her mother was sold a couple of times, sold like a horse or a mule. My mother's father was a Indian, Aaron Phillips. He was from Kentucky. Mama had a brother named Aaron and one named Sylvester. Sylvester's last name was Jeeter. They had the same mama but different daddies. Sylvester married a lady called Irene Hills and they had one girl, Katrine. Aaron and his wife had Magnolia, Joseph, Eddie, T.C., Arlo (we called him Man Son), Daniel, Riley—they had fourteen kids. I used to go to sleep over at their house and wouldn't have nowhere to sleep! All us kids would sleep on cotton sacks on the floor. Aaron's wife, Cornelia, was the only somebody who ever called me David.

They always called me Honey, all the time; white and black called me Honey. When I was trying to walk, just toddling like a baby, Mama and them said my older sister Lessie said to me, "Come here, baby. Come here, baby," trying to make me walk. And I tried to take a step and run and she said, "Mama, look at little old Honey!" That's what they told me; that's why they started calling me Honey. When I started to recording I gave the name of Honeyboy, but my people only knew me by Honey.

Mama also had a sister, Beatrice. We called her Aunt Daughter. And Magnolia, Aunt Mag. They was Jeeters. Magnolia had four sons, Quincy, Nathan, Mannie, and Elijah. And one daughter, Sarah. Beatrice's daughter is Willie Mae. Me and Willie Mae was raised up together till I got grown, running all up and down the roads.

The Phillips was all of them real yellow with straight hair. Except Mama, she had black curly hair and she was red. I don't know how we got so black; my mama was red. She could play guitar and harp. She'd put a guitar across her lap with a pocket knife and play "Par-a-lee" on it.

The site of Honeyboy's childhood home, outside of Shaw, Mississippi, 1993.

We was all kind of musical people. Didn't none of her family but her play music, but on my father's side was musicians. He played violin and guitar but he got rid of them after I got up to be a little size; he quit playing.

Papa used to hold country dances on a Saturday night, sell whiskey and play guitar at the house. Sometimes he'd go off to play at jukes. He got in a fight one time at one of them Saturday night dances. My daddy got to fighting and hollering with a guy and they run out of the dance and into the field. My daddy had a plaid shirt on and this guy Jack shot at him with a Winchester rifle. The bullet just missed Papa, but it shot a hole through his shirt! Then he quit playing.

I can remember when I was four years old, just as good. I can remember back before 1919, when my daddy moved over to the Dave Bishop

Plantation and over to a place called Meadow Place. Guy Dean run that. That's out from Shaw. I can remember in 1920, when my sister Altie was born. I was five years old. I can remember that. Me and my sister Blanche was on the stairs, looking. Matty Scott, the midwife, was catching Altie.

All of us was born at home. My grandmother waited on me, my mother's mother. My grandmother was a midwife. That's what they told me. My grandmother was my granny. Back then we called a midwife a granny. A black midwife caught my sisters, but Dr. Field, a old white doctor, he waited on my mama with her other kids.

When I was real small there was bears, panthers. When I was small out there on the Bishop Plantation, Mama and Papa used to go to Shaw and my daddy used to have to wear a headlamp, a old hunting light, when he come through that part of the country called the Deadening. That's where a lot of woods was, before you got to where the farming was at. Come through the Deadening and them panthers be in the trees, you had to watch for them. They'd be up in the trees at night and you shine your light and see their red eyes shining back at you. They'll jump! You had to know what you was doing with them panthers and bears out there then. But I was real small then. After '22, they started to cleaning that up.

I remember when I was a little boy, about six years old, at Christmas my mother used to buy us toys. The toys they made back then wasn't like the toys now. They made them out of wood. I had a truck with wooden wheels, a little bed, little man sitting up in there. And the dolls the girls had had a hole in the top of the head you could put your hand in, to hold that little head up. They told me there was Santa Claus. I lay down in the bed one Christmas night, I never will forget it, and Mama said, "You go to sleep and Santa Claus will come to you if you go to sleep early." I went and jumped in the bed and listened at my sister and my mother putting up the stuff, the toys. And I heard my mama say, "This for Hermalie; this for Altie; this for Honey." I said, "Where mine at?" She said, "You bastard, get up from there!" She thought I was asleep! "You bastard, get up from there!" She was trying to hide Santa and I'm laying there watching! I always been funny like that. When you say that's mine, I want to see it! We used to have funny times back then.

Honeyboy's sisters Hermalie (left) and Altie in 1970.

I was seven years old when my grandmother died. I can remember that night in 1922. My mother walked out of Shaw, about three miles to where my grandmother lived over in Sunflower County. When they called on my mama and told her that her mother was dead she left there crying. I never will forget it. She put on her yellow jacket and walked out of Shaw, went on over to Sunflower, where her mother was. My grandmother died in 1922, and that's the year Mack Henry was born, my brother.

Papa didn't make no money. He was a sharecropper. He rented once when I was eight years old. He had two mules and a cow then. That was in '23 and '24 in Dubbs, Mississippi, between Lula and Clarksdale. In '24 he moved to Coahoma, stayed one crop in Coahoma, then he wasn't doing no good. Sharecroppers move every year to make a little money. How it works, the white man would furnish the sharecropper with money all the winter to take care of himself. And in the fall the sharecropper would have to pay him back that money. A few sharecroppers would raise their own food and hogs, and wouldn't owe the man too much, but if they didn't want to do that they'd have to go to the white man for everything. So that made him owe the white man at the end of the year.

You would work the white man's land, and sharecrop means when you make cotton, if you make twenty bales, ten go to the white man and ten go to the sharecropper. The white man sells the cotton, and out of the sharecropper's ten bales, he had to pay off the money he got all that winter. When I pay the man out of my ten, I ain't got nothing. I might clear two, three hundred dollars, a hundred dollars all the year to feed that big family. Clear nothing, go somewheres else. Papa left Coahoma and went back to Dubbs, stayed one year, 1925, and I went to school.

Sharecroppers, they don't cut no money one year and don't like the boss, they carry the contract out and jump up and try to do better somewhere else. Renters could get ahead of the sharecroppers. Renters had mules, tractors, because they had enough money to take care of theyself—they didn't borrow the white man's money. When they made something it was clear. And then they raise a lot of hogs, chickens, and the only thing the renter would have to buy then sometimes was a little flour and a little rice. I knew just one man who started working sharecropping and come out making some money, got to be a big renter. Lawrence Johnson, that man would eat dry bread. If he cleared two hundred dollars out of his crop he had that next year when he'd make another two or three hundred dollars. He kept on like that and that man bought himself two mules, and then he started to renting, started selling his own cotton. He went to Leland and bought eighty acres and got a tractor, and that's when he was on his own. Had a car, wagon, mule, everything. But that was by starving himself to death, near about. But most, they never did do better, do worse and worse all the time. But they wasn't in the same place doing worser. So Papa shift around.

Papa always got a double house when we moved. In a single house, on them plantations, they'd have one big room for the family and a kitchen. But a lot of people on the plantations would have big families and get those double houses, have a couple of rooms. The boys would sleep in one and the girls in another. And have a big porch to set on and talk all night long. All we had for light was lamplight, oil lamps that set on the mantle, and to keep warm we had them old potbellied stoves. In the summertime we would cut oak wood for the winter. And to keep us warm at night, Mama would make quilts. Mama would go to town and buy scraps and then after the fall of the year, she'd have quilt parties.

Four or five women would come over and they'd sit up all night and quilt and drink and tell lies. Sometimes they'd get through with a quilt in one night. The next night they go to another woman's house and make one there.

When I was nine years old I was working in the field. I was running a plow behind the mule to drag the grass out of the middles. Then when you get out to pick cotton there ain't no grass in the middle of the rows. My daddy, he'd put me behind a mule, and I used to just hold that plow and go right down that row. I get to the end and say, "Whoa, yea," and that mule come right on back, go right down the next one. I been in fields when I was small, I did. So I know all about that farming thing. I helped Mama trying to pick cotton out in the fields with a little old flour sack around my shoulders. Wasn't no real cotton-picking sack, just a little old sack I'd fill up, then I'd go and put my cotton in her sack.

Us kids would have a good time, though. I learned how to swim when I was around ten years old. My cousin Riley throwed me in the water out in a big old deep hole, called a blue hole. The boys would get on a tree limb hung over the water, get up on that limb and jump off and dive. And Riley got me up there and chunked me off. I come up drinking water and fighting. And he just laughed; he just killed himself laughing. I started swimming then. I could swim any way, on my back, any way. I learned how to do all that.

I fished a whole lot, too. I used to like to fish when I was young. We'd dig around the house blocks to get baits, night crawlers. We'd fish with them and fish with crickets, too. Put it on your hook, they be flying around and them fish would grab them. We used to muddy, too. When the river get up real high, it would spill out in the branches and over the land. Then, when the river go back in the bank, the fishes would still be over there flopping around in them shallow holes. We called them gully holes. We go there and muddy them gully holes. When you stomp around in the water, the fish come to the top to catch some air. We get in there and muddy the water, and them big buffalo catfish rise to the top. We'd just stick a gig in them or reach in and pick them up. You got to ease behind him, catch him behind the head so he won't see you.

I'd hunt, too—take my papa's shotgun and go out with my dog Joe and hunt birds and possums and coons. Coons you hunt at night, but you find the possum in the daytime. Kick over them old stumps where they lay out during the day and he's sitting back there grinning at you. My mama would singe his hair off and soak him and bake him with potatoes.

Mama raised chickens in the yard. My mother used to bring the eggs to town to sell, fifteen cents a dozen. And chickens, yellow buff chickadees, fryers, pullets, she'd sell them chickens for thirty-five cents apiece. That was money! She'd get two or three hundred little old biddies for two or three dollars a hundred, order them from Sears Roebuck, from Chicago. She'd get the chops and grind from the corn what they raised in the field, put it in her apron, and feed the chickens in the yard. And in the spring and summer, we'd sell them fryers. Mama would carry them to town, sell them to the little stores and restaurants for thirty-five cents apiece. She could take two dollars and get enough groceries to do for us. When she get ready to kill those chickens she'd feed them with chops all the week, clean them out. She wouldn't let them eat all them worms and bugs then. Give them clean food all week then she kill them on Friday or Saturday.

That's like you do a hog in the country. We would put the hog on the fattening floor, like to kill him for Christmas, two or three months before. Build a pen for him on a wooden floor and then you feed him slop, corn, and when you get ready to kill that hog, he's so fat he can hardly walk. He ain't laying all in his mess, he's on that wooden floor. That song, about the "killin' floor," that mean they got you so down you can't do nothing for yourself. I been there!

After you kill that hog, you cut all that fat off him and rend it up for lard; that's your cooking oil. And Mama take all the trimming come off the side, put it in the sausage grinder, and make sausage. The women would grind sausage all night long. Then we wash them hams off good, take that green meat and salt it, and hang it up in the smokehouse. You get some hickory barks, oak barks, let that burn in a old tub, and that smoke cooks that ham. The smoke is curing it up then. You can cut it loose and it's just as red and pretty. Put it in a skillet, let it cook low. That ham was sure enough good. You could smell it all down the road. We eat that all winter long.

In the spring, there was dewberries growing across the fields. Mama would take and wash them, cook them down in a pot with sugar and lemon, put it up in a jar with them good rubbers on them, and tighten them up. Put them in the pantry and when you get ready, just get a jar of berries and make a berry pie. And peaches, she'd peel peaches for days and cook them down for preserves. Mama had hundreds of jars. Mama didn't buy nothing back when I was a boy. We raised corn and took it to the gristmill to grind it into meal. Have it ground coarse and that was grits, fine and that was meal for cornbread. You would give the man at the gristmill one third of it for payment. The only thing she bought then was flour, because they didn't raise wheat in Mississippi too much. And rice, had to get the rice. Arkansas always been a rice state. And sugarcane from Louisiana, down in the bayou.

The light bread man, Wonder Bread man, used to come through there. We used to get bread from him, and that bread was so sweet. It was a dime a loaf. We'd be out in the field and Daddy would look up and quit, saying "Yonder bread man." And we'd go across the field and meet the bread man on the gravel road and eat that dry bread — it was so sweet. Just a solid loaf, wasn't no sliced.

All the people from out in the country would go to Shaw on Saturday afternoons, to shop in the stores. The Chinese immigrated into the Delta and they run stores in them little towns. They got real plentiful around there. You never saw the Chinaman working out in the field, but you would see poor whites working in the field sometimes. In Shaw, the Italians had a lot of the little jukes and restaurants; they come to the Delta and brought some money with them. They made gardens and sold vegetables and opened stores. They got to be so strong in my hometown that what they said got done. They had the sheriff all tied in. Money rules it and they had the money. Everyone went along with what they said.

I would go to Sunday school for Bible lessons, and I would go to church; my mother would carry me to church. And we all went to the revival when it was in town. I used to ask my mother, "Mama? If I was to die now, would I go to heaven?" She said, "You would go to heaven. Before twelve, the sin is on me and your father, your sin is on us. After you get twelve, you on your own. You die with sin then, you go to hell." Older people would tell children that.

They started the revival in the spring. I would go to revival and sit on the mourner's bench. That's the place you go and pray, called the mourner's bench. And we would go out in the woods, go hide in trees, for hours at a time, praying, trying to get converted. What converted means is that you'll be safe when you die.

I prayed and I can remember I had a feeling one time I never had before. I was just turning into twelve years old. I felt light and like something had lifted up off of me, a burden had lifted off of me. And if that was any sign, then I got converted when I was twelve years old. You never have that but one time. Once you got it, that's something, because God don't give you nothing and take it back. You have that until you die because that's what He gives to you in your younger days. You've prayed enough and He forgives you. That means you got converted of sin. You never get that but one time; He gives that to you one time. You may neglect and not go to church, but you lay awhile and you can straighten up with God. Because you already been converted.

The black people long ago in the South, they would feed the preacher after service on Sunday evenings. They made the children sit back and they feed the preacher first before the kids could eat. I remember one Sunday evening the preacher was eating at my friend's house, eating and talking and grabbing up all that chicken. He was reaching for the last piece, saying, "This sure is some good chicken," and my friend-boy hollered out at him, "Preacher, you're a God damn greedy son of a bitch!"

Musicians and preachers are just alike: they ain't no good! They always want to start some junk. Another preacher was at my Aunt Daughter's house all the time. He likened her. He used to sit around eating and laughing at her house and tell her, "Oh, Sister Beatrice, this is a good dinner, and you sure got some pretty legs."

My mama went to church on Sundays but my father, he'd go to town and buy him a paper and sit on the porch and read the paper all day. He'd read the paper all day, and then he'd go across the field and watch the crop, see how the cotton and corn coming up. He'd have his hands behind him, walking along the field in the hot sunny day.

Mama left Dubbs after Christmas in '26 and carried us, me, Hermalie and Altie and Mack, back down to Shaw, Mississippi, where her brother Aaron was at. Mama made a crop by herself that fall, in '26, and my father made a crop further down the Delta by himself. I remember Altie and Mack was too small to be much help but me and Hermalie helped Mama in the field. At the end of that summer, Papa give his crop up to the man. He made it but he didn't gather it. He give it to him, and the man, that's all his, proper. Papa come to Mama. All of us was chopping cotton in the field. I had my flour sack. My mama looked across the field and saw my daddy coming. She called my daddy nigger. She looked up and said, "Yon come nigger." We put them cotton sacks down then, quit out the field, and went on home to the house. Mama cooked chicken and everything, we rejoiced over Papa, and we didn't work in the field no more that day. My daddy stayed there all the rest of the year and helped my mother. And my mother was pregnant when my daddy come home, pregnant by another man. But my daddy accepted her.

Mama got her crop together that year and there was $250. That was a whole lot of money for us, those dollars counted then. My mother bought my dad a black broadcloth suit of clothes, had it tailor-made, and paid forty dollars for it. Broadcloth is thick just like a mole, real black and slick. We buried him in that suit. She bought it for him in '27, when the high water was.

Chapter Two

The water overflowed
her heart.

Nineteen twenty-seven, that was the year of the high water. I was coming up on twelve years old. It rained for months, all winter, and the levee went down in April. The water broke through the levee over by Scott. And all that water come back around Shaw, around the bow. We had to come out of the country then, come in to Shaw.

The water broke out in the morning time. We could hear it when it broke, just like a "Boom!" It busted that levee through. And the water was coming. We could hear the river roaring. People was hollering, "The levee broke! Get ready and get out!"

Mama was far along with that baby. The boss man had a old truck; it was just a box built over a gas tank to sit on and a big body, just like a wagon body, behind. He put Mama on the back there with some quilts and we all sat on there. They was taking us out of the country, carrying us along the gravel roads to town, to high ground, to give us some shelter to stay in.

And before we got to town, the little truck got stalled. Water was trying to seep way up. The men had to push the truck, and it started raining again and Mama got wet. The water was coming up the sides of the truck; it was rising. Mama got wet and she caught cold, a cold whilst she was carrying that baby. And that cold sopped up in her. They took her into a little old hotel down in Shaw, and the rest of us they took to a boxcar on the railroad tracks.

The government sent boxcars from Memphis so the people coming out from the overflow could stay in them. The Red Cross took care of everyone. We lived in the boxcar for a couple of months. They built a mess hall for all the people from out in the country to eat at. And they had something like a pit built. They'd get whole cows and cut them up and put them big pots on and make beef stew. When they get ready to serve dinner, all the people what was living in them carboxes, they was a ding-donging to let everybody know their dinner was ready. Then everybody would go down to that big long camphouse. There was long tables, just like a prison camp. You'd go by one man wearing a white cap with a red cross on it, a big white apron. He got beans, a great big dipper; you'd go by him and he'd dip in and give you beans. Go by another and he'd give you meat. We'd eat good because they had them whole cows, had people steady cutting them up, putting them in the pot. By the time they get through breakfast, they put dinner right on. They didn't let the pot never get cold.

From all over the country people sent us clothes, secondhand clothes. They stacked them up and divided them by plantation, and each plantation got so many clothes for their people.

We stayed out there while Mama stayed at that little hotel in Shaw. My mama had her baby there, a little girl. Mama couldn't take care of the baby and Papa, he had all of us and he couldn't tend to her. A woman friend of Mama's took the baby, but the little girl only lived about two months.

We went back to the country at the end of May. There was water everywhere. Mama wasn't getting well. It was too late to make a crop of cotton. That low land was so wet, the water had been up so long, that we couldn't plant a crop in '27.

Mama had caught the dropsy. Her legs swole up, her face swole up— she was sick. Mama was about thirty-two years old then and walking with a stick. My daddy carried her to Cleveland, Mississippi, to find a doctor to tend to her. They tapped her for her water, got all the water

**High water near the confluence of the Ohio and
Mississippi Rivers, 1994.**

out of her, and in about three weeks she come back with that same
water. The water got so high it overflowed her heart and drowned her
heart out. And so she died. She died, all that from childbirth, in 1927.
In July. In Shaw, Mississippi.

She died at home. I was twelve years old. The undertaker from Shaw
come out there and they put curtains up at the door. They cut her and
drew the blood from her. And they bathed her in a number 3 tub, the
big old tubs we used to bathe in out in the country. They bathed and
dressed her, and they laid her out on a cooling board. A cooling board is
something like chairs with a board across them, they laid her out on
that. Then they got the casket from Cleveland. She was buried nice.
She's buried at Green Grove Church—that's out from Shaw. The graveyard where she was buried at, they raising corn and beans on it now. But
I know the spot.

I was in a sadness then. I had nobody to go to. I missed my mother so much. I can remember everything about my mother. I loved her, but she was kind of rough. She had two babies wasn't none of my daddy's. She had a boy early on, but he didn't live and I don't know much about him. And this baby during the flood. Mama would go out and Papa wouldn't say nothing but "OK, Pearl." My mother had a boyfriend with a old car, a old T-model Ford. I would get in the back with them and ride. I knew what was going on. One night they carried me to the Ringling Brothers show in Shaw. At that time when the Ringling Brothers go through a country town that was a big attention. Merry-go-round, round and round, people on the stage telling lies, lips painted red, cracking jokes. Them country people hadn't seen that before; that was good to them! See the elephants walk around with their long snouts, man riding atop his head—that just opened them country folks' eyes up!

My daddy loved her but he didn't pay no attention to where my mama go. He'd sit down, watch us kids, just wanted to be quiet. Kept to himself. My mother, she would play on my father because my father, he just acted like he didn't care about nothing.

After burying Mama, the fall come in then and we was picking cotton out there in Sunflower. The people out in Sunflower County in the high land, they made crops that year. And when the cotton opened up, the cotton-picking trucks come and picked all us people up what had the backwater and took us to the crops in the high land to pick cotton.

Last of the fall in '27, Papa moved to the Wildwood Plantation, over around Greenwood. It run from Money clean back to Shellmound. One quarter mile and across the river from Wildwood was the Bledsoe Plantation, and next to him was Willie Bass. Papa made a crop there, sharecropped, in '28. I worked the field with him, doing everything. I followed the plow. We all picked cotton. And when we made that crop, the boss man took that money back out of there. Every year when you settle up at the end of the year, you settled up with the boss. "Well, you done good this year, old boy. You come out $250 in debt." That's behind. That's the truth! Then he turn right around and ask, "What you want, boy, for Christmas?" That's to hold you for the next year! "How much you want for Christmas?" "Well, Mr. So-and-So, I need about three, four hundred dollars." That's the money you should have cleared

**Honeyboy's sister–in–law, Alice Edwards, holding a portrait of
his mother, Pearl Edwards, 1994.**

out from your crop. But he doing that to hook you for next year. He let
you have that, and you laugh, go on into town, get a lot of candies,
cakes, and stuff, drink a lot of whiskey. And we stuck for the next year.

The white folks run it down there. Some of those big plantations was
just like little towns and the man who run it just like the mayor. You
wouldn't always see the owners. If it was a big plantation sometimes the
owner would just come out once in a while in his big car to tend to the
money. For the work, he would hire a agent—he would be out there
telling you what to do. And some of them big plantations had riders,
would ride around on horses overseeing the people. There was a big
plantation in Scotts, Mississippi, that had hundreds of people living on
it. They called it the Syndicate Plantation. That plantation was so big it
had three cotton gins. In the fall of the year after the cotton harvest, car

dealers used to drive old cars down from Memphis and park them on the road just outside the Syndicate and sell them to the sharecroppers. Those people had no sense; they didn't clear much money but they was going to have one of them cars. If a guy didn't have enough money to buy one, he'd go to his boss, "Mr. So-and-So, I want me a car." "Boy, you want a car?" The boss is going to get that car for him, too, because then he'll have that son of a bitch hooked for two or three years. Next year he can say, "Well, you didn't clear any money and we come out even. But you know I bought you that car, now."

In '28 my sister Lessie died. She had come up from Missouri with her husband in that open truck, hauling corn and stock. She slept out in the cold on the back of that truck, just sleeping under a tarpaulin, and caught pneumonia. She come to my daddy. He was the backbone, everytime something happened the kids would come in to him. Lessie got so weak she trembled. After a few weeks she died.

I had a good daddy. I never heard my daddy cuss; he was easygoing. But if you make him mean you couldn't hardly quiet him. He never bothered about nothing unless it come to him. I never saw him laugh, never saw him cuss. When he laughed, he turned his head off and smiled, "Humph." Then he was through with it. He didn't mess with nobody, didn't have many friends to sit around with, laugh, and talk. He was self-conceited or something. He was a good man, though. He used to play that violin and guitar and with that good education sit on the porch and read his papers. Nobody bothered him; he don't bother nobody else. He didn't care who come to our house, he was just to himself.

Except with women. I think before my mother died, my father had eyes on Miss Sue. Miss Sue was dark, with big eyes and a little gap in her front teeth. She was living with her daughter over by Shaw. So that last of '27, when we moved over to Wildwood Plantation, he carried Miss Sue with him and they married when they got over there. They wasn't together too long because she went to losing her mind. She was over there till about the last of '28, then her daughter come and got her and carried her back over to Shaw. Then Papa got acquainted with Miss Virginia Mitchell. She already had two grown sons. Miss Virginia was a yellow woman, mulatto, with good hair and a big mouth. He married her later in '29. That's one thing my father didn't do, when my mother died, he didn't do without a woman. He married twice after my mama died, he sure did. Married Miss Sue and married Virginia Mitchell.

In '29 Papa moved to the back acres of that same plantation, Wildwood, Mr. Jeff Wilson's place. He thought we could have a good cotton crop because all the land was rich back there. It was a big plantation, chopped up in parts. And in the back was a lot of black, rich soil. Papa cleared money that year, Papa cleared three hundred dollars in the fall of '29. They had the best cotton crop in years in '29. Right around then was when he married Miss Ginny. He took me to Greenwood and bought me a little old suit. And he bought me a guitar too, a used one from a neighbor. And right after that the Depression fell out.

The banks went down and the plantation owners got broke. Some folks was out there killing theyselves! I can remember that! Everybody was equalized; didn't nobody have nothing much. The troopers come from New York, come to Mississippi, and got all the money out of the banks and carried it back. And the people what had money in the banks, they went down. They was broke. The only people who had any money then was them white people in the country who had sewed up the money in the beds and put it in pots and things. A lot of them old, simple people, they'd bury their money, keep it in them big old iron pots. And them what worked with the bank, had loans and everything, the bank went down with their money. Those state troopers come, got that money out of the bank and put it on them trains and took it back to New York.

There on Wildwood Plantation we picked cotton for thirty cents a hundred. And the year before we got three dollars for a hundred! The Depression was so bad people, if they didn't raise their food, they wouldn't have nothing. But we got by.

We'd go in the cornfield and get these old whippoorwill peas that grow in the corn. We'd eat them and eat fatback. The meat we would buy out of the store, it was so fat there wasn't no lean in it at all, so we called it fatback. When we couldn't get food to eat I'd get my shotgun and go to hunting. And we'd steal hogs.

The white folks had a lot of hogs, shoats, and they would let them run out in the wintertime to get whatever they can to eat in pastures. Those shoats weighed about 100 pounds, 150 pounds. Us kids would catch them by the leg, tie them up, and to keep them from hollering we'd put them in the henhouse and give them something to eat. They start to eat and then we take a ax and hit them in the head. Put on some hot water, drag them in the house and have meat for three or four days. We had to do something like that; if we hadn't done that we'd starve to death! Sometimes a hog would get under the house, by the chimney. They'd get under that chimney to keep warm. And we'd take a ax and cut a plank out of the house from the inside, take a shotgun, and shoot them right there. Then drag them up through the hole. Have fresh meat, cooked onions. The white folks never missed them because they had so many of them running in the fields. And we had to eat!

Back on that plantation there was a old man, Mr. Green, who come out of World War I and bought himself a old T-model Ford. And he couldn't drive it. I was only fourteen, but I taught myself to drive this man's car and would carry him all around to Greenwood and other places in that car. It didn't even have a clutch! We'd go down those gravel roads where there wasn't nobody but us and I'd pull them valves out and we'd go about twenty-five miles an hour. He'd hold on to my arm and tell me, "Cut her down! She's too fast! Cut her down!"

I went to school a little while there out on Wildwood Plantation. Wildwood was met up with a plantation called Sweet Home Plantation. We went to the Sweet Home school because that was the closest school to us. There wasn't no schoolhouse. Kids would go to school in the church house, at the church sitting out in the country. They'd clean the church up Sunday when the people quit having the meeting and they'd have school all the week in the church.

All the grades went to school together but they got called at different times up. And they'd have different teachers for different classes. At that time, if you didn't learn, our school teachers would beat you. They'd get those willow sticks and ply them! I had a teacher, Miss Beasley; that woman put some knots on my head. She'd whup me and then I'd go home and get another beating at home! When the school got out on a Friday, the teacher made the kids clean up the church for the preacher on Sunday. We had to mop up, clean up, get everything ready for church on Sunday. Many Saturdays I done it. Then on Monday, come in early and clean up before school started again.

**1993 photograph of Sweet Home Missionary Baptist Church
near Money, Mississippi, where Honeyboy
attended school as a child.**

Back in Mississippi most all the girls have got more education than the boys. They went to school longer than the boys. The boys would have to go and work in the fields in March. They have to cut stalks. Girls still went to school. Girls went to school till the last of May, and they had two or three months longer than the boys. That's the reason they got a better education than the boys got. But I didn't stay in school long; I got mannish and left. I didn't learn nothing much more than how to spell my name. It wasn't till later that I learned that stuff on my own. I needed to learn to read and write to get around. But at that time I had got that guitar and that's something I wanted to do.

Chapter Three

I kept that guitar
in my hands.

There was a man, a sharecropper, who stayed across from our house, and his name was Clarence McDaniel. He ordered a guitar from Sears Roebuck. I think he paid twelve dollars for it. Cost you a hundred now, or more. It was a good guitar, called a Stella. Every night when we come out of the field we'd go over to his house and he'd sit down and play. That's the first time I got interested in the blues and tried to know what it was. And I fell in love with the blues. I'd pick up the guitar and try to play, and I couldn't play nothing! Clarence played that guitar till about the middle of the fall, then he got tired of it, and that's when he sold it to my father, for eight dollars.

Well, I started to playing that guitar and I learned how to play in late fall of '29. I watched my daddy play that guitar, and whenever I could I would pick it up and try to strum on it. I used to sit up and play one tune so long Daddy would say, "Boy, why don't you get out of that tune? Don't you know something else to play?" I started to change little things around, playing in E natural, playing in D. That's how he played. Before then, I was playing in Spanish, doing lots of fool stuff with the strings. He'd say, "Boy, get in natural key! You won't make a guitar player playing in Vastopol." He told me right. Most all of the musicians back then, if they played the violin or mandolin, they had a guitar player behind them playing bass. That was called the complement. Daddy showed me; he run a few lines bass behind me. My daddy taught me how to play guitar. And I learned some pretty good strokes on it.

One night a crowd of people staying across the field from our house gave a party. Back then they would give country dances at a different place every Saturday night. They'd fry fish, drink white whiskey, dance. And this night they was dancing to one of them windup gramophones and they fooled around and broke the spring on it. And they said, "Man, we ain't got no music. Know what we'll do; we'll get little Honey over here. He can play pretty good!" And they come over to my papa's house and got me. I guess I played one piece and sang a hundred songs all night long, fast and slow, fast and slow!

And that was the first time I ever drank any alcohol, because those people kept bringing alcohol around. I didn't even want to drink! But they said, "Get you a drink. You'll feel a little better." I wasn't nothing but a kid; I wasn't but fourteen. And I fooled around that night and got drunk. I went in home before day and I was talking all out of my head. I can remember just as good! My father said, "Boy, you been drinking that old rotgut, ain't you?" I said, "Yes, Papa." He said, "You better leave that stuff alone." And I was singing a song about "The rooster crow before day" and I was just drunk, singing some kind of song rolling across my mind. And from then on I started to playing the guitar.

Daddy had some songs he played, songs like "Joe Turner Blues" and "Stag-O-Lee" and "John Henry." Them was some damn good numbers. Daddy would sing,

> John Henry fell dead with his hammer in his hand.
>
> He was a steel-drivin' man.
>
> The woman John Henry loved, she wore a dress of red.
>
> She said, "I'm goin' where John Henry fell dead."
>
> John Henry fell dead with the hammer in his hand.

Wildwood Plantation, north of Greenwood, Mississippi, 1993.

I used to play all of them different damn songs. Back then, in the country, we played all the older stuff because there wasn't nothing new come out.

When the phonographs come along about '28, '29, my sister Blanche bought one. It was a windup; it had the horn and a needle to go right around the spool. Sears Roebuck come out with that windup, and people could dance by it. My sister used to have a record by Blind Lemon Jefferson, "Blues Come from Texas." Blind Lemon Jefferson was a big star back then. She used to play that song over and over again; we'd sit up and listen to it all night. Before that phonograph come in, the only music we heard was what we made on pianos and guitars, violins, fiddles, mandolins. That was our music.

It was out on Wildwood Plantation when I first met Tommy McClennan. Tommy would come out there and play the guitar a while and bump on the piano. He could play the guitar pretty good, but he sure wasn't no piano player. He threw the people; he had them dancing and hollering. He had about two or three pieces he'd play on piano, and they'd dance all night to them two or three pieces. But he could play that guitar, and he could holler; Tommy had a big mouth. He had two brothers, Carl Richie and Boonie, and a sister Katie. Their mother was Miss Cassie. They come from Yazoo City; that's where Tommy was born at. Miss Cassie brought them up around Greenwood and they stayed in Greenwood for years.

And it was in '29 when Tommy Johnson come down from Crystal Springs, Mississippi. He come to pick cotton by the hundred. The crop was so good that year they had to get the people out of the hills to come and pick the cotton in the Delta. That's why Tommy Johnson and his brother Clarence come out in a old T-model Ford. On the plantation they had a great big old double house like a camp house where people who come from the hills stayed at. Some had beds, some had bunks; they didn't care what they was sleeping on. At nighttime we'd go there and listen to Tommy Johnson play. People would sit around on the cotton sacks and drink white whiskey and eat hot tamales. And listen to Tommy play the blues. He was just a little guy, tan colored, easy-going; but he drank a whole lot. Listening to Tommy, that's when I really learned something about how to play guitar. Tommy Johnson was a great guitar player; he had his own style. He had beautiful chords, kept them together, kept them up tight. That made them sound pretty good. Tommy Johnson, he could play anything.

And I remember the first time I met Sonny Boy Williamson. His name was Rice Miller. It was in 1929 in the summertime. It was hot. Across back the river from Wildwood Plantation was Shellmound, a little plantation town with a little old post office and store together there and a filling station. There was a little café there too, Peg Leg Jim's, under a sycamore tree. It was just a old shack, Jim's café, and Sonny Boy used to gamble in there. That's where Sonny Boy lived at, on the Bledsoe Plantation. One day I went over there; I was fourteen years old. I was standing beside the road and he was playing on a store porch. He had his overalls on, one suspender broke loose and his apron hanging down.

He was real tall, kind of light skinned, big nose. He was playing a song called "Pot Likker Train," playing that harp. He was a country boy!

Sonny Boy's brother's family stayed over on Bledsoe. His brother, Madonia, was a big, tall guy like Sonny Boy was, and he had a wife who was tiny, look like she weighed about ninety pounds. People said he beat her all the time. One evening she was drinking in Shellmound. All the people from all around had come out from the country, to eat at them stores and gamble at the café on the riverbank. The people from all the plantations around there would meet up in Shellmound, come in their wagons and buggies and have a good time whilst they were there. And that Saturday evening Madonia's wife called to him and said, "Come here. Let me tell you something." He thought because she was drunk she had got pleased with him, but she had a razor. She cut his throat, that little woman. She killed him! You can't beat people like that, them are the people that hurt you, coward people. People that are scared of you, them people kill you.

I saw lots happening. I once knew a boy out in the country who was on the same plantation as my uncle, called him Quack. His wife was pregnant. One Monday morning he come up early to the barn to get permission to go to the doctor for his wife, and the agent said, "Get that bush ax and go down and cut them bushes down there." Quack said, "My wife is pregnant and I'm going to town to Dr. Field and get some medicine because she's crampin', she's hurtin'." The man said, "You're goin' nowhere but to cut them bushes." Quack said, "No, I'm not ei-ther." So they got to arguing and fighting and the agent shot this boy twice with a little old .32. And Quack took the gun from him and shot him three times. The white guy tried to run. Quack took that ax and hit him on top of the head, said, "You ain't goin' nowhere"—killed him dead. He hid for a while then he went to his house and a gang of white men was there, beating his wife. He come out of the woods then and said, "Don't beat her. Here I am." They started to shooting at him then. Those men tied Quack behind a old A-model Ford and drug him down from out in the country clean to Shaw, drug him with a big grass rope. He wasn't nothing but beefsteak when they got into town. Old Dr. Field, the old white doctor, he said, "Well, this nigger's eyes are shot out; he won't see his way to hell." See, he had killed that white man but that white man made him kill him! That was some bad times back when I was a boy.

In August, in 1930, right after vining time, we had just come out of working the cotton, trying to clean the vines out of it, and the cotton opened up the same week. The boss, old man Kerr, he wanted us to get a sack and go right back in there and start working. And my daddy said to him, "No, my kids is not goin' back in. We got to have a week's rest or somethin'. We'll be pickin' cotton next week. We'll work the fields then." Mr. Kerr told my daddy, "Henry, if you don't get in the field by the time I come back, you better not be here."

I never will forget it. My dad put a shotgun behind the door. Old man Kerr went down the road on his old horse, and my daddy stood there right in the doorway, chewing tobacco. He put that double-barreled shotgun inside of the door, and if Mr. Kerr had said anything more to him, he would have blowed his head off. See, at that time, people didn't care nothing about dying if they killed the one they wanted. They'd say, "I know I'm goin' to die, and I'm goin' to kill this son of a bitch while I'm goin'." A lot of black folks was like that. Some was scared and some not—would just as soon be dead. Life was so bad for them they didn't care about anything. And my daddy was one of those. But he had a lot of sense. He didn't put the gun where old man Kerr was going to see it. And that man come right by the house and didn't say a word to Papa, just rode right by on his horse. I was so glad. If he said something, my papa would've killed him.

So we moved to another plantation over by Greenwood, to Fort Loring. My father had married Miss Ginny and us kids was loose, just loose. Because he had got him another woman. He always took care of us, but he didn't care too much what we do. He wasn't tight on me going no-where. Matter of fact, he wasn't tight on the girls, neither. He give them respect, but he wasn't tight on them. So we raised ourselves, near about. We cooked for ourselves and Miss Virginia cooked for my daddy.

Fort Loring was just a small cultivation. It was right along the river and alongside the railroad, a few little shacks and the owner's big white house. Boats used to come right by us there. In '32 there was another high water, and one of them great big steamboats come up the little river. That was something to see. A little diesel train run through there,

**Train trestle crossing the Yazoo River near the Fort Loring
Plantation, outside of Greenwood, Mississippi, 1993.**

a short run, just had one or two little coaches on it. On the front of the
train was yellow and black stripes; it looked just like a bug. We called it
the Doodlebug. And the Southern used to come through there. It run
twice a day, from Greenville in the morning to Columbus and then
from Columbus back to Greenville at night. Runnymede was just two
miles down from there, and Itta Bena was a mile from Runnymede.
They was little flag stop towns—you'd flag the train down at those stops.
Many a time I walked down those tracks and across the railroad trestle
and through Walter Phillips's plantation right into Greenwood.

Tommy McClennan was staying in Greenwood then and I got good
acquainted with him. I started staying at Tommy's house more than I
stayed at home. I used to lay by their house just like they was kin to me.
I was just like that; I liked to hang around grown people at that time.

Tommy's wife Ophelia was always cooking a big pot of something to eat. Tommy never worked much; Ophelia worked most of the time. Tommy played the guitar and gambled, shot dice, played cards. He and Ophelia had two kids, Bubba and Carrie; they was about six and seven years old at that time.

Tommy was dark and had big eyes like a frog. He was real little, about four foot and ten, just touched me right along about the shoulder. Tommy didn't weigh a bit over 115 pounds. There wasn't no hat would fit Tommy's head! His hats would be coming down around his ears. He was a funny guy. He'd pull his hat off and comb his hair down and look in the mirror and talk to it, saying, "Good! Now you got all night to rise!"

I and Tommy, we be together all the time. And when he wasn't with me he was with Robert Petway. Robert was a funny guy. He was married two or three times; he wouldn't stay with nary a woman. In Greenwood was a lot of sanctified, church women and Robert would want one of them and get right into church and play his guitar there, till he get her. When he get her, he jump right back out, start to playing the blues again! Then he's back on the streets with Tommy. Tommy and Robert was about the same size. They'd come down the street with two guitars, looking like midgets. Now Robert could beat Tommy playing but Tommy could holler more than Robert. Tommy had a big mouth! He could holler loud. You'd think it was a big man playing when you heard him. Robert had a soft, tinny voice. I learned a few licks from Tommy, a few numbers he made. He made "The Bullfrog Blues" and Petway made "The Catfish Blues."

"Catfish Blues" is Robert Petway's song. He just made that song up and used to play it at them old country dances. He just made it up and kept it in his head. You call that mother wit. He remembered every verse he ever sang; didn't have to write down nothing. I learned the "Catfish" from Robert. Robert and Tommy McClennan and me, we'd be together all the time. On days when we wasn't out playing at the whiskey houses or on the streets; we'd be at Tommy's house drinking and playing cards, and one of us sitting in the corner practicing some song. Just sitting around the house. Tommy would run out and get some whiskey and his wife Ophelia would cook a big pot of soup. Bubba and Carrie Mae was little, running around the house.

Tommy, he wasn't really a guitar picker; he was mostly a frailer, and played a few chords in the key of C, running chords with that big loud voice. It all hooked up together there. Everybody said Robert Petway could beat Tommy McClennan on guitar. Well, he picked it more than Tommy. The people likened what they was doing. People liked Tommy.

Tommy McClennan played a raggedy and rough guitar, played a lot in G and C. He could put a feeling to his music that way, but when I got to learn to play, those chords in those keys didn't put a feeling to my music, that C wasn't attractive to me. Now Tommy Johnson, that guy had a lot of attractive chords. The key of D is the sweetest key you want to play in the blues—if you know how to play it.

Tommy and Robert, they played at Three Forks, right outside of Greenwood. Two lanes come into Greenwood, one from Shellmound, the other from Itta Bena, and there was a little juke house at that crossroads, called it Three Forks. They played all them places around Greenwood. I had my little guitar and was just learning to play. I'd be following Tommy around. They'd see me coming and they'd say, "Yonder come little Honey." And they'd dodge me! I was so worrisome! "Yeah, yeah, let's go," and they'd dodge me!

Around then was the first time I saw Rube Lacy. He lived on our same plantation, out there from Greenwood. He had gone to Chicago and made that little old record "Hambone." Then he come back down and stole a man's wife and brought her back up to Chicago.

I used to stand around and listen at him. He was playing the "Hambone and Gravy Blues." After he cut this little old record and it got on the jukebox, everything was, "Rube Lacy! Rube Lacy!" He was staying with this man out in Greenwood, and I would go to this house where he was staying. We'd gather up every night and we'd give him nickels and dimes. That's the way he made it. We'd work all day for seventy-five, eighty cents a day and then at nighttime we'd go over there and give him those nickels. He made it playing his guitar. And when he left there he carried that man's wife with him; he brought her back to Chicago with him. He did! Musicians always will steal women! She was a good-looking woman, too. Rube Lacy left overnight and that woman left with him.

In '31, at Christmastime, I was walking down Johnson Street in Greenwood with some of my friends, pushing each other along like boys play.

I had my guitar on my shoulder with a little cord string. And Lester Lucas, he run up against me and pushed me, and the cord string broke and the guitar fell and busted all to pieces. And I like to die. Lester tried to pay me for it. He said, "I pay you for the guitar." He worked two days, paid me a little, but times was tight then and I didn't worry him no more about it.

I couldn't make any money to buy another guitar. But out there in Greenwood my sister Blanche had met a man with a guitar. They married. His name was James Son Davis. He was half Mexican. His mother was a black woman but he took every spit after his daddy. He had black, big curls in his hair, them big old brown sleepy eyes. He had a little old guitar, had a broken neck on it. And I used to sit down and play that guitar. I couldn't even go down to the bottom of the neck because the neck was broken. But I stayed up on the high frets and played that all the time. Son, he would play all night long. We'd roast potatoes, parch peanuts in lye, play the guitar. He used to play "Poor Boy, Long Way from Home," "Rollin' and Tumblin'."

It was around that time in '31 that I saw Kokomo Arnold playing on the streets in Greenwood. He was sitting on the porch of somebody's house, playing "Milkcow Blues." The people was all ganging around him. I didn't know who he was till after he got through playing and he told the people his name. He looked to be in his middle thirties, and he wasn't from the Southern states, he was from back East somewhere. I think he had come from Georgia. He played that song "Sweet Home Kokomo." He was playing a big Martin guitar and it had a pretty good sound up and down the streets; it was loud. He stayed in Greenwood a couple of weeks; he was doing pretty good around there. He stayed around and got known pretty good and then he left there. I don't know which way he went. He made good money around Greenwood because he had a different style of playing. He was hustling and made a lot of nickels, dimes, and quarters. He was a traveling musician, trying to make it, hoboing around, catching freight trains, and laying around in town till the next train came through.

Honey can play now!

When I was about sixteen years old, I thought I was a man. I found myself looking at girls. I couldn't get no money to buy no shoes and I was tired of working on the farm. I was just a child, but I thought it was time for me to make something for myself! In '31, that's when I left Greenwood, hoboing with a boy called John Henry. That was the Depression; times was tough and you couldn't get no job. Me and John Henry caught a freight train to Memphis. We hopped off south of town and found work at a farm. We stayed with a old lady called Miss Lucy on her farm south of Memphis. She didn't have no kids. We helped her out, tended to her cows. After a while I got it into my head to come back home. She was just feeding us peas and beans and I was getting hungry!

We caught a freight train home and it was full of hoboes. They was all over that train, white and colored, hanging all over the side of the cars trying to get somewhere where they could find something to eat. It was bad then, that's the truth—it was bad. You couldn't get no work. Hoboes would go to a house to beg food, and the people would have to say, "Go back. I ain't got nothin' to eat." If you was lucky enough to get a job, you'd work all day long for fifty, sixty cents.

I was going back home on that freight train and about ten of us got pulled off the train in Glendora. The local police pulled us off when that train stopped and carried us to the plantation store. They had one of them plantation judges sitting there; he was just a farmer with a big hat on. A judge at the store and they called that the courtroom! He was sitting there with his eyeglasses on, tapping the side of his head. "Uh, don't you know you is trespassin'? That it's against the law to ride a freight train?" The freight train didn't belong to them, but if they catch you in their city, they'll pull you off and give you time for trespassing.

There used to be railroad dicks, men who would ride the train. They'd pull you off the train but they wouldn't give you no time. They'd pull you off and wouldn't let you ride. "Y'all can't ride the train. Y'all got to get off now." Sometimes they'd try to shoot you off! You just wait and catch the next one. But these guys were local cops, waiting to catch you coming through their town. The train would stop to take on water or freight, and they come up there and get you. "Come on. Come down. Come on down, y'all. Don't you know you're trespassin'?"

They put me on a county farm, a cotton farm. That was in June and I stayed all of June and July, and they turned me loose in August. Weldon Willis ran that farm; he was a cotton farmer. I did everything on that farm: worked in the field, chopped cotton, dug ditches barefooted with shovels. It was something like a penitentiary. They run us from daybreak till sunset, then locked us up every night after we was done working for the day in a great big old building, a prisoner cage.

Sometimes guys got away. When I was there two guys got away. They never did catch them. They'd run them down with horses but they couldn't catch them after they crossed those lakes. And after a while they wouldn't look for them. The prisoners there was only small-time, serving thirty days, ninety days. They didn't have no guys there for murder or nothing like that. People for murder went to the state penitentiary, went to Parchman. But people on the county farms, that's for when you jump contracts on the plantation, or steal, or commit some misdemeanor. They just let that son of a bitch go. He just lucky. He got away; wasn't worth catching him.

They would have a gunman and a driver. The driver, when a man wasn't doing right or wasn't working right, he would beat him. He'd say,

Cotton harvest in the Delta, 1993.

"Get down," and take a big leather strap with holes in it and sling it and beat you. That's a driver. The gunman would stand back off from the prisoners, holding that rifle and keep an eye out, keep you from running.

I seen guys out on that county farm, if they couldn't keep up they'd beat them so bad they'd go back to the camp and lay down and die. The driver would take that strap and turn a guy's butt from black to white. There was one guy who jumped a contract on a plantation. He owed the boss money. He got caught and put on the county farm. They beat him so bad in the field one day till he couldn't get up, then they threw him over a little horse and carried him back to the cage. By the time they got there he was dead. They hit him too hard with that strap and busted his heartstrings.

When people died they just put them in the ground, didn't even no-tify their people. They had a place they called the Potter's Field, and they had a carpenter would build boxes to bury you in. He built a box and put a little black cross on the top with nails. They put a couple of quilts in there and lay you down.

I got so sick out there. I was barefoot; I didn't have no boots or noth-ing. I had malaria fever, and I wouldn't eat because the food for the prisoners wasn't nothing but potatoes cooked with no grease in it and not even any salt. They just cut up an onion in it. They gave us that and old cornbread, sometimes some chicken necks and crowder peas, little old brown peas cooked with fatback meat. The grease would be so thick on top of the peas, you'd have to rake through the grease to get to them. I was so sick I couldn't eat that stuff. I fell off and got so little, locked up in the cage. Captain Willis come over and asked me one day, "How you feelin'?" I said, "I don't feel good." He went to town, bought me some sardines, some tomatoes, stuff to bring my appetite back. He done that for me, sure did.

Then they turned me to be a trusty. I didn't go to the field to work no more. I was a prisoner still but I didn't go out on the farm no more to work. I was like a handyman around there. I'd get up at four o'clock in the morning, get the stove good hot and ready to cook. They had a big eight-eyed iron range to cook for all them prisoners. I'd start the fire and help the cook start to cooking. After we all ate breakfast, daylight come and then they got all the prisoners out to go to the field. When they leave with their sacks to go to the field, I'd go out in the field and gather up corn and feed the mules and hogs. So I had it made for a little while.

Everyone there called me Little Greenwood. They give you a nick-name when you go to penitentiary. I was the youngest man there, me and Coonhide. Coonhide, they caught him stealing coon hides from them trappers. The trappers left their hides out to stretch and he'd go out there and steal them.

There was a boy working on the farm, W. C. Walker, who got freed before I did. He knew my sister Blanche, and he went back to Green-wood and told her, "Honey's out there on the county farm," and she told my daddy about it. And my daddy and his boss, they come up to the county farm to get me. They got there on a Saturday but I had been turned loose that Friday night. Captain Willis had come to me and said, "Little Greenwood." I said, "Yes sir?" He said, "You're a free man today. You can go home or you can stay and work by the day and stay right here at the camp and I'll pay you seventy-five cents a day. You're free." I said, "Well, Cap'n Willis, I appreciate that but I want to see my father. I been gone a long time and I want to go home." He said, "Well, do what you want to do." They gave me some new blue jeans to wear home, with yellow pockets on. I got up that Saturday morning at four o'clock, and lit out, left walking. And I walked from that county farm over to that same place where they took me off the train in Glendora, walked through the country, and caught a ride from Glendora over to Money, Mississippi, near to my daddy's home.

They turned me loose and my daddy come to get me that next day. But I'm glad I was gone because if they had come and got me then my father would've had to pay to get me off the farm. You come to get someone, it cost one hundred dollars. But they turned me loose. It was lay-by time, there was nothing to do on that farm till August. In August they'll catch a new set of people. They worked us to death; it was time to get a new set.

I lost so much weight working hard on that farm; I was so poorly. They nearly killed me out there. I was raggedy as a can of kraut. I stayed by my sister Blanche's for a time in Greenwood and she had me tending the yard for a white woman she worked for. That woman gave me some old clothes, fed me. After a time, I come home to my daddy's house. It was coming up to August, and time to pick cotton.

I stayed by my daddy's for a while when one day Big Joe Williams come through there hoboing. There was a woman staying on our plantation at Fort Loring called Black Rosie and she run a juke house. Black Rosie gave a dance one Saturday night. It was a little before Christmas in 1932. And Big Joe Williams was playing at Black Rosie's dance. Joe wasn't nothing but a hobo then, running down the streets. I went over to Rosie's and there he was playing. He was in his thirties, had a red handkerchief around his neck, and was playing a little pearl-necked Stella guitar; he was playing the blues. He played "Highway 49" and I just stood and looked at him. I hadn't heard a man play the blues like that! I was standing up in the corner looking at him and he said, "Why you lookin' at me so hard? Can you play?" I said, "A little bit!" He got a drink of whiskey and said, "Play me a little." I was ashamed and shy but I strummed a little. I played a little number or two for him. He said, "I can learn you." Just like that! So I hung with him then, I wanted to play so bad. I stayed with him all night that night. All night till daylight.

I come home Sunday morning and Joe come up with me, with his guitar on his shoulder. My dad was a musician and he would take with musicians. I brought Joe to him and said, "This is my father." I said, "He used to play, too." So Joe sat down and played the blues for my father, and my sister cooked a big chicken dinner for him. After Joe got through eating, he wanted to go out to Greenwood where he could stop at the whiskey house, make a little money around the bootlegger's house. He asked my daddy, "Well, Mr. Henry, can I carry Honey with me? It looks like he's taken a likin' to me. I can learn him how to play." My daddy said, "He can go if he want to. It's cold and dead out here in the wintertime. There ain't nothin' to do on the farm. Just come back when the weather breaks." My sister's man, the one we called Son, had that little old guitar with the neck broke on it. We fixed that guitar and that's the guitar I played with Joe. Son said, "Honey, take it on with you." Joe tuned it up for me. I was playing in the key of E, low, and he was playing high.

So I went to Greenwood with him and we played at a good-timing house on Avenue F. Man, we played. Women was flocking, giving us nickels and dimes and quarters, and we kept the house lively.

Fridays, Saturdays we'd be on Carrolton Street, at a white man's grocery store called Mr. Russell's. That's where all the people come out of the country in their wagons to buy their groceries. That's where they do all their trading, at that store; that was a meeting point for the people. Me and Joe would sit in the back on cottonseed sacks and play our guitars. All them country people coming into town to buy their groceries gave us money.

Saturday nights we'd go out to different whiskey houses. We'd go out with our guitars, try to get a good shot of that white whiskey and feel good. Then we'd start to holler the blues. People would be pouring in. We done had a good time around there.

Then one day we left down the river, me and Joe left there, hitchhiking and hoboing. Back then when a musician was on the road with a guitar, cars would stop and pick you up. "Where y'all goin'? Play me some music, y'all!" We'd fall in the back and play the blues. Sometimes they'd stop and get us a drink, buy us a sandwich.

And Joe Williams would catch trains. Joe wasn't nothing but a hobo! He couldn't write his name! But he had a lot of sense, mother wit sense. He could go to any town, get off at a corner and look around. He'd say, "Well, let's go to such and such a place." And when we come back there and you think, "Hell, was this where we was?" he'd say, "Uh-uh. You go down further." He knew. He couldn't read or write, he didn't know his name hardly when he saw it. That's right! But he knowed the spots that he went by. And he'd be right, too.

Me and Joe stayed together about eight or nine months. We come to Jackson, Mississippi, and we come to Vicksburg. I met quite a few musicians. Frank Haines, he was a guitar player; he was in Jackson. Johnny Young was down in Vicksburg, playing the mandolin. He was real young, working with a fellow named Blue Coat who played violin. We stayed with a guy who run a riverboat and sold whiskey, he kept a good-timing house. We left Vicksburg, crossed the Mississippi River to Tallulah. Went to Rayville, a little town that stayed up all night and all day barrelhousing. Then we went to West Monroe, played over there. They had a big paper mill over there, and we went to the paper mill quarter and played. And when we left there we went to New Orleans.

I stayed with Joe till I got plumb good. Joe Williams would play in high Spanish with a capo on his guitar, and he run me down in E, open key. When I played open key behind that high Spanish, it sounded just like a bass behind a mandolin or something because of that high tone of his with the capo. And I got a low tone in the key of E but it's the same key. Nine strings, he always had those nine strings on his guitar. That's something he invented himself. He bored holes at the top of the neck of the guitar and made himself a nine-string guitar. That's the way he played all the time.

He was playing "Brother James," all them old numbers like that. "Brother James," "Highway 49," "Stack O'Dollars." "Stack O'Dollars, keep a-knockin', you can't come in. Stack O'Dollars, you can't come in." "Baby, Please Don't Go," "Milkcow Blues." He played all them old numbers. Some songs he made up, and I just played second guitar behind him. He'd just make up songs on the spot, and they'd be good songs, too. And we got pretty good; we made money. Because there wasn't a whole lot of blues players in the streets then. They was scattered around; it was hard to find a good blues player. You could find anybody to sit up and holler and go on. But to find something with life and a sound, you couldn't run up on that every day.

Joe was the first man that learned me how to hustle on the road. He could go anywhere, and he knew how to hustle with that guitar. I was following Joe, because Joe was like a dog. He knew everywhere, knew every train. Joe was the laziest man you ever saw; he wanted to work no way. I don't think he'd work in a baker's shop if you gave him a cake every time the pan came out. He played that guitar and made enough nickels and dimes and quarters to get rooms.

At that time, you could get rooms anywhere for three dollars a week. It wouldn't be a nice, classy room, but you had somewhere to sleep and eat at. Sometimes we'd pay six dollars a week and get board, room and board. The woman would cook you two meals a day. You get your breakfast, hot biscuits, bacon. Most of the people then raised hogs and had all that ham hanging in the smokehouse. Them old womens would put a couple big slices in the skillet, make the rice, put that ham gravy on the rice. Have bacon and rice and biscuits. That's six dollars a week. And that didn't cost them much because they raised that meat.

We could go on a Friday night, get two dollars apiece at a little country dance. In the daytime, in a set on the streets, we pass the hat around and sometimes we'd make up five or six dollars apiece. That was natural money. With a couple of dollars in them country towns, you could do alright. Nickel and dime, go and change it up for some greenbacks. We hustled—we gambled with them guitars.

He learned me how to go on the road, he learned me how to stand on the streets and make nickels and dimes and learned me how to hustle in barrelhouses. I learned under Big Joe. He'd take me in them places when I wasn't old enough to go in there and people let him bring me in.

When he wasn't playing, Joe would be messing around with the women, getting drunk, having fun. I remember one time he was in a

**Honeyboy performing in 1992 at Blind Willie's in Atlanta,
sixty years after leaving home with Big Joe Williams.**

room with a woman and he broke her bed down! That woman was
saying, "Mister, don't tear my bed up!" and he said, "Well, this bed just
ain't no damn good!" Joe, he didn't gamble too much but he drank and
played with the women. I'd be out shooting marbles with some boys on
the streets. I loved to play guitar but I was still young; I had childish
ways. He'd say, "Come on, Honey, get your guitar. Let's go." And he fed
me, gave me a little money to keep in my pocket. I appreciate that, he
kept me out of the field. He changed my life and I'm glad of it.

In New Orleans, that was good hustling there. I always did want to
come to a big city. We stayed with a Creole woman of Joe's in the French
Quarter. It was something to see them bright lights. There was street-
cars and the Canal Ferry was running then, men loading banana boats
on the river, people everywhere on wagons and in old cars and on horses.
It was beautiful.

We was the only ones playing blues around there then. New Orleans always been a jazz town. But the people got excited over the blues we was playing. Me and Joe would play around Rampart Street at the little joints, go in the bars, get chairs, and set down and play. In New Orleans in them bars people didn't drink white whiskey. They'd sit at a table and get a gallon of wine and a pitcher of ice. They let me play in the bars even though I wasn't but a boy. Things wasn't so strict and I'd sit behind Joe. We'd play in them bars, serenade in the streets, play for the whores, play at the train station, different places all over New Orleans.

Joe started drinking heavy in New Orleans, started drinking heavy on the pint. I was young, I didn't weigh but 110 pounds, and Joe started wanting to fight me. So I slipped off and left there walking. Slipped off one day and left Joe sleeping. And I come out of New Orleans and hit number 90 Highway, coming down the coast. I had my guitar on my shoulder and I'm wondering what I'm going to do because I hadn't been by myself before. I caught a ride to Bay St. Louis and got out on a bridge where there was people catching crabs. Some guy stopped me. He said, "Can you play that guitar?" And I said, "Yeah, I can," and I started to play it a little bit. "You're good!" I didn't know how good it was, but I was trying to play like Joe. This man starts to throwing me dimes and I thought, "Hell, I don't need Joe."

I come into Gulfport and I went to the music store there and found a little old harp rack. I started playing the harp and guitar and that was sounding alright.

I hitched a ride from Gulfport to Columbia, Mississippi, with two white men in a old black Ford. Friday come up and I played at the mill quarters there, at a big sawmill. All the people lived at the mill, in those section houses. I got up at the barrelhouse, playing my guitar, and them old women got drunk and started to hollering, going on, chunking that money at me. I played there for about a week, made a little money, and finally pulled up for home.

I lit out hitchhiking and got to Greenwood in a couple of days. When I got there, all of them, my sisters and them, was standing around me like somebody they never seen before. They said, "Honey can play now!"

Chapter Five

I wasn't going back to them fields.

I went back to my father's but I didn't want to work on the farm no more. I was plowing out in a field and wore the sole out of my boot. Anytime you wear the sole out of a boot, it's time to leave there. That Saturday the boss asked my daddy, "Henry, where's Honey at?" My daddy told him, "Well, Honey's a young man. Honey's gone now and I don't know where he is." I left; I cut out.

Joe changed my life and I was glad of it. I didn't want to be in that field from sun to sun, can to can't, can see to can't see. I was going to make it with the guitar. I could make more money playing than picking cotton.

I got in a gambling game with a iceman, a boy going through the country selling ice for a dime a block. He was a white boy. We started to gamble and I beat him out of about eight dollars, all the money he had. He said, "Nigger, you got a black cat bone." I didn't have no black cat bone, I was just throwing the dice so good! So pretty and so smooth. I took that money and hitchhiked to Greenville and went on Washington Street and bought me a brand new guitar, a little Stella. That was a hell of a guitar—it played good.

I played around Greenwood at the different houses, on the streets. Greenwood was divided, white and black. Tommy McClennan and me played on both sides of town. We used to serenade in the white neighborhood. We'd walk down the street amongst all those old houses, strumming our guitars, and we'd see them curtains fly back and they'd chuck nickels and dimes out into the street for us. We'd play "Tight Like That," little jump-up songs for them. Then we'd go back across the river where we come from, raise hell and drink, holler our asses off all night long, singing the "Cotton Patch Blues" in them shotgun houses in our part of town.

Tommy could raise hell. He was a funny guy, always had folks laughing, but he would get drunk and raise hell. One night there in Greenwood he tore up this guy, Buzz. They got to arguing over a skin game and Tommy hid behind a house, and when Buzz come along Tommy took a bar to him and messed that man up! Tommy hit him and run. Little Tommy, he'd say, "If I hit you, I'm goin'. If I miss you, I'm gone!" He knew he couldn't whup you so he was gone either way! "I'm not goin' to stand there and let him fight me back!" I jumped on Tommy one night myself and hit him in the nose. Tommy had been messing with me and I went wham! and Tommy was bleeding all over. The next day I went to their house and Tommy had got over it but Ophelia asked me, "What you want to hit Tommy for, Honey?"

Tommy and me had a good time. We'd run the streets with my girlfriend, Baby Peaches. She was a little older than I was and she was a rough old gal. She was light-skinned, had kind of a big mouth, a big ass. She lived with her mama, her and her sister Sweet Roll. Me and her and Tommy would drink that white whiskey and sing "Rocks in My Pillow" up and down Johnson Street.

> I got holes in my pocket, baby
>> Got patches all over my pants.
> I'm behind on the house rent
>> My landlord wants his money in advance.
> I got rocks in my pillow, baby.
>> I can't rest easy no more.

That was some tough times then. All we could do was play the blues and drink white whiskey. There wasn't no money. We felt good off of that, though.

In the South they had that vagrancy law, that hog law. I got pulled for that a number of times. That means better have a job or don't be seen on the streets. The police pick you up in the street during the day when everybody's working. "What you doing walkin' around here? Get in the car!" They carry you in to jail and they give you four or five days, and that time was spent out in the fields, working the cotton. "Don't you know so-and-so out there, his cotton growed up with grass, and he can't get nobody to workin'? You could be out there workin'!" But he didn't want to give nobody but a dollar a day and nobody wanted to work all day in the hot sun for a dollar. The way to get by all that, stay in the house all day long. I was like a groundhog. Come six o'clock, I'd take a bath, come out like I been in the field. They don't know whether you been in the field or not then. That's the way I done.

When I was young and just running around and living in Green-wood, all the police knew me because it was a small town then. Chief White and Captain Hayden, I knew all the police around there. And if they come some Monday morning and ask me, "Honey, what you do-ing?" "Nothin', sir." "Come on boy, get in the car. My wife wants you to cut the yard out there for me." I'd cut the yard, trim the hedges. She'd give me a dollar, sometimes a dollar and a half, and when she cook dinner, she give me my dinner, steak or chicken, something I wasn't used to getting. And I go back where I'm staying at. If I ever get arrested I call one of them, they be the first somebodies I call. "Turn him loose. That's Honey, that's Chief White's nigger." I was kind of slick. Always, if the whites would ask me to do something, if I know it wasn't for long, I'd go out there and do it. If I get into something they'll help me get out of it. You got to have somebody to speak for you at that time.

On the plantations, the owner was law and he would speak for the people on his plantation if they got in trouble. On every plantation there's somebody people was kind of afraid of; "That's so-and-so. That's the bad nigger here." Every plantation had somebody who built their little rep up, shot one or two guys and everyone scared of him. But if he was a good worker, if he'd get out there and work hard, the man would take care of him. "That's my hardworking nigger." If you was a good worker, you do what you want to do. All the boss wants is you be out there Monday morning with the sun. If you get into something, them police carry you to jail, there come the white man saying, "Turn my nigger loose!" If them police come to the white man's door looking for that bad nigger, the white man come out with his big cigar, jaw sticking out, and say, "What you want?" The boss man would always say, "I'll tend to this. My nigger, he ain't going nowhere but to chop that cotton out in the field in the morning. You talk to me; don't bother my niggers."

White folks run it down there. The boss always said, "When a nigger dies, hire a nigger. If a mule dies, buy a nigger." That's right! On Saturday nights at them country dances, making white whiskey, guitar playing, all them women dancing and drinking all night, cutting and shooting each other sometimes, the man tells the niggers, "You stay out of the ground, I'll keep you out of jail."

If you killed a black, generally wouldn't nothing much happen to you. I knew a boy, Nathan, who killed his stepfather. Nathan's mother and her husband had got to arguing and he saw this man fighting his mama and he went and got his shotgun and killed him. But he didn't have to go to the penitentiary. He was driving his boss's car around Greenwood the next day. The white man could get you out of any kind of trouble except if you're bootlegging whiskey. That's a felony—if they catch you with that he can't help you then.

My brother Mack, when he got a little older he drove a tractor for Mr. Johnson in Shaw. One Saturday evening him and his friends was driving on the highway and had two gallons of corn whiskey in the car. The police arrested them and carried them all to jail. Locked them up in a calaboose. Sunday morning, Mr. Johnson come to jail and got Mack. He told the sheriff, "I come to get my nigger." He said, "I'm not goin' to drive that tractor tomorrow. He got to drive it! Turn him loose!" "There's two or three more with him." "Turn them all loose!" Them farmers got all them police in there by voting for them. They tell them that, too. "I voted you in there, I can vote you out!" "All right." Mack and them had no trial, no court, nothing like that. Just, "Go on home, boy. Get in that car and go home." And the next morning Mack was back on the tractor, tearing that field up.

BUREAU OF IDENTIFICATION
POLICE DEPARTMENT — DETECTIVE DIVISION
MEMPHIS, TENNESSEE

COLOR__b Black_____ No.38377

NAME DAVID EDWARDS

ALIAS "Honey"

DATE OF ARREST Sept. 11, 1946

DATE HANDLED Sept. 12, 1946

ALIAS

CHARGE Inv.(Vagrancy & Loitering) VAGRANCY-LOITERING.

RESIDENCE 905 Arkansas

HEIGHT 5'8" AGE 31 WEIGHT 179 EYE Dk. Mar. Br.

COMPLEXION V. Dk. Br. BUILD Medium OCCUPATION Unemployed

HAIR 6-28-1915 MARRIED No TEETH 2 Up. Front open Face 1 All Gold

BORN Shaw, Miss. OFFICER White & Forrest.

ARRESTED WITH Jesse Spats, No. 38378

MARKS, SCARS, MOLES, ETC.

I:- Small blot scar Forearm Front at Elbow. II:- Two inch cut scar Forearm Outer midway. III:- Small cut scar at Outer Corner of R. Eye. Small cut scar at Inner corner of R. Eye. Operational cut scar at Inner Corner of L. Eye. Three inch cut scar bridge of nose extending to L. Wing of nose. Three inch cut scar Forehead to L. of M. Line at Hair Line.

DISPOSITION

9-12-46, fined $50.00 & $1.00 costs for Vagrancy; fined $25.00 & $1.00 costs for Loitering.

CRIMINAL HISTORY

F.P. CLASS (23) 17 U ECO 16
4 W OOI 15

F.P. REF.

**Copy of Honeyboy's arrest record from 1946, when he was
charged with and jailed for vagrancy.**

They treated us like we was property. Come all through slavery time and they still wanted us to be slaves. If them farmers couldn't get nobody to chop their cotton they'd have the police enforce that vagrancy law and get you to work a few days. They'd find a reason to pick you up and carry you out in the field. When you're through working they give you what they want to give you and say, "Go on home, boy. I'm goin' to turn you loose. If you don't catch them trucks to go out in the fields tomorrow mornin' we're goin' to lock you up again." In '32 they picked me up and had me working on the levee during that high water, toting cement bags and piling them up to keep the river from overflowing the town.

And it was always "boy," they always call you "boy." Up to about thirty, thirty-five years of age, black men in the South are called boy. When you get older, they call you uncle. They don't want to call you by your name! I had a white boy for a friend when I was a child, D.B.; we come up together. When we got to be about fourteen, his papa told me, "Well, D.B. gettin' to be a young man now. It's time you put a handle to his name. You call him Mister D.B." And here I used to go in his kitchen and eat!

And when the black folks started voting down there, the boss man would come around in his pickup truck. "Honey?" "Yes, sir?" "You votin' tomorrow?" "Yes, sir." "I want you to vote Democrat, you hear?" And you better not go in there and vote the wrong way!

But not all the white folks was bad; on both sides was some good and some bad people. I'd play at white parties and they always treated me nice. There was some good white folks, some Christian white folks.

Leaving my papa's home and playing that guitar, I thought I was a man. I was fooling with them girls and drinking, getting into gambling games. I made a couple of girlfriends in Greenwood: Baby Peaches, Virgil Mae, Cleo. Oh, them Greenwood gals with dust on their toes! I stayed with Cleo at a little place by the train depot. I used to steal coal from the railroad yard to heat our apartment with. I stayed with Virgil Mae, too. She was working, cooking for some white folks. She'd come home bringing all the food the white folks left from dinner. I'd lay up in her house all day and then she'd come with those steaks, pork chops, sweet potatoes, good muffin cornbread, they always had good food. I'd eat for free—that's the way I made it. Nothing out there for me in that hot sun! We'd go out walking at night, promenade, go to the picture show on Johnson Street for a dime if I wasn't playing.

I liked a girl out in Fort Loring, too, Anna Mae. One night I went with Anna Mae to listen to the preacher at the little church out there. The preacher was there from Greenwood; the people out in the country hired him to come out and holler at their church. They paid him with chickens, some of them would give him cured ham. He was hollering and preaching and going on about "Jesus say so," and I was in there thinking about how to get that gal out of there. I was ready to go. I went outside and around by the window and started crowing like a rooster to let that preacher know it was time to get out of there! That's true! Had to crow like a rooster to get him to leave!

I was going with another woman called Bigfoot Clara and one night, Bigfoot Clara caught me with Virgil Mae. She was drunk and so was I. Somehow she got straddled on me right there on Fulton Street. She pulled out a knife and drawed it back and said, "If you wasn't a young, crazy son of a bitch, I'd kill you! But I ain't goin' to kill you." I'm not lying! She could've killed me, too.

With what I learned from Joe, I started going to the small towns all around Greenwood and playing the streets by myself, towns like Ruleville and Drew. People start to coming out of the country on Saturdays about one o'clock, come to town and get drunk. I'd be there playing my guitar by the train stations. I'd be a little scared because I didn't really know how to handle the public. But I got so I could talk to them and ask them what they'd like me to play. I had a lot of fun.

And I'd play for them little old parties on Saturday nights, those country dances. Some guy out in the country have his house, get four or five gallons of corn whiskey, catch some fishes in the mudholes and wash them with that pumpwater, kill his own chickens and make fish and chicken sandwiches. He'd have a party and call in some musician to play. There wasn't no electricity out in the country then, and it'd be so dark at night. When they have a party, they would take Coca-Cola bottles, put kerosene in them, put a wick in them, and hang them up in the trees. Have two or three lights hanging on the porch. You'd find that house by the lights shining in the trees—you could see them from far away. You get about a quarter mile from that house and you hear the piano and guitar thumping; you start to running then! Oh, we enjoyed ourselves out in the country. We'd start to playing around nine or ten o'clock at night and when the sun rise at five o'clock, we're still stomping. Women laying across the tables, drunk. We played all night long.

I always circled around Greenwood at that time; that was my home base. I'd go to them little Delta towns and sometimes up into the hills. Greenwood was just close to the border of the hill country, east of there and you come out of the Delta. It was a rough kind of country. Some of them towns were like little western towns still, everybody carrying guns, riding horses. The first town you hit in the hills out of Greenwood was Carrollton. It had a courthouse made out of logs, with a little place next to it to hook up horses. That was something to see. I was lucky to see all that old stuff, and I liked it too.

My sister Hermalie married in 1934. She wasn't but sixteen years old. My sister got out quick after my mama died because she didn't want no stepmother. They married on the plantation back then, would have the preacher to come to the plantation. Get all dressed up in little suits, have the rings, just marry like you marry in a church except in the house. Give the preacher two dollars and now you man and wife.

And then have a party. Eat baked chickens with dressing, fruit, cake. They dance, have whiskey and beer and dance. They give them some kind of presents sometimes but it wasn't much, what they could give back in them days.

A lot of times the girls didn't stay with the husband that night. They had to stay at home, talk to the mother, and the mother would tell her what to do. How to carry herself and her womanhood, how to treat her husband, tell her all about the life that she went through. And so, he didn't get it that first night. He had to go home, leave that and go somewhere and look for it that second night!

So Hermalie married and moved to Ruleville. My papa and Miss Virginia and Altie and Mack moved out to Itta Bena, to the Lake Henry Plantation. And I got hooked up with a traveling medicine show. I played all the fall of '34 for this show. I was hanging around Greenwood with a boy called John Henry Simpson. He was playing harp and I was playing guitar on the streets. This Dr. Mahala saw us and asked us to play for his act. Dr. Mahala come out of Missouri. He had come to Greenwood in a little old car with a trailer. He was a stout, tall white guy, crippled in one leg. He drove all around to different towns to put on a show and sell liniment, salve, and all sort of other jive stuff. He'd rub folks' faces with that salve, tell them, "You goin' to be alright after while." Those people would duck their heads and say, "Yeah, I feel better." They didn't feel no better; they imagined that. Voodoo stuff! Cheating people out of their money!

Eddie's juke joint in Helena, Arkansas, 1994.

We'd go to them little country towns and he'd talk to the sheriff or whoever owned the city to get permission to perform. He'd go and notify people ahead of time of the show, put out little handbills all out through the country. We'd set up and play on flatcars on the railroad tracks. We'd set up there on the platforms and play different things, tell jokes and lies. Me and John Henry would play them old songs. I'd play a few Lemon Jefferson songs like "Blues come to Texas lopin' like a mule, brown-skinned woman hard to fool." I used to play that pretty good. "Lay me down a pallet on the floor, make it down by your door." I used to play all that old stuff like that. We picked up two girls from Belzoni who danced on the stage. We had a pretty good setup. All the people would come out from the country to hear us play, and Dr. Mahala would sell little boxes of candy to the crowd for ten cents a box. And in that box of candy, there'd be a number. If you get a lucky number then you'd win a blanket. Nobody ever once got that lucky number, though! He sold his tonic for twenty-five cents a bottle. Sometimes he'd make around twenty-five dollars a night in them little towns and he'd give us a dollar a night to play.

I stayed with Dr. Mahala all the fall and at the end of the year, a little before Christmas, I come back to Papa. That was November, the last of '34, when I left that medicine show and come back to Greenwood. It was a little before Christmas and everything was closed; the streets was quiet. I caught the Doodlebug, the little train out of Greenwood, to Itta Bena and come to where my father was staying in Lake Henry. I thought I'd lay up and rest, cool out for a month or so, help him a little bit, meet some of my country friends.

And I was walking down the road to my father's house and I looked up and saw my father come a'walking. I could tell by the way he was walking that something had happened. He saw me coming with my guitar hanging down my back and come up to meet me in the road. When he met me, he fell upon my shoulder and went to crying. And he said, "Honey, Son killed Blanche. Blanche got killed." My older sister was dead, killed by her husband. That was my daddy's oldest child, by his first wife. He was crazy about Blanche, that was his heart. We stood in that road together and cried.

My sister was a hard worker. She was cooking for Chief White, the chief of police in Greenwood. She kept a nice apartment. Son only worked when he wanted to. And he was going with another woman. Blanche had got over to it, had heard about it. A man who lived in their building, Mr. Willie, he told me he heard them when they started to arguing about it. Blanche told Son, "Son, get on up and go. I don't want you no more. Go on where your woman's at. I don't want you no more." They fought all night and then they went to bed and kept on fighting in the bed.

Son kept a little shotgun behind the bed all the time. They kept fighting and Blanche got up and intended to run out the door. Son jumped up and grabbed the shotgun. He shot her right there and broke her neck, little Blanche, lodged up against the screen door. Mr. Willie come out and told my father. My daddy went to Greenwood and got Blanche and buried her. Son got fifteen years in Parchman Penitentiary for killing Blanche. Then he died the year after he come out. You can't never tell what a person will do. Times was bad back then.

I stayed with my father the rest of that year and then left for Memphis. After my sister got killed I didn't have no more desire to call Greenwood home.

Chapter Six

The world don't owe
me nothing!

Right after New Year's in '35, I come to Memphis, thinking I could make more money up there. I was only nineteen years old, just a skinny, young, raggedy boy. Memphis was a happening place for musicians back then, that was the headquarters for musicians. People out of Mississippi, on a Saturday night they'd drive to Memphis. People over in West Memphis, Arkansas, they'd drive to Memphis. People way up in Cumberland and Ripley, Tennessee, they'd drive to Memphis. And they come right to Beale Street Park, that's where all the music was playing.

All the old guys was in Memphis at the time: Jack Kelly, Raymond Payne, Frank Stokes and his son Little Frank Stokes. Big-Eyed Willie B., he played harp and guitar. Later, Big-Eyed Willie and me had the same woman, Arla Mae. I took her from him. Floyd Jones was there, Will Shade, a little old bright woman played the violin called Lilly. Ukelele Kid and his brother out of Jackson, they was pretty popular around there. They come into Memphis red-hot! Blind Roosevelt Graves, he stayed drunk all the time. And had three blind kids with him.

Memphis Minnie would be in and out of there, people called her Kid Douglas. She come from Walls, Mississippi, and she was playing around the park, at the different little barrelhouses. That woman was a good guitar player and good-looking, too. She was pretty rough sometimes, always wanting to fight and carry on. "Bumble Bee" was her best number back then; she played that on her National guitar. Here she was in Memphis and just a little while before I was a boy standing in the streets in Greenwood, listening at a boy play that "Bumble Bee Blues." When I first heard that song I said to myself, "I'm goin' to play that thing one of these days."

Sleepy John Estes was out in Ripley but he come into Memphis all the time, and always was drunk. He could see a little bit; he wasn't plumb blind. He was walking with a stick. Him and Yank Rachell were both from Ripley—that's about thirty-five miles out of Memphis. It's big, flat country like the Mississippi Delta, where they pick a lot of cotton and corn. John Estes and Yank and Allen Shaw, all them used to come in and play. Tango, Allen's son, played, too. And there was a boy named Moody; he was a big, chunky dark boy, used to play harp with Joe Williams. We all called him Bit. Bit Moody, he was a good harp player, too.

Little old Buddy Doyle, he was out there. He was drunk all the time, a old red-eyed drunk with two or three gold teeth. He was a midget. His legs was so short that when he sat on the bench to play the guitar he couldn't pat his feet. He had to just bump against the seat, his feet would be that far off the ground. He'd get to playing the blues and just bump, bump, bump. His wife, Hedda, was six feet tall. She used to play with him a little. She was a good guitar player in the key of G. There was just a gang of people playing in Memphis then.

And all of them played in Beale Street Park. That was the place where all the musicians would play because it was sitting in the middle and everybody coming down Beale Street and Third used to come right by the park. When they'd hear that music they'd come right in the park and start throwing that money at the musicians. Then next they'd go right over to the drugstore on the corner of Third Street to get some whiskey.

I knew a lot of them musicians. Up until the forties they all hung around the park. And they had been playing there way before I come into Memphis. Memphis got started as a music town with W. C. Handy,

Train yard in Memphis, along the Mississippi River, 1995.

and then The Memphis Jug Band come right behind him and everybody started coming to Memphis. I was a lot younger than they but I met all of them. I was fifteen or twenty years younger but I was right behind them. Them guys had recorded and done everything. I was lucky enough to have come through then and to get to know them.

That was in '35 and things was tough. In Memphis people was working for fifteen cents an hour, ten cents an hour at the hotels, peeling potatoes. And if you was making fifteen dollars a week, that was top wages. People walking the streets then was hungry. There wasn't no relief; you'd work all day for nothing. You could get food from the Red Cross, they'd give you split beans, a little short rice. There's a "Red Cross Blues," goes "Red Cross folks say they goin' to treat everybody right. Give them a can of pork and beans and one little can of tripe. Yeah, baby, I got to go back down to that Red Cross store."

I remember one day this little sporty guy up at a hotel got himself a steak dinner. Another guy was sitting back looking at him, a old hobo, he was so hungry and watching him. The man went over to the counter to get a RC to drink and when he got back to eat his dinner this hobo was sitting down eating it. At the One Minute Café the women would come in and say, "If you buy me a sandwich, I'll turn you a trick." Them prostitutes would turn a trick for a quarter, things was so bad. Memphis was the worst town you ever seen. If you could make it in Memphis you could make it anywhere. If you come out of Memphis, you was alright.

I got hooked up with some of The Memphis Jug Band and played with them in the park. Will Shade, we called him Son Brimmer, he played guitar. He wasn't a hell of a guitar player but he was a good chord man. He smoked cigars all the time and all the time sang this song about "I'd give a thousand dollars just to have a big name." He tickled me. Jack Kelly played guitar, too. Dewey Corley played that big bass can, a big tub with a cord running through the bottom of it and a cut broom handle. Dewey come out of Arkansas. He had bags under his eyes, light brown skin, and a long nose. He could clown with that can; he could play. There wasn't too many drummers at the time, mostly musicians playing washboards and jug. Noah Lewis played jug with us, and played harmonica, too. We all drank that white whiskey together and talked and played. They recognized me and took up time with me. And I learned a whole lot playing with The Memphis Jug Band.

Dewey and Son Brimmer was some of the first part of The Memphis Jug Band. They played a lot of ragtime stuff like "Bring it on to my house, baby, ain't nobody here but me." "Nickel's a nickel, dime's a dime, I got a house full of children and nary of them mine." Stuff like that. And "Careless Love," "St. Louis Blues." I used to play a lot of stuff like that, we had to play that stuff to make a living. Even "Coming 'Round the Mountain": "I be comin' around the mountain, I bring chicken and dumplin' when you come." White folks was crazy about that stuff! It was so hard you couldn't get no jobs and the white folks had the money. We didn't always play the blues. Mostly we played a lot of that old ragtime stuff with the kazoo and tub.

That song "Bottle It Up and Go," I learned that from Dewey; that was Dewey's number. "Old lady down, sittin' on a rock, with a forty-dollar razor trying to shave that knot. Got to bottle up and go." Later, I went back down to Greenwood playing that number and Tommy McClennan learned it from me. Tommy recorded that song a few years later.

So I started playing with Son Brimmer and old Dewey. I was young and playing the blues pretty good and Dewey picked me up. I was playing guitar pretty good—Joe Williams had learned me a whole lot. And by me being new Dewey thought I could make more money for them; he saw a good thing in me. We would play for the kitty, a cigar box we called the kitty, and then Dewey would split up the money. We'd make a mess of money and divide it amongst three or four people. But every time he count out the money, he'd give you a dime and take him a quarter! Always come up messed up. Musicians would steal from each other! We'd split up the kitty and I'd get a dollar.

Dewey got me a room with him and his wife, Alma, and I'd give him money for rent. Dewey had a stepdaughter, Cenolia. She was half white and good-looking. She had long, black, curly hair. And old Dewey sicced his daughter on me and she got the rest of my money! He had that hooked up, that Dewey was slick! I was paying three dollars a week to stay at his house and Cenolia got the rest. I was working for the house! Folks used me a lot when I first come to Memphis by me being a greenhorn. Her curly hair, I fell for that.

Big Walter Horton was sometimes playing with The Memphis Jug Band then, and that's how I met him. Big Walter was young but he was playing good harp then already. Big Walter started playing harp when he was only five years old. And he was the best. He played so much harp and he was so young at the time that people would always flock around where he was playing at. The older guys would want to play with him, because they'd make some money, too. Big Walter could play more harp than anyone. And play in more keys. He could play any kind of harp in any style. And every guitar player in Memphis, Walter knew them, near about.

That's when I started playing with Big Walter Horton. Me and Big Walter, we probably grew up together in one way. I was nineteen; Walter was about sixteen. Walter was skinny and tall and had the longest fingers. Walter was always kind of funny-looking. Walter was half retarded but after he got grown he grew out of a lot of it. He had good sense, he wasn't crazy, but he was always rocking. That's where he got that name, Shakey Walter. Sometimes he would shake so bad he couldn't steady himself. I could always find him sitting on the porch at his mama's house on Gayoso Street, rocking.

Walter carried me to his home one day to meet his mama, Miss Emma. She said, "Walter, this young man, this is who you're supposed to play with. Why don't you leave them old people? You all work together and save your quarters and dimes, and I'll keep your money and give it to you as you need it." Because Son Brimmer and Dewey was taking all of Walter's money, too. So me and Walter hooked up. And them older guys like Son and Dewey and Jack Kelly, they missed us. They said, "Where's Honey and Walter?"

We'd get started around eight o'clock at night. We'd go to Hollywood and play out there, come back and wind up back on Beale. We used to go in the lobby of that Hotel Leclairs and serenade.

We got ahold of this little boy, Junior. He was only seven years old and he could dance. His mother let him go with us, and every evening we'd take him to the hotels, Hotel Leclairs, Hotel Peabody, Hotel Cordoba; we'd go from one to the other. Junior would tap-dance. Everybody liked that.

That was directly after the Depression and times was tough, but the white folks in Memphis always had plenty of money. They had them big Lincolns and Cadillacs and they had chauffeurs then. In the evening time, before five o'clock, the white folks would sit out in the hotel lobbies and we would go by and start to serenade. We'd play a piece or two, and then Junior would step out there tap-dancing. He'd be clowning, jumping and dancing, kicking up his feet. Junior could dance, turn the flip, and they liked to see him do the monkey shine out there. That would start them to laughing and to chunking that money, too. Every Wednesday in Memphis there used to be amateur nights at the Daisy Theater. We'd take Junior there, too, and he used to win prizes at the amateur. We would give him some money and carry him back to his mother. Carry him back home and hit them whiskey joints.

That's when me and Walter would walk along the riverfront, on Front Street, down amongst the whorehouses all around there. That's where the boats from the Mississippi would tie up. And that's where we made our money at. Them white farmers, we called them honkies, they would come out of Mississippi and Arkansas with hogs and cows, and they come to the stockyard in Memphis to sell them. Them farmers with four or five cows, selling them for sixty dollars a cow, that was a lot of money. And then they leave the stockyard with that money and break and run down to Front Street. And all them whores just down there waiting for them! Them honkies down South always was crazy about them black women. By the time they get back in that pickup truck to go home they ain't got a quarter! Go home and tell their wives somebody robbed them!

Me and Walter would go down where those hustling women were at, all drunk and ready to spend their money. We'd walk down the streets playing and people would call out, "Come here, play a couple of pieces. I got a quarter for you. I want to hear a little music!" We'd walk up to the house, play two or three numbers, walk down to the next place. They'd chunk them quarters at us! Them white guys all drunk and laying on the couches, turning all red and saying, "Give that boy another dollar!"

We made more money in the streets than you could make at a club. And you could eat a square meal for fifteen cents then. We'd make money there, come back and have four or five dollars to give to Miss Emma. Walter was born in Horn Lake, Mississippi, right out of Memphis. Miss Emma, she was in her forties then, she was kicking forty. Miss Emma was a nice-looking brownskin. She had a big mouth, little freckles on her face, she was kind of chunky. She was a prostitute. She worked in restaurants, cooked, hustled for her children. Snook and her other children were down where their daddy was, but Miss Emma, she kept Walter because Walter was the baby and he was like he was. After we started to playing together, Miss Emma she'd work in the daytime and we'd go to her room and sleep. One room with a little stove, make a pallet on the floor. And on the weekend me and Walter slept in Handy Park most of the time because she had company. We'd throw blankets down and lay out on that grass and sleep and the police didn't bother us. The park was full of people. Then we'd get up and go to the One Minute Café to eat breakfast, be out on the streets again. That's how we made it. Me and Walter both come up the hard way.

Walter was a great harp blower. Miss Emma told me Walter started playing harp when he was five years old. Everybody wanted to play with Walter. Floyd Jones would walk from Marianna, Arkansas, to Memphis to get Walter to play with him. In later years I'd come to Memphis and go down on Gayoso Street and say, "Where's Walter at?" Miss Emma would say, "He gone off with Floyd somewhere." And if I didn't get him next, sometimes Johnny Shines picked him up. We all wanted to play with Big Walter. He was the best. He could play four or five different positions with just one harp. He didn't need a whole set of them. He'd put one in his pocket and say, "That's all I need to carry with me," and we'd hit the road. I stayed friends with Big Walter all through the years. We traveled together and played together all over the South and in Chicago, right up until he died.

There was a guy who used to run a shoe shine parlor on Beale next to the Daisy Theater, and after we finished serenading we'd come in nigh on twelve or one o'clock at night and we'd give him fifteen cents to keep our things so we wouldn't have to worry about them. He'd lock up our instruments and then we'd get out on the streets walking and drinking and having fun, go to the restaurant and eat, and go out and get us a woman.

I met a girl, Arla Mae, she lived on the north side of Memphis. She was a cook for white people. She was good-looking, yellow. I was playing at a little old club on Gayoso and she come in one evening. We drank beer, got high, and I made friends with her. She lived in a chauffeur's apartment in a great big house. She worked every day till about three o'clock and then she was off work till seven in the morning. And I'd be laying up there waiting for her in that nice old bed with the inner spring mattress! She wasn't my only girl there either. I was going at the same time with two Arla Maes. Black Arla Mae, she worked at the same restaurant where Walter's mama worked at. She was a cook. I'd stay up north with bright Arla Mae for a while, then come to the restaurant to see black Arla Mae. I kept them apart. Black Arla Mae, she was Big-Eyed Willie's woman but she would come to the park and bring me blackeyed peas and ham hocks. "Where you been? You hungry?" I was young and good-looking. I had all the fun I want to have!

A Memphis juke joint, 1993.

Another girl I knew in Memphis I met right on Beale Street there. I walked down a alley one day and there was a girl back there, sitting on the porch of a building. Her name was Arlene. She had just gotten out of the hospital, had an operation. I used to go back there many times and talk to her. I was awful nosy about talking to people. She was real nice, about my age, and I liked her. She was real good-looking, a light-skin, with a small waist, and kind of heavy. I'd make a little money on the street and I'd go back there and carry her a Coke, cigarettes, food, whatever she wanted. After three or four months she started to get well and I started staying back there with her. Her house was right behind the Midway, at Fourth and Beale, the club where Memphis Slim played at.

Memphis Slim, he was at the Midway and Roosevelt Sykes was playing at Chicago House. Those two places was only four or five doors apart. You could go out of one and go in the other. Those guys was only getting a dollar and a half a night. A dollar a night, a slat a night, back in those days! Sykes had patches on his pants! He'd wear a clean shirt and have his pants creased in front but when he stood up you could see it was all patches behind. We'd go see them; we'd put our guitars up and go to the piano dives, go to where they'd be thumping the piano all night! Oh, we had a good time down there!

They was both good piano players. Sykes was a better piano player than Slim was. Memphis Slim had a good name, and made a few little numbers pretty good, but Roosevelt Sykes was a hell of a piano player. That man was hell. He was the best. Roosevelt Sykes had a uptempo country blues style. He used to do a lot of flying chords—he could play. He'd play "The 44 Blues" and "West Helena Blues." And when he got done with one of them hard, cramped plays, he'd grunt coming out of it, "Humph!" We'd come in late at night, come off the streets around midnight and them dives stayed open till three in the morning. Women would be sitting all on top of the damn piano, drinking white whiskey. We'd just get drunk then, try to get us a woman to carry home with us. It was plenty of fun. Musicians have plenty of fun. My God, the world don't owe me nothing!

Chapter Seven

I was just up and down the road.

I stayed in Memphis till the summer of that year, 1935. Then one night in the middle of the night I woke up, and my mind told me to go back to Greenwood. I had been laying in the bed and I got a chill and then a hot feeling come over me. I was sick as a dog. Sweat jumped off my face as big as the end of my finger. The first thing that fell on my mind was my father and I said, "Somethin's wrong. Somethin' happened." I got right up and caught the first train that morning and went to Greenwood.

Virgil Mae, the girl that I had been shacking with, was standing at the station when I got off the freight train from Memphis. Just like she knew I was coming. She said, "Honey, did you get that letter? I didn't know where you was stayin' but I wrote a letter to Memphis. And didn't nobody know where you was. They couldn't find you. Your father died." I said, "I knew somethin' happened." You can feel these things, that somethin's not right somewhere in your family. She said, "I tried to reach you. I tried everything. I couldn't get you."

A friend of mine, Bo Booze, was there and we walked out to the country where my kin was. My father and my stepmother were out on

Claude Redick's Plantation, out west of Greenwood. I walked out there that day and Gin, my stepmother, she started to crying when she saw me and she said, "Honey, Mr. Henry died last week." She had been washing and there was my father's pants hanging on the line. She said, "We buried Mr. Henry Thursday." My baby sister Altie and my brother Mack had been living out there with my father and stepmother, so Hermalie come and carried them back to Ruleville. Hermalie and her husband raised them.

My papa suffered so hard. He had prostate gland trouble. You get that now, it ain't nothing. They take your water, push you in the bed, put IVs on your arm. But they didn't know that stuff then. The doctor that knowed that, we couldn't get him. Rich white folks had him because they had the money to pay him. The doctor we had was the same doctor that went to the mule. That's the truth! When you're a sharecropper, working for them white folks, you have a doctor come to you about twice. If the doctor talk to your boss and say, "Well, he ain't goin' to get well," then the boss quit spending money on you.

My stepmother had gone out and caught a whole lot of fish and had big old pans of fish frying to feed everybody. I stayed out there a couple days with them, but I couldn't stay out there too much after I lost my father, for thinking about him. Me and Bo left and after that, after my father died, I was just up and down the road. Hermalie had Mack and Altie and I knew they was alright, so I left there. I kept in touch with where my sister and them was but I couldn't stay still. But I never will forget that time. I knew something had happened, just like somebody telling me, near about.

I just run astray after that. I was only twenty years old. I run all through the country, hoboing and playing my guitar. I rode the freight trains. At that time they had a lot of coal-burner trains. I'd find a destination where the freight trains would take on water and coal and stay there till some train come through. I'd go from Greenville on the Southern over to Columbus, Mississippi; that's the Alabama border. Then I'd cut out of Columbus and go into Tupelo and from Tupelo into Decatur, Alabama. I rode in through Birmingham, Alabama, and I rode from Jackson, Mississippi, to New Orleans. I used to go to all them places.

**Honeyboy packing his belongings in a Chattanooga,
Tennessee, hotel room, 1993.**

I got up to Cairo, Illinois; I made the Mason-Dixon line. There was a hobo jungle up near there, in Effingham where one track goes off to St. Louis and another to Chicago. All the hoboes would come in there from different places: Tennessee, Arkansas, Missouri. There was a big tent there and pots and skillets hanging on the walls. When the hoboes would come in they'd cook, wash up, and leave them for the next crew that come in. There was a big sign there, it said, "Clean up." We'd get us some big old logs, build a fire, go to town and hustle up some pig's feet, throw them on the fire. We'd wash our clothes out in the mudhole with bar soap and hang them out to dry in the sunshine. Or lay on them so they got pressed while they dried. You had to stay clean. If you're too dirty, people won't talk to you.

All the hoboes would tip each other off: "Watch yourself in such and such a town. They'll pull you off there." They'd pull you off and make you work, give you thirty days to punish you for riding that train. There was a big pea farm in Cairo and they'd pull you off the freight and put you to work on the pea farm. The North wasn't much different from the South back then, they'd lock you up and make you work. They'd keep you till the crop was all in, then let you loose.

Memphis had a big freightyard, too, and all the hoboes would sit there in the shade of the trees and watch the engines hook up different cars. When the train got ready to go, we'd see the brakeman step on and hear them pull the whistle twice, "whoo, whoo," and we'd get ready to jump.

There wasn't too many cars or trucks going a long ways then. You had to ride a freight train to get around. And I didn't have enough money to ride the cushions! I'd only have two or three dollars, so I'd ride the freight train and when I'd get there, I'd have something to buy me a sandwich till I can hustle. Sometimes I'd carry a blanket, a roll, sometimes just a newspaper to lay down on so I don't get dirty. There was a lot of baker shops back then, and you could wash pans for them and they pay you in day-old bread and sweet rolls. And the stores would give you meat they couldn't keep no more. I was young; I didn't have sense enough to be worried about how I was going to eat.

I learned how to hobo. I traveled like that for years. In the winter, when it was cold, I'd go to Louisiana, run around Monroe and Tallulah, Rayville, all through there. In the summer I'd come on back to the Mississippi Delta, go to Memphis, St. Louis. I know every train and every stop between Chicago and New Orleans.

There was a gang of men and boys hoboing then, white and black. Times was tough and nobody could find a job. So many people was on the trains, the cops quit bothering them. I saw a white man on the train one time who had his whole family with him. He had a mattress in the carbox! He put the mattress down and his children lay right down there. Somebody asked him, "Where you goin'?" and he said, "I don't know, I'm going some damn place where I can get some bread to eat."

I'd always look for a carbox so I could lay down and sleep. You got to ride a couple hundred miles, you'd get an empty carbox and spike the

**Illinois Central train pulling out of Greenwood,
Mississippi, 1993.**

door. Take a railroad spike and jam the door so nobody could slide it open, just leave a little space so you could look out good. That way, nobody on the outside can push the door open, not unless you pull the spike out. So when the dicks come and holler "Come out!" I'd say, "You come on in here!" He could holler all he want, he ain't going to get to me. When that train is through taking in water, we going to go then. I ain't got to worry about that dick, he can't get in there! "Come out of there!" "All right!" And the train starts to blowing "whoo" and I leave him right there. Sometimes those agents would ride the trains, and if they catch you they put you off. I'd get off and lay out in the bushes and catch the next train that came by. And dodge the next agent.

One time I caught a freight and was riding on top of the car and the train went through a long tunnel, about six miles long. I saw that tunnel coming and laid down on my face and held my guitar at my side, and I thought before I got out of that viaduct I'd suffocate. That was a coal-burning train, and that smoke like to have strangled me to death. I was smutty with coal dust when we came out of that! Sometimes I'd ride the rods, too, underneath the train, because the cops would never look down there for you. The rods are kind of rough, though. Sometime the train be running so fast it would throw rocks up and they'd hit you. It was dangerous riding them freight trains. I know a couple of guys got killed trying to catch freights, being careless.

I'd ride the blind, the mail car, and I used to ride the reefer, too. What you call the reefer, before they got so many refrigerator cars on trains, they'd have a hole in the back end of one of them carboxes where they put two or three hundred pounds of ice to keep the cargo cold. Like the banana cars up from New Orleans, before they load them with the bananas they'd put two or three hundred pounds of ice in there to keep that whole carbox cool. So when you catch one of them reefers empty, you jump down in where they put that ice at and pull the handle down and close the door. Now you got the handle inside and ain't going to let nobody in there! Oh, I used to ride them freight trains. If I had in quarters the times I rode freight trains, I'd be rich.

And in all them little towns I went to there was always people wanted to hear music. I'd sit by the train depot and people would gather around and throw me nickels. Or I'd play in the country stores, the stores would sell root beer and cold drinks to the people, and there was always a place in the back to play. Sometimes I'd serenade in the white neigh-borhoods, but the whites didn't flock in the streets too much. They'd stop now and then and listen to a hillbilly song. Mostly I'd get where the black folks was gathered and holler them blues. I'd be at all them little train depots, and on every plantation somebody had a juke, selling a little whiskey and having a dance on Saturday night.

I'd play blues; I'd play shuffle; I'd play them old songs like "Corinna," "Tight Like That." I'd play anything anybody asked for because some-times you had to get on both sides of the street, play whatever the people want to hear. Because they'll give you that money! I'd hear one of them old records on the Seabird, listen to it about twice, all them old differ-

Train yard in Tupelo, Mississippi, 1993.

ent blues Satchmo and them would play, then if people say, "Play that and I'll give you a quarter," I could play it, I could make that quarter.

All them little country towns I went to was so crowded, so full. I knew a time in those Delta towns on a Saturday you couldn't walk up the streets. People had to come sideways to get through the crowd, there be so many people in town. Now you be glad to see a dog cross the street. Every plantation was full of people, one would have forty families, another thirty-five. All them people, they would get in them old cars and wagons, leave at seven in the morning to come to town, carrying pecans and eggs and things to sell.

I'd just switch around, go to all them little towns at different times, so I could make that money. I wouldn't stay in no place when it got dead and I couldn't make nothing. Sometimes I go over to Clarksdale, the next Saturday I be in Drew. I be kind of new then, when I go back to the people. Next Saturday, I go back to Shaw where I was born at. Come back to Cleveland. All through there all the time. You wouldn't go to the same place every Saturday; you go to different towns. And every one of them little countries had different people and the same people wouldn't see you all the time. Like you play here today, this Saturday, "Well, I won't come back here next Saturday, I'll probably go down to Moorhead, where the Southern cross the Dog. Then come on back up to Sunflower." Then you never got old in one town, where everybody knows you in every town. That's how I made it. I didn't stay nowhere where I got old. "I sure miss you." "Come back, man." "Where you been the last two, three weeks?" People treat you just like you was a preacher when you're playing the blues, "Come on, go home with me. My wife will fix dinner."

It would be a long time sometimes before I'd see my people. I'd visit my sisters and brother in Ruleville sometimes, or go to Shaw by my Uncle Aaron's home, or stay with my Uncle Sylvester and Auntie Irene in Coahoma.

When I started playing music and going all them different places, that opened my eyes up a little bit. I was learning how to get around, how to make it on my own. I taught myself how to do my figures and my letters then, so nobody could take advantage of me. Whenever I saw a paper or a book I'd sit down and study the letters and practice and write and copy things. I wanted to do that—I had to do that.

I started doing pretty good. I learned how to make it in the streets and after I made some money, the first thing I do would be get a little room. Rent a little room by the week and then go to a grocery store and get some cans of beans, buy some sardines, fill up a box full of groceries for two dollars and when I get hungry I go to cutting them cans! Sometimes when I was playing somebody would say, "You need a room? A place to stay? You can stay with me." Folks down south are like that. Musicans always had a place to go.

That guitar kept me rolling a whole lot. I went everywhere I wanted to go. But I wouldn't stay nowhere long. I'd be in a town, not be intending to go anywhere, take up my guitar and start to playing, and think, "Well, it's time to move on out of here." I'd start to thinking about somebody who's somewhere else and I'd get up and go. I'd have my harp and my guitar and hit the road. I'd play for a while in one little town and jump and go to another place. I might meet a girl in one place and go back and see her once or twice. After I see her I get her off my mind and go on somewhere else.

Chapter Eight

I had three ways of making it.

I was hustling all through the country. I been a hustler ever since I was
big enough. I learned by watching people in the country play cards
and throw dice. I got so I played with them dice so much they'd do
whatever I wanted. I could roll! I hardly ever got beat. When I was
fourteen years old I'd be out in the cotton house shooting dice with the
boys from town and winning. We didn't have nothing to gamble with so
we'd gamble for our caps and things. One day a boy would be wearing
my cap and belt and the next day I win them back and I'm wearing
them. And when I got older, that's how I got by. My guitar was my meal
ticket but how I got by good was gambling. I had three ways of making
it: the women and my guitar and the dice.

When I first left Big Joe and started traveling around to them different towns by myself, I was riding a freight train with a one-eyed nigger
who got me in a game and beat me out of all my money. He was a good
hustler. We got off the train near Batesville, Mississippi. There was a big
lock and dam job going on there. They had houses for the workers and
a barrelhouse there. I got to that barrelhouse and I was broke. I was sure
enough blue then! I played the blues that night and made about five or

six dollars. A girl come and sat on my knee and fed me whiskey. She said, "Stay with me tonight."

This fellow, this one-eyed nigger, he was there and said to me, "Come here." He said, "You little old nigger, I like you. You're smart. I'm goin' to learn you somethin'." He said, "Tell this woman you're my brother so I have somewhere to stay tonight, too." So I said to her, "This my half brother here." And she said, "Well, he can stay, too." I went and laid down with her that night and when we got up, she fixed breakfast. And that's when this one-eyed nigger taught me how to cheat.

I said to him, "I'm in bad luck. I can't make no money." He told me, "You're a good square gambler. You ain't bad. You're a fool, that's all." He got out a big sack of dice and showed me how he had weighted them so when they fall, they're going to fall on a certain spot every time. You always know what's going to come up. He taught me how to play with straight dice till you get where you have a good bet up, then how to switch them dice and get satisfied.

A lot of times you couldn't get a job, and the people that had a job, they'd die before they'd turn that job loose. I had to make my money off the public. Everywhere down south, I looked for where the money was. Sometimes I'd look for a levee job going on. A levee camp is where the river breaks and floods the land and men put up a barrier to stop the water from coming over into the flat countries. The men live there while they're working on the levee. I'd hear from other musicians, "Well, so-and-so pays off next Saturday at Rosedale," and I'd go to Rosedale when they paid off—I'd be right there. When them niggers get paid there's prostitutes coming out and whiskey flowing, and I'm right there playing my harp and guitar. I'm going to make enough money to stake a gamble with.

When I get me a good gambling stake, I put my guitar back in the corner, jump right down to a game, make me some money and I'm gone. Then I can drink some whiskey, pick me a girl, and have some fun. Next Saturday, these people that I know down by Duncan, I go down there and meet that payday. Probably the next one be down by Rolling Fork at the levee down there. I knew the paydays, when they paid off up and down them levees, up and down the Mississippi clean to

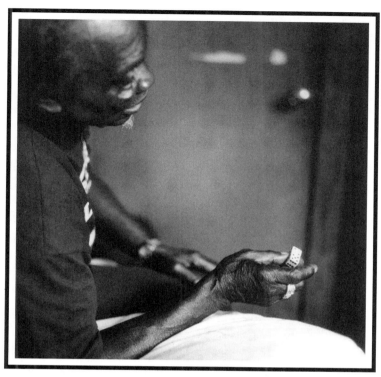

**Honeyboy demonstrating dice tricks in a Clarksdale,
Mississippi, hotel room, 1992.**

Vicksburg. I didn't work but I knew when they got paid off. I kept that in my book.

All I'd need was one or two hot dollars to get in a game. Those men worked all the week, getting that forty cents an hour. They didn't make much money. But the games would get real hot sometimes and you'd be surprised what guys would bet. I'd say, "Shoot fifty cents. Shoot the dollar," and they'd say "Shoot two!"

I was so good, I'd take a blanket and put it down, smooth it out, and take them dice and roll them down to the end of that blanket, and they were going to come out on seven. That's called even roll. I could take them and roll them at the end of my hands and pinch them, and they're going to stop wherever I want them. Five-deuce or six-ace or four-tres.

Dice was my game. I love the dice. I got so good, I could take a pair of drugstore dice, square dice, and win.

And all that's free money! Then I would get on away from there. After I won a lot of money sometimes I'd pretend I had to take a piss. I leave a twenty dollar bet on the table and say, "Oh man, I got to go to the bathroom." I leave that twenty dollars just to get away and sneak on out of there then.

Sometimes there would be a guy across from me doing the same thing. He look over at me, I look at him. We both know what the other was doing but all around us was fools! So we don't bet against each other. Every which way one bets, the other guy bet the same way. A person that's got knowledge about gambling, he's not going to get up and holler. When the game's over, he's going to say, "Man, you're good." We both keep the fool from knowing anything. The fool, he might want to kill you but he don't know just what it is you was doing! The man who knows the same thing you know, you beat him and he'll say, "You're the best."

I have been in bad places. I have been in places where I had to watch myself. When you gamble, you look for the danger spots. That guy drinking and having fun, can't see, spitting and slobbering and going on, you know that's some free money! He'll be cleaned out of that in a minute! But people do get mad. They don't know nothing about gambling too much and when you cheat one of them, they don't know what you done, but they know something's wrong. And people will kill you about that. He don't know what it is but he know it ain't right. I have gambled with one hand on my gun, then if anybody jump up, I say, "Now you sit down there. Get back and let me out." When a guy wants to start a fight or cut me, "You sit right there, man. Get back." I always had to be ready for something like that.

One time in Fulton, Mississippi, me and a friend of mine got in a crap game at the sawmill. Boxy, he was a hustler from his heart. Every one of the guys we was playing was white and we broke them clean. We made about a hundred dollars. We overheard them saying the police was coming and we left that mill and started running through the thickets. We didn't know how to get away from there! It was a woods, a thicket, about a mile from the highway. We went through those woods and fi-

Sawmill in West Helena, Arkansas, 1995.

nally come up to the highway through a swamp. We started walking down the highway and here come a taxicab, coming from Tupelo going to Fulton. We got in the middle of that road and flagged him down. He stopped. We said, "What do you charge to take us back to Tupelo?" "Fourteen dollars." We said, "Turn around!"

I didn't want to hurt nobody, do nobody harm. I always hustled smooth. Every payday on the levee or in the log camp, I'd be there. I had to study that stuff, sleep and eat it. I'd go in there and play guitar and gamble and then I take that money and drive the blues away. I don't want to play guitar now till I get drunk and want to hear the blues. That's how I made it, gambling and shooting dice. I had to win! If I could beat, I could eat. I wasn't going to work for nobody all day long for three dollars a day in the hot sun, not me. I could make that in fifteen, twenty minutes! My cousin, Man Son, he told me once I ain't done nothing in my life but rob people's money. He said, "You son of a bitch, you're my cousin and you ain't never been any damn good!" He thinks I'm lazy, but I wasn't lazy. I know what I done: I made it.

The other place I would always be at was the bootlegger's house. At that time in the South there was a lot of men out in the country with stills, making bootleg whiskey. Many of the towns was dry, wasn't no whiskey in the stores. The bootleggers made all the money then. They paid the police off so they could be free to sell the whiskey. And they had crowded houses, wide open, with gambling and music. The bootlegger would always have a guitar player at his house. I'd be playing on the street, drawing a big crowd around me and some guy would come up saying, "How long you goin' to be here? I run a whiskey house. Why don't you play for me Friday and Saturday night?" He'd pay me a couple of dollars, make me drunk, give me all I want to eat. Then I got a gig and someplace to stay.

All the people would come in and buy whiskey. The police come by and shake him down now and then, get their payoff and don't tell other police nothing about it. The only somebody that they have to really dodge, that's the Internal Revenue. Now, if the revenuers come into town, they let the city police know they coming. And the city police runs to the bootlegger and warns him, says, "You better clean up!" The revenuers come in and they can't find nothing! Because the police been paid off, and they done come and told.

The bootlegger would buy whiskey by the gallon from the whiskey maker. The whiskey makers had stills all over out in the country. They'd take chops, that's corn ground up real thick, and put that in one of them big wooden barrels and put water in it with a little yeast and sugar. You let that sit about four or five days and it gets hot and that stuff starts working, then you put it in a still and run it off to be white whiskey, pure white, just as strong as you can get. Drink that, then you start talking trash! Sometimes they take that plumb white whiskey and give it some color. They take a bread pan full of peaches and dry them in a stove, parch them real brown. Then take a number 3 tub and pour that whiskey up in there with them peaches and that whiskey changes color so it looks just like whiskey come out of a store. Sometimes they'd take that white whiskey and add a couple of drops of gin flavor. They was slick.

I had three ways of making it.

83

Then they'd ask you, "What you want, whiskey or gin?" But it's the same thing!

My hometown, Shaw, was dry. We used to have to go over to Leflore County to get whiskey; it was dry all the way to Cleveland. They catch you with a pint of wine and put you in jail then. Once I was in the woods with my uncle's gun, hunting rabbits, and I run up on a man cooking whiskey. I just threw the gun down and sat down on a stump and got me a cup and started drinking. All at once a airplane come over. We saw it but we didn't pay it no attention, didn't have sense enough to know it was the revenuers. They flew on to Clarksdale and come back out to the woods in about a hour, right out to the spot where we was. We heard the bushes cracking and creaking but we wasn't paying no attention and then it was, "Don't y'all move!" By me being kind of young they didn't arrest me. But they carried that whiskey maker to jail and he stayed there about a year or two. He come back out and made it again—he never quit! You couldn't stop him running that whiskey. That was his big hustle!

Them bootleggers and whiskey makers in the country, they made more money than the common guy. Bootleggers always have money and new cars. You work all day for a dollar but a whiskey maker, he's doing alright. He could run off thirty-five, forty gallons of whiskey and retail it out for three or four dollars a gallon. When he got that, he got a lot of money in his pocket! And that's why all the women would flock to them bootleggers and whiskey makers. There was one bootlegger in Jonestown, Mississippi, called Son Collins. He didn't even have a chin and that man had the best-looking woman in town!

A musician couldn't make no money in dry towns because people wasn't getting drunk and feeling good too much. I would always look for a wet town; you could always run up on people to give you something there. Go to the bootlegger's house and people be there, a whole crowd, sitting around drinking and having fun. That's where the musicians would be.

In the fall of the year, all the hustlers, all the gamblers, all the piano players and guitar players, they played the Delta. That's where all the money was after the cotton harvest. In the wintertime there wasn't nothing happening and all the hustlers played the hills, like Tupelo and

West Point, Jackson, even into Alabama. We'd go to the sawmill towns all through there, play them sawmill towns because they had paydays every two weeks, just like the levee camps. There was a lot of sawmills in Mississippi back then, all over the hills because in the hills was a lot of pine trees. In the heat, in the summertime, the gum would run in the pines and you could smell it everywhere. The big upright mills was like little towns. They had big boiler tanks and big steam engines, 100, 150 men working. But there was a lot of little sawmills—we called them groundhog sawmills, just small little places out in the country, too. They wasn't big operations; it might be just a few guys working in a shed.

We knew their paydays, and when they paid we was right there. We're going to leave with some money, too! The sawmill paid off at West Point one Saturday, next Saturday would be in Tupelo, next in Kilmichael. And there was always some guy on the mill job who run a craphouse and sold whiskey. Always somebody was hustling. We'd come in and work with him, the houseman. In the summer and fall I'd play on the streets; in the winter I'd hit them levees and sawmills. Always following that money!

I met Sunnyland Slim when I was hustling through all them little towns. He was working in a levee camp over around Friars Point. Jim Powell was in charge there, a big shot white guy, wiry, tough, always had a cigar in his mouth. The workers was living and eating in big tents along the levee. Sunnyland was working for Jim Powell driving a tractor on the levee and playing the piano at the camp Friday and Saturday nights.

Sunnyland was driving the big machine, one of them big Caterpillar tractors. Sunnyland, he was a big man and he always had them big, heavy jobs. Driving that thing, he made a little more money than most people—everybody couldn't do what he was doing. He always had a good job and always played piano. Sunnyland was a musician since he was real young. So I went there, all raggedy and dirty; I was only twenty-one at the time. I met Sunnyland and he got me a little job toting water to the men, and playing on the weekend.

About seventy-five, eighty men worked that levee, driving wagons and bulldozers. I would tote that water to all of them. It was all men, but women worked in the kitchens. They had a big mess hall and they'd cook on a big stove, have great big pots of spaghetti and meatballs. They'd feed everyone at the same time. Come dinnertime all the workers would sit at them big long tables and eat.

On Friday and Saturday nights they set aside a big tent, like a revival tent, and had a wooden floor inside and a platform for the piano. They'd barbecue hogs and all that stuff, and people come from all around to drink white whiskey and have a good time. It was beautiful. They'd make a whole barrel of lemonade and drop a big block of ice down in there. Get a ice stick and bust it all up. Have that hog all mopped with that good sauce, cooking slow all day. Take a nice slice off and make sandwiches, barbecue sandwiches. Eat, drink, and gamble all night. Oh, we had a good time.

Sunnyland hustled all over the Delta, working and playing piano. He was a great piano player and the women was crazy about him. He was big and tall, nice-looking, had brown eyes, straight teeth. He could hustle and always knew where he could get some money. He used to come to Memphis a lot, too. He worked for a sheriff in New Madrid for a while, as a cook. He had that man all buttered up, knew everything that was going on in town. He cooked for the high sheriff and would drive his car and wouldn't nobody bother him then! He played all by himself all over them little towns. He played at them big country barrelhouses in Hayti and Braggadocio, and always drew a big crowd with that piano. Some of them barrelhouses would have a little microphone sitting on top of the piano and he could sing, too. He didn't need no band out in the country.

Sunnyland got his name from playing "The Sunnyland Blues." That blues was about the Sunnyland train. That train didn't have its own track; it used to run over the Frisco line, coming from some part of Tennessee, into Memphis. But he was faster than the Frisco.

Hush, hush, hush, children, I thought I heard that Sunnyland whistle blow.

Blowed early this morning like it ain't going to blow no more.
Sunnyland, Sunnyland, running over the Frisco line.

Take that picture, hang it up in a frame,

Everytime I look at it I think of that Sunnyland train.

Hush, hush, children, I thought I heard that Sunnyland

whistle blow.

The Sunnyland train would come through those small towns picking up Coca-Cola bottles and paper. Sunnyland would sing that all the time.

Later, Sunnyland run a little club on 61 Highway betwixt Hayti and Portageville, Missouri. He was working for a man that had a ferryboat that would cross the cars and passengers from Tennessee. This man had the ferry and a big cotton farm, and Sunnyland used to drive a truck for him out there. Sunnyland opened up a little piano joint in a shack and run the place for this white man. I'd go out there and play now and then. Sunnyland would run some hot gambling games. And when the games got dead, he would start playing that piano and draw the crowd back.

One time he was playing with some loaded dice. Sunnyland drilled some dice and made extra holes in them, filled them with mercury. And when he went to throw those dice, the mercury popped out! Those blank dice was laying there and the mercury was popping all over the table! The eyes popped right out of them! He said, "Honey, pick them up. Them cheap old dice I got at the drugstore ain't no good. I'll have to take them back." We scooped them up before anyone discovered the cheat! We have laughed many times together about that. We used to have a nice time. It was a long time ago. Can't call it back but it was alright.

In playing music, I slept in carboxes, I slept in empty cars on the road, sometimes I slept in nice beds, sometimes I slept in hotels. Sometimes I'd meet a woman with a nice house, a clean house, and I'd stay there, take a bath, wash out all my clothes, lay up with her for two or three weeks and then I'd get lonesome for leaving. Get myself cleaned up, rested up real good and be gone again. I wasn't going to work. And I wasn't making enough money playing music to take care of anyone else at the time. I made enough just to take care of myself. I didn't make enough money to get a woman what she want so I didn't get tied up in that. I'd just get up and go.

Sometimes I think I was too fast, running too much. I ran so fast nobody could ever catch me, but sometimes you want to get caught! There come a time when I was wanting to record, to get something out there to make a name for myself, and I missed some chances for that. I missed Lester Melrose when he come through Greenwood looking for musicians to record. He was looking for me and I was gone, out running down the road. He picked up Tommy McClennan then and Tommy recorded "Bottle It Up and Go" for him. He recorded Tommy, Robert Petway, a gang of musicians through the South. He asked, "Where's Honey at?" and Tommy told him, "Man, Honey's on the road. You can't catch up with Honey." I missed that recording boom because I was staying nowhere. But I wouldn't slow down. Running was the only way I could make that money. I didn't have a wife to work and take care of me; I didn't want that. I stayed on the road all the time and the only thing I carried with me was my guitar and harp and those dice in my pocket.

Chapter Nine

Everything sounded good to me.

When I was young in my hometown of Shaw, I used to stop by the Chinaman grocery store to listen to the Moore brothers play. Andrew Moore used to make guitars out of white oak he'd collect in the woods, and those guitars were so good, had such a beautiful tone, you wouldn't know them from factory guitars. He was a hell of a guitar player; he was the best guitar player I heard when I was real young. He was great. His brother Tom was real good, too. They played a lot of ragtime stuff. I learned the song "Big Kate Adams" from them; that's a song about a steamboat used to run from Memphis into New Orleans. They had a fellow named Spence Walker playing bass viol—he was a one-eyed guy—and Hacksaw Harney used to play with them, too. They sounded so good! I'd hear them play about that "Katie Adams blowin' just like a man, way up river and on a bank of sand" and when they'd sing about that whistle blowing, it would thrill me. They'd play on a Saturday evening and the store would sell root beer and people just crowded in there. They never recorded. Andrew Moore got killed in the early forties. He was messing around with a black woman who had a white man going with her, too. One night he was driving home from her place in his A-model Ford, and that man and his friends stopped him in the road and killed him.

Hacksaw Harney was a piano tuner and would go through the country with his guitar on his back, going to different towns tuning pianos for three dollars. And he'd play guitar for parties. He stayed over at Money, Mississippi, not far from Greenwood, and many times he'd come to town when I lived there, and me and him and Tommy would go to the whiskey house and play. Tommy got that song "Cross Cut Saw" from Hacksaw. Hacksaw could play any kind of music. He was a good chord man and would play behind us. He could run them chords. He'd always play a song about "If I catch you in my house again I'm just going to tear it down." That's a ragtime number. He used to play the saw, too, the hand saw. He'd bend it and play it with a bow.

Pinetop Perkins was from my hometown of Shaw, too. He was born in Belzoni but his family moved over to Shaw. I been knowing Pinetop Perkins since I was a boy. Pinetop knew my mama! Pinetop grew up just a half mile from my home, him and his mama—we called her Little Bit—and his stepfather, Cornelius Shepherd. Pinetop learned how to play piano from him. They lived out on the MacLemore Plantation. They had to come out of the country just like we did during that '27 flood. I remember there was a woman used to have a juke house outside of Shaw. Her name was Molly, and when Pinetop wasn't but fourteen years old he'd walk out there and barrelhouse. He sure did! And when I started traveling around I'd run up on Pinetop in different places. We played for a while together in Tutweiler, at a juke joint there. Pinetop was going with the wife of the man who run that place. All us musicians did that. Those men didn't always know it but they shared that stuff with us!

The most famous guy when I was young was Blind Lemon Jefferson. When my papa first moved over to Wildwood Plantation, Lemon Jefferson come through there. He had placards posted all around that he was going to play at a little school out by Itta Bena, play for a big dance. They was charging seventy-five cents to come in. I sure wanted to see him but I couldn't make that seventy-five cents! I used to play a few Lemon Jefferson numbers—everybody did. I sure wanted to see him. One man I did get to see, though, another musician who was the leading guy, was Charlie Patton.

I had been hearing about Charlie Patton for a long time when Hermalie married and moved to Ruleville. And that's when I run up on him. Ruleville's only about two or three miles from where Charlie lived. He stayed at a farm betwixt Cleveland and Ruleville on number 8 Highway called Dockery's Plantation. Dockery's was Charlie's nest egg for a long time; he made a lot of money there. He didn't make that money working, but he stayed in good with the boss and made it playing that guitar. Charlie was the leadingest musicianer in Mississippi at that time. I was lucky to be around at that time, to know Charlie Patton. I was only seventeen or eighteen years old.

I went to Dockery's a few times and saw him there. I wanted to see him and learn what he was doing. Charlie Patton was playing on a Silvertone guitar, and he had some pretty chords he made in Spanish and in D. He was playing "Pony Blues," "Tom Rushen," "Pea Vine." I learned how to play them "Pony Blues." People would ask for Charlie's numbers; people really liked "The Pony Blues." Everyone wanted to hear that "Pea Vine," too. That song was about a short railroad line, the Pea Vine. It run from Minter City over to Rosedale. That was for country people. Folks would stand all along the railroad tracks waiting for the train to take them to the little country towns. I remember a lot of them old numbers he played.

He had a big voice—he didn't need no mike. To hear him singing, you'd think he weighed two hundred pounds. He broke them country houses down! I used to go out there to Dockery's when that plantation didn't have no houses; they was putting up carboxes from the railroad tracks for people to live in. They had a commissary, and Charlie would play there on the store porch.

Every once in a while I'd meet him in Ruleville and see him playing in the streets. He used to come there and play on Greasy Street every Saturday evening. I'd play on Greasy Street, too. That's where all the niggers would go on Saturday evenings and eat them greasy hamburgers, stand by the railroad station, and listen to music. Charlie would play out there on the streets so drunk sometimes, he'd be slobbering. He stayed drunk all the time. He loved his whiskey!

Then he'd go out in the country and play at some juke. He didn't play on Dockery's all the time. Charlie stayed nowhere—he'd go all over the Delta. He'd go to Scott, Lula, Rosedale, Merigold. Play on the streets and make nickels and dimes. Go out in the country and play for them people giving the country dances for three dollars a night and all the whiskey he could drink. He'd put on a big show, take that guitar and play it behind his back, clowning around!

He was a yellow mulatto with curly hair, little bitty and low. He wasn't no size. He had that good heavy voice and yet he didn't weigh but a hundred and some pounds. Charlie never dressed up; he was always just wearing khakis, blue jeans. He liked to fight and get drunk. He was a hell-raiser, always drinking a lot of whiskey and fighting, every Saturday night. He'd even fight at his own dances, when he was playing. He didn't win nary a battle, though! Charlie, he was like a banty rooster, he was so small.

Charlie left Dockery's and was living around Merigold for a while, that's up on 61 Highway. He had a woman in Merigold, she was a whiskey seller. I used to go to his old lady's house. I played for her many times. Then he left there and come to Holly Ridge, moved with his uncle, Sherman Martin, to Holly Ridge.

Charlie had recorded and had a big name for himself out in the Delta. He recorded with Mr. H. C. Speir. In 1934 was the last time he made a record. That's when he was married to Bertha. She sang on a couple of cuts with him then, the "Bo Weevil" and "The Yellow Bee Blues." Charlie had been wounded kind of bad right before then. He had been cut in the throat; he had a mighty bad scar, clean all around. I heard some guy cut him with a razor, cut him about a woman. Then he caught something like pneumonia. You can hear it in his recording, his voice was kind of staggered.

Charlie died in '34, around about the last of April. The way I found out about it, I left my father's out in Itta Bena on a Friday, hitchhiking, and caught a ride on a truck. The man put me off over at Holly Ridge. It was raining and the wind was blowing strong. Holly Ridge wasn't nothing but a plantation store and a few houses, a little juke. Charlie's Uncle Sherman, he run the little juke house there. He was a bootleg-

**Cemetary where Charlie Patton is buried in Holly Ridge,
Mississippi, 1993.**

ger, always running a house everywhere he go. He played guitar, too, a
little bit, but mostly he was a bootlegger.

I come to Holly Ridge with my guitar on my back. When I got there
that day, I walked up to the little country store. I think I had thirty cents
in my pocket. I was hungry so I went in and bought me some bologna
and some crackers to eat and went back out on the store porch. Some
men out on that store porch saw my guitar and said to me, "You know
Charlie Patton, boy?" I said, "Yeah, I know him." They said, "You see
that new grave down there where that fresh dirt is at?" There was a little
country graveyard right there by the store. "That's where Charlie's buried. He was just buried there last week." That was sad news to me. I
went by the graveyard and looked. On Charlie's grave was a lot of mud,
gumbo mud, hard and black-looking clods piled on the grave. And he

had a little cross, with a paper wreath on it. I looked at the grave a while, then I walked over to Sherman's house.

Sherman lived in a big double house sitting in the field. Sherman said, "Charlie died last week. We lost Charlie last week." I said, "Yeah, I heard." He pulled out a jug of whiskey and give me a shot. We sat around and talked a while. He said, "He's gone and I hate it but we got to carry on. I'm givin' a dance Saturday night. Why don't you stay around and play for me?" So I played for him that next night. He didn't hold up for nothing. He said, "Well, there's nothin' we can do; he's gone. Still got to go on. Time goes on." So Sherman gave a dance that Saturday, had a lot of white whiskey, fried a lot of buffalo fish and hamburgers.

Bertha was out there, Charlie's wife Bertha. Bertha told me Charlie woke up one morning and then laid back down and died. She said he suffered sometimes but he would always play. Musicians are hard to give it up, but Charlie probably killed himself with the way he was living. Bertha was only about eighteen or nineteen years old; me and Bertha was the same age. And Charlie was forty-three when he died. He was like all men, liked those young women.

Charlie always had a lot of women. Charlie always had good-looking women, too. Men didn't like him much because all the women was fools over him. A musicianer, he's not got as many men friends as he has women, and sometimes the only men friends he has is other musicianers, or a man who ain't got no woman.

Sherman had a good-looking wife too. Sherman had a wife named Ada, tall, little in the waist, had a great big butt on her. I started going with her a few years later when they was back over in Ruleville and I was playing for him over there. One Christmas he gave a big dance and there was two of us guitar players playing that night. Whilst I was on my break, Ada and me met out in the garage and I got a little of that. Then Sherman moved to Shaw and when I went to Shaw I wanted to play for Sherman all the time! I knew Ada a long time. I've had my fun. I had nothing but good times. Charlie did, too, he was a hell of a guy. He'd clown and drink and carry on with them women. Charlie Patton was a hell-raising kind of guy. I was lucky to come up in time to know him.

Who else I saw back then was Son House and Willie Brown. It was around that same time I heard they was playing out there at Flowers

**Honeyboy tuning his guitar backstage before his appearance
at the 1994 Chicago Blues Festival.**

Plantation out in Coahoma County, up near Robinsonville. I cut on
out there and they had a big crowd at the barrelhouse on the plantation.
Willie Brown was kind of a big, husky fellow; he was heavy. He worked
on the farm and played with Son House. Willie Brown was a great guitar player. That man had some beautiful chords he made in the key of
A. Son House had a rough guitar style on that National guitar of his. He
was a rocking, rough slide player. He was a good singer and a good
hollerer, a good entertainer with his guitar.

I first saw Howlin' Wolf in '32 in Greenwood. He come walking into
town with his high top shoes on and we called him Foots. He had the
biggest feet—he wore about size 14! He called himself Buford, too, but
Chester Burnett, that's his real name. He come by my daddy's house,
along the river, walking. He had a cap on his head, one of them winter
caps, thick, with some little bitty eyeglasses, like Blind Lemon used to
wear. He was a young boy, too. I was seventeen and Wolf wasn't no
more than twenty-two. A little fat black boy. But he said, "Hey, man" in
that rough voice, he always had that voice.

Howlin' Wolf was trying to play guitar back then. He always was a
good singer but he never was much of a guitar player. In the country at

that time you could play any kind of music if you had a good voice and your guitar was tuned up. The country people went for it because they didn't have no other kind of music but that. Wolf could phrase it and make a few chords, and he had that good, heavy voice. He played for some country dances around there. He'd set himself down on a cane-bottom chair and play and be scooting all around the room in that chair. When he'd get through scooting he'd be all around the other side of the room! He'd tap that big foot and you could hear it all over, like a drum.

He discovered for himself that he wasn't going to make a good guitar player with them big old fingers. Then he took up the harmonica and made a headway with it. He made his way through with the harp and that voice. Wolf had his own style with harmonica and that big voice of his. That set him apart. That made him Howlin' Wolf.

Now that name Howlin' Wolf was from a record that was popular back in the late twenties. It was kind of a famous number, by Funny Papa Smith. When I first met him, Wolf was singing that song, "I'm the wolf that digs my tail down in the ground." Yeah! And sing, "I want everybody to hear me when I howl." That's the number he was playing then. He liked that song and wanted to name himself The Howlin' Wolf. I can remember that number. That Funny Papa Smith had a hell of a voice on him, too. He could holler so loud and his voice was so heavy, when you'd play that song on one of those windup gramophones, it would shake. Wolf was playing that, and trying to play Blind Lemon numbers. He was playing some Tommy Johnson too, "Cold Water Blues," and a few Charlie Patton numbers.

There was a lot of good musicians back then never did get on wax. Musicians who was stone good, too. The Moores. A fellow named Man Ship, he lived out of Greenwood, played a Martin. Tom Toy. My friend J. C. Robinson, we called him Popcorn. He used to run around the Delta a whole lot; he learned guitar from Joe Willie Wilkins up in Hushpuckena. All of us country boys would visit each other, set down in the house, and play for nobody. That's how we learned to play the guitar, just sit in the house, play all the evening, play to yourself till you sharpened up and could play at those country dances.

Back then musicians didn't all play the Delta blues. They played a older style of blues like "Stop and Listen," "Sitting on Top of the World."

People played violin and guitar, had little string bands. Blues has changed. Blues has always kept a'moving. Back in the thirties, guitar players just played like a horse, trotting all the way through a song. Then things started to change up a little bit. The blues started to changing. The blues come out with a little turnaround to it. Joe Williams come out with that "49 Highway"; that picked things up. And Robert Johnson, everybody come behind him trying to play in his style. I was lucky to come up right in the middle of all those musicians. I come up when Charlie Patton was playing and stayed around long enough to see all the young guys playing the uptempo blues. I run up on all those musicians and everything sounded good to me!

Chapter Ten

Robert was crazy about women and crazy about his whiskey.

I met Robert Johnson in Greenwood in 1937, in the fall. He was traveling around through the country all the time by himself, playing country dances all through them little Delta towns like Indianola, Leland, on over to Greenwood. He was hustling. He had made a few little records, and more probably the quarters and nickels and dimes was easier for him to make because he had a little something on wax. His songs was on the jukeboxes and everyone was listening to them for a nickel a crack.

When I first met him he was on Johnson Street near Main in Greenwood, playing right back on the alley. He was right outside of Emma Collins's—she kept a good-timing house and used to sell whiskey, too. He was standing on a block and had a crowd of people back in the alley ganging around him. But they didn't know who he was! I didn't know at first either, and when I first walked up I thought he was sounding a little like Kokomo Arnold. I walked up with my little old guitar, put mine on back and started listening. He was playing the blues so good. One woman, she was full of that old corn whiskey, she said, "Mister, you play me 'Terraplane Blues'!" She didn't know she was talking to the man who made it! She said, "If you play me 'Terraplane Blues' I'll give you a dime!" He said, "Miss, that's my number." "Well, you play it then." He started playing and they knew who he was then. He was playing and trembling and hollering.

It was a little after noon and the people was coming out of the country, coming to town. He had the street blocked with all the people listening to him play. He was dressed nice, wearing a brown hat. He wore a hat most of the time, broke down over that bad eye.

I got acquainted with him when he finished playing. We started talking and I found out he was from around Robinsonville, had just been through Tunica. I asked him did he know my cousin there, Willie Mae Powell, and he said, "That's my girlfriend!" And I said, "That's my first cousin!" So we started to laughing, chatting it up a little bit and we kind of hooked up and started drinking and hanging around together. That's how I got attached with him. I met him and found out he was going with my cousin.

That same Saturday I first met Robert, this man saw him playing on the street and asked him to play at his house. All them big whiskey sellers would come to Greenwood and pick up musicians. That's why all the musicians would play on the streets on a Saturday. Big whiskey sellers would come to town then and listen at them and hire them for their dances and jukes. It was the only way to reach musicians; nobody knew where they was living at. They'd see them in town hustling and say, "You want to work with me tonight?" Them bootleggers would try to get the best guitar player, then you get the biggest crowd following him. So this particular Saturday, Robert was playing and this man come up and asked him, "I'd like to get you workin' tonight. I'll pay you three dollars." And three dollars was a lot of money then. Robert said, "Alright." Robert stayed in town a few more hours and made a little money on the streets. The man come back and picked Robert up about nine o'clock.

This guy was a big whiskey seller. He made a pretty good buck. He had a big gambling house out at Three Forks. It was about three miles out of Greenwood where Highway 82 runs into Highway 49, in a big house in the middle of a field. Three Forks Grocery was facing Greenwood, and behind the store was the big juke house this man used to run. That place got blown away in a tornado in 1942. They sold white

**1993 photograph of the Greenwood, Mississippi, alley where
Honeyboy first met Robert Johnson in 1937.**

whiskey, hamburgers, hot dogs, had a big gambling shack in the back. The man kept a crowded house.

And Robert played a long time for this man, every Saturday and Friday. I was hustling on my own at the time but if I didn't have nothing to do, I'd hang around where he was playing, play a few numbers, get together and have some drinks. Me and Robert hung out together there and would go to Tommy McClennan's and different places in Greenwood. We'd go to Emma's over on Johnson and drink white whiskey and have a good time. Sometimes we'd go to the good-timing house on Avenue F. Some folks called the Lemons run a craphouse back over near there, too. We used to go back there and play the guitar for nickels and dimes and drink. We got pretty tight together during that time.

I played around with him many times that year, would go over to his room, sit down, hit a few chords behind him.

He was a quiet type of guy. Robert didn't associate with too many people. Now, I know he stayed with Willie Brown and Son House. They knew Robert pretty good. And he played with Johnny Shines. Johnny Shines traveled all over with him, and he played with Robert Junior Lockwood. Robert Johnson used to go with Robert Junior's mama when Robert was just a boy, twelve or thirteen years old. Robert Johnson was just a few years over Robert Junior but he lived with his mama. She was a pretty woman, nice shape, looked like she might be part Mexican a little. They lived out in Marvell, Arkansas. Robert Johnson and Robert Junior would run around together, and Robert Junior learned a lot of stuff from him. I know Homesick James run up on him here and there, too.

Robert Johnson was a great blues player and had his own style. He had a different style than any other musician that was playing back at that time. All the rest of them like Rube Lacy and Tommy Johnson, all of them had that bookity-book Delta style. Robert Johnson come out with a classic blues style, with mostly a lot of minor chords. He had a lot of seventh chords in his blues and it sounded better than just playing straight. And that took with the people, because he had a different sound.

Robert was a nice person. He wasn't a hell-raiser. He wasn't violent. I never heard him arguing with nobody. All I know Robert to do, he liked to drink. He loved whiskey and he was crazy about his women. That's two things he was crazy about. And that was his downfall. But anything else, I never knew him to fight or argue. Robert wasn't no hell-raising young man.

When the wintertime came I left for further south. I went to Vicksburg and New Orleans and I stayed down there a long time. Summertime, getting warm then, I got back up in the Delta.

Now this guy that Robert was working for, he had a wife. A nice-made woman, nice-looking, brownskin. Robert was rooming with some people over in Baptist Town behind the little old fire station, near where my sister had got killed at. He had a little room in a house over there, at Pelican and Young, for around three dollars a week. And what happened, Robert was whorish. All musicians like women to some extent,

Crossroads in Sunflower County, Mississippi, 1993.

but you're not supposed to get too crazy about them. But he was whorish and the man had this good-looking wife, chocolate brown and hair way down to her ass, mixed up with Indian a little some. And she had a sister lived out in Greenwood, near where Robert was rooming at, and every Monday she had to go see her sister. And would lay up with him all day. She kept doing that every Monday. The man thought, "You go see your sister every Monday." And someone, his friends, whispered, "She layin' back there with Robert." Robert should have left her alone—he would have lived longer.

When I come back to the Delta, Robert was in Greenwood playing for this same man. And one Saturday a bunch of us went out to Three Forks on a old flat-bottomed truck. We was all high, ready to ball all night long. When we got there, Robert was sitting in a corner with his guitar under his arm. He was sick. And the women jumped off the truck, come in, and said to him, "Play me 'Terraplane Blues.'" "Play me 'Kind-Hearted Woman Blues'!" He said, "I'm sick." And they said, "Have a drink of whiskey. Have another drink and you'll feel alright."

But Robert had got poisoned. Robert was crazy about whiskey and this man was mad about Robert going with his wife. He had a friend lady give Robert a glass of whiskey that had poison in it. People would do that. They poison you rather than shoot you, get you in a smooth way. That way people don't know what you done. All the folks kept on hollering, "Play!" "Play!" "Play!" He tried to play once or twice but couldn't and said, "I'm sick. I can't play." They took and laid him across a bed in a back room. And everything got quiet then. Before day, some guy who had a old car carried him back to Greenwood, to his room in Baptist Town.

Robert stayed sick and lying around for two or three days. I didn't go see him Sunday or Monday; I really thought he would be alright. But when I went to see him on Tuesday, he was really sick. I talked to him but he wasn't able to talk. He was bleeding at the mouth, heaving up and going on. There wasn't nothing I could do for him. I was young. I was twenty-two years old, and I didn't know what to do. Folks, his friends, was giving him home remedies, trying to heal him up. People couldn't call the doctor. What black person had any money then? Doctors charged them and there wasn't no money. So he just died for attention. And here I thought he would just get over it. But Robert died. He was buried by Wednesday. They say at the end he was crawling around, crawling around like a dog, and howling. That's the way they say he was.

Some people say that had something to do with Robert selling himself to the devil. I've heard that, about Robert selling his soul at the crossroads. People say he wasn't any good playing guitar until he went out to the crossroads and sold his soul to the devil. They say after that Robert could play any kind of music. I have gone to the crossroads myself, and played out at night in the country. In the country where the air is clear, with the stars and the moonshine, it's as bright as day in the night. I'd walk down them gravel roads with a bottle of whiskey in my pocket, get to a crossroad, and sit down and play. I have played the crossroads. I used to carry scorpions in my pocket, too, dried and sewed up in a bag. That's like a mojo, for luck. And I used to put a nail up above my bed and hang my guitar up over my head when I go down to sleep at night. That way I don't forget what I learned that day, keep it in my mind. My daddy told me to do that. That stuff was our nature. That was our thing at the time.

It may be Robert could have sold himself to the devil. In the way he was, the way he played and the way he acted, he could have felt that he sold his soul. A special feeling could have hit him like he done that and that feeling come out in his music.

That stuff Robert done more than fifty years ago, it was a hit with the people, but he didn't get nothing much out of it. Now he's dead and people are making money off his music, trying to get everything they can. The man is dead and people are trying to dig up everything they can dig up about him. It's money they're making off of it or they wouldn't fool with it.

Robert's more popular because he died, like everybody else who dies young. But he was a great musician. He innovated his own way of playing. Robert had his own style and he held with it till he died. He wasn't out there too long but he changed everything. Everyone tried to follow Robert Johnson's style.

Robert's sister come down from Chicago to bury him, but when she got to Greenwood it was too late. The county had already buried him, put him in the ground. Back in that time they didn't let you stay on top too long. They went on and put him in the ground, and she quick had him dug right back up and put him in a casket and put him down in the same place, put him in a decent casket. He was twenty-six years old.

Chapter Eleven

We was all just country boys.

I played that guitar all the time and was getting better and better. All I wanted to do was meet more musicians and learn from them. All of us was up and down the road, trying to make it in them little towns. I met Homesick James sitting at a train station in Tunica, wearing overalls and carrying his Stella guitar, on his way to Memphis. His name is James Williamson, but he said, "Call me Homesick." Folks called him Lookquick then, too. I met Little Brother Montgomery at a sawmill in Canton, Mississippi. I met Little Milton playing at a poolroom in Greenville and Robert Junior Lockwood hanging around Helena, just starting out. He used to play a lot by himself, then he hooked up with Sonny Boy. We was all just country boys and glad to see each other.

I first met Sonny Boy Williamson when I was only fourteen. That was out at Shellmound on the Bledsoe Plantation. He must have been around thirty years old then. He was picking cotton and playing around at different places, hustling all over the Delta. Before that he come from Glendora. But by 1932, '33, he got a little popular playing and he didn't have to pick cotton no more.

Sonny Boy played all over, all by himself. That man could entertain a crowd, too. He would holler, play that harp, bucking and jumping and going on. He was a show all by himself. When I first knew him there was no electric harps, he was just playing dry harp. He had a belt all around his waist with slots cut in it carrying the different keys.

Sonny Boy moved to Greenwood with a woman named Mandy and was running around town with those harps all around his waist. We hooked up there and I played with him many times. Sonny Boy was kind of a fractious guy. When I first started playing with him, I was playing with a capo then. He took it off and said, "Take that choke off your guitar!" and he threw it away! He didn't like it and he didn't want me to play with no clamp on that guitar.

There was a small riverboat on the Tallahatchie River in Greenwood, and Sonny Boy and me used to play for the white man who owned that. All the white men used to come there, park their cars and come on the boat to gamble and have a nice time. It would run up and down the river and they would play blackjack, cotch games. The man that owned that riverboat, he had a wife, a redheaded woman. And she was always wanting us to play "Careless Love." We'd play that "Careless Love," and she'd come and sit on my lap and cry and cry. I don't know what was wrong with that woman. It made me scared, though, having that white woman sitting on my lap. I'd call out to her husband and say, "Come get your wife, man." And he'd say, "God damn it. That's my wife. And if she wants to set on your lap, you just let her set there!" I let her too, but I didn't want her there!

I remember one night me and Sonny Boy stole their damn car! We got drunk and took that man's Buick! Sonny Boy was driving, we had a bottle of wine, and drove around all night long. Come dawn, we come back and left it at his door. We had a lot of fun with those white folks.

Me and Sonny Boy caught a freight train one time, and we was coming to Tchula, Mississippi, into the little train yard there. They was bad about putting you on the county farm there and we knew it, so when the train come to the yard we jumped off it and landed in a woods. I got lost of him and he got lost of me. It was dark night. I couldn't see anything, and I couldn't tell where Sonny Boy was, crashing through them trees. And we didn't want to holler out too loud and get caught. Sonny Boy made it to a gravel road on the other side of the woods and then I heard him blowing that harp, "Whaooo," calling to me. Sonny Boy was

Forest along the banks of the Mississippi River, 1992.

playing that harp, low in the dark woods, to lead me to him, just like saying, "Here I am!" I had to feel my way and each time he blew his harp I knew I was nearer to him.

I caught up with him on that gravel road and we started walking. We didn't have nowhere to stay. Right before we got to Tchula was some section houses on each side of the road. We started to playing the blues walking down the road and doors started flying open, "Hey!" "Play us some blues!" "Come here!" One man called us into his house and everyone come there. He had a gallon of whiskey and we played there all night long and the next morning he cooked breakfast for us.

A few months later I went back there by myself and I got a baby by that man's wife, Annabelle. He was digging ditches out in the field and I got in the bed with her, right beside the window so we could keep an eye on him outside. I found out later what come of that when I saw her brother in Greenwood one day. He said, "Man, you got the finest boy by my sister you ever seen in your life. He looks just like you."

One time me and Sonny Boy and Tommy McClennan, we went to Jackson, Mississippi, and into Yazoo City. We played together with a fellow named Bear from Grenada, Mississippi, who beat planks to sound like a drum. They hired us down at the Chevrolet dealer's in Yazoo City; they gave us two or three dollars to play. And one night we got to shooting dice and gambling and I broke all of them!

I broke Tommy, I broke Sonny Boy, I broke Bear. We all made this money together and then started gambling and drinking whiskey at this woman's house and I broke them all. I went downtown and bought myself some new shoes, got me some corduroys, a heavy shirt, and I was ready for the women. Sonny Boy, he got mad and booked up and left us then. I didn't see Sonny Boy for a good while, two or three months, after that.

In 1938 me and Big Walter Horton went to Jackson, Mississippi, to find Mr. H. C. Speir. He had a furniture company in Jackson and re-corded a lot of musicians, too. He recorded Charlie Patton, Reverend Cotton, Tommy Johnson. The old man was good. He was a nice guy, used to talk kind of low, never raised his voice. He knew good music when he heard it. A lot of good musicians recorded for H. C. Speir. We got there right before Christmas and everything was closed so we couldn't make a recording. Sonny Boy showed up there, too. So we got together, me and Big Walter and Sonny Boy, and we left together. We hit number 80 Highway, that's coming out of Jackson going into Vicksburg. We walked along the highway, hitched rides. We'd stop in the little towns and play together, two harps and one guitar.

How they would play together, Sonny Boy would dip in every now and then and Walter would dip in every now and then. Walter was trail-ing Sonny Boy. Walter had been a good harp player all his life, and he knew the chords that would mix with Sonny Boy's chords. They played in and out together and it was sounding good.

We come to Vicksburg together and played on the corners, at little taverns. Sonny Boy was a good harp blower and he'd been out there a long time before we, playing and making money by himself. That man

**1993 photograph of boss and cotton workers at the site in
Shellmound, Mississippi, where Honeyboy first met
Sonny Boy Williamson 2 in 1926.**

could do more with a harp. He'd take that harp, keeping time with his foot and people could dance to it! He could hold a crowd with that harp! He'd holler; he could holler pretty good. The people liked that. But Big Walter was a hell of a harp player, so young and so good, Big Walter was playing so much harp and by him being so young the people gave him the praise! Everybody said, "That little boy's hell, ain't he?" Sonny Boy was good, too, but they give Walter that praise because he was so young. Sonny Boy didn't like that.

We left for Tallulah, Louisiana, and we stopped at a country store beside the highway betwixt Vicksburg and Tallulah. It was a big planta-tion store. People was settling up, getting their Christmas money from the boss man. Everyone was drinking and having a good time. We got us a drink of whiskey, started to playing, and the country people was gathering around us. After we got through playing, we was drinking and laughing and talking. There was a place behind the store to shoot dice and gamble. After about half an hour back there, me and Walter looked around and Sonny Boy was gone! He slipped off and left us, didn't say nothing. He knew he could do good by himself.

Later, in 1940, I come to Helena, Arkansas, and played on the streets and at the little whiskey joints, and I'd see Sonny Boy over there then. Joe Willie Wilkins come over to Helena from Hushpuckena and Sonny Boy picked up with him. Joe Willie was a pretty good guitar player. And Willie Love come over from Tunica and started to playing with them. They all just hooked up, got a band started; that was somewhere around '41. They played on the radio every day, on 1245, that KFFA station. That radio show come on around twelve o'clock noon. I can remember all the people used to come out of the field to catch them playing on that radio station.

Robert Nighthawk broadcast on that station, too. Robert Nighthawk had been playing and living out on John McKey's Plantation in Friars Point since before '37. Him and his brother used to drive around in a A-model Ford, playing different places. His name was Robert McCoy then. Robert was a plantation boy. Robert Nighthawk played the smoothest slide there was. When he played that slide, he was just as smooth and clear as water. In the forties, Robert started a little thing and called himself Nighthawk and that's when he would broadcast on the radio in Helena. He had a boy playing with him, a crippled boy from St. Louis, who played a four-string electric guitar. That poor boy got burned up in a building in Helena. When I first met Kansas City Red, he was playing with Nighthawk, till Robert stole a woman from him. Them country people would break down the house to get to the radio to hear Nighthawk broadcasting with his band. Then the musicians would announce where they was going to play on Friday night and people would get spruced up and go on over there.

That's how Wolf got his name out there, by broadcasting over the radio out of West Memphis. Wolf come from Aberdeen, the same place Bukka White come from. That's betwixt West Point and Tupelo, Mississippi. It's a small town, a sawmill town. Wolf come to the Delta and he stayed in the Delta a long time, then he moved to Blames, Arkansas. He left there and went over to West Memphis, Arkansas. Still I knew him at that time because all of us musicians would go to Memphis to all the clubs and Wolf was over there. We all kept up with each other.

Wolf stayed in that little place called Blames at his grandfather's home. I used to go up there and visit him. He'd work his grandfather's crop for him, working that plow. Wolf wore this old straw hat, like a Mexican hat, walking behind that plow. I'd go to Blames to see him and we would go to Ruleville on a Saturday and hit the streets. We'd play on the streets and I'd go back on a Sunday morning to his grandfather's house with him, sit around there. He had a woman down on Highway 49, sometimes we'd go down to her house and we'd drink beer and play cards. Sunday night I'd come back to Ruleville where my sister was, and Wolf would go back out and plow them fields. Wolf never dodged no work, he was a hardworking man. Howlin' Wolf didn't get no rest till he come here to Chicago and started recording for Chess.

I saw Tommy Johnson again in '37. I went to Jackson and inquired about him. He was out on Farish Street and when I went out to his house he was glad to see me. Tommy was pretty easygoing, nice to get along with. He was a heavy drinker, though. His wife worked for some white people and Tommy would play a couple nights a week. He didn't do a damn thing but play that guitar, dip snuff, and drink canned heat. He'd rather drink that stuff than whiskey! We'd go to the drugstore and get us a couple of cans of canned heat and some orange pop. We'd melt it and squeeze it through a thin rag, mix that alcohol with that pop and it made us as drunk as can be! We'd sit and drink that canned heat and get our guitars and start to playing the blues! He'd drink that stuff and sing, "Canned, mama, canned heat is killin' me." Yeah! He likened that. A lot of people used to drink canned heat—Tommy just drank more than anybody. Tommy just broke the record!

I met Elmore James in 1937 in Doddsville, Mississippi. He was playing acoustic guitar, he had a little old Stella, and he had that out in the country sound, that hollering, squalling sound. Elmore James was a pretty good guitar picker when he wanted to, but he just loved to play that slide. He was playing mostly blues he'd made up and stuff like Texas Alexander and some Lonnie Johnson. He was getting a dollar a day driving a tractor on a plantation and he played on the weekends for a bootlegger named Grady Sharkey. I'd hang around with him; we'd go fishing. Me and Elmore, we'd eat off the same plate. Elmore fooled around playing there for a long time and left and come to Memphis and that's where he got discovered.

I met B. B. King back then, too, when he was just a small boy. B.B. used to live betwixt Indianaola and a little town called Inverness, right alongside a little creek. Christmas of 1937 I was playing on the streets in Inverness and I made fifteen dollars in dimes and quarters. People, by being Christmas, some of them had money in their pockets. I noticed a young boy, standing there listening at me play. The next day I was going down the road walking and this boy was out in a field plowing. He come over and talked to me, said, "I saw you playin' on the streets. My name is Riley King and I play the guitar, too." That was B.B. He was singing with the choir then and nobody knew nothing about him. The next time I saw him was in Memphis, and he was the Beale Street Blues Boy.

It was sometime in '38 when I found my way over to East St. Louis and run up on Big Joe Williams again. I didn't see Big Joe for a long time after I left him in New Orleans, but I would always hear talk of him coming through places. When I come to St. Louis and run up on him, he was glad to see me. Then I had somewhere to stay. He had a old lady and she fixed up a bed for me in their back room and I stayed with them. I stayed with J. D. Short sometimes, too, Jelly Jaw. J. D. Short is my cousin. My Aunt Cornelia, Uncle Aaron's wife, and J.D.'s mother was sisters. I used to hear Aunt Missy talk about J.D., her son. And when I went to St. Louis, Big Joe said, "Let's go down to J.D.'s house." When we met and got to talking, he asked me where I come from. We found out we both had people in Shaw and found we was cousins.

I got acquainted with a few musicians in St. Louis. I got acquainted with Blind Darby there. He played the banjo. He was a good banjo player. We left St. Louis one day hitchhiking, thought we'd go to Memphis to make a little money playing in Beale Street Park. That was around '38. We left St. Louis hitchhiking down 61 Highway in Missouri. Darby was carrying his banjo, I had my guitar, and we saw this white farmer coming down the road in his pickup truck. We flagged a ride from him. And that man picked us up and carried us straight out to his plantation

**Honeyboy after a 1992 performance on KFFA's
"King Biscuit Time" radio show.**

in the country and put us out in the cotton field! We couldn't get off the truck! We stood out there in that field and he handed me a cotton sack and handed one to Darby, too. The farmer said, "You put them machines, them guitars, right over there by my house and get to pickin'." The cotton was just as pretty and white out in the field. Blind Darby said, "Man, I'm blind. I can't see to pick no cotton!"

Darby sat down on the man's porch. The way he was, I figured there wasn't nothing the man could do to him. I picked up that cotton picking sack and went out in the field. And the farmer left again in his pickup truck. I watched that truck until I couldn't see it no more, and when he was back down 61 Highway I set aside that sack and grabbed my guitar and ran across the field. There was a railroad running alongside the highway there and I ran across a couple of fields to get to it. And there come that farmer on the highway. He saw me. He tried to chase me down but I got away from him and ran all the way to the state line.

I ended up in a little town in Arkansas and stopped at a white lady's house and asked for a drink of water. She gave me a drink and a sandwich and I told her what happened. She said, "Well, I never heard talk of this happenin' in Missouri before." I said, "Well, it happened to me!" I saw Darby in St. Louis a few weeks later and he said, "God damn, you left me!" We laughed about it, though.

Lots of musicians were in St. Louis, and Big Joe knew them all. He would take me around to meeting everybody. I met St. Louis Jimmy. I met Jim Brewer there and played with him at the whorehouses in East St. Louis. And Peetie Wheatstraw. Peetie Wheatstraw lived in the redlight district. He had a white old lady and a little white dog, too! He was a big shot down there, got dressed up every day and walked that dog down the street on a little chain. We'd go around to Walter Davis's sometimes, too. He was managing a hotel down there on Delmar Street. Big Joe recorded with him; they made "Number 13 Highway" together. Walter Davis had a left-hand bass like no other piano player had. He could kill you with the sound of that left hand.

Me and Joe, we'd get on the streetcar and ride it from one end of St. Louis clean to the other, playing the blues and passing the hat around. We had a boy called Prosperity who played washboard with us. We'd be sitting in the back and the streetcar would get full of people and get on its way, and Prosperity would jump up and holler, "Elevate me, mama, five or six floors down!" People would look! Prosperity would start the crowd off, and then me and Joe would join in playing while Prosperity played that washboard all over, even down betwixt his legs. We'd play for one group and on the next run we'd have a whole new set of people and we'd play for them.

Joe took me to meet Muddy Waters in 1939. I run into Joe over in Leland and he said, "Come with me. I'm goin' down to Muddy's house." Joe knew everybody! Muddy was staying out in the country at the time. He was a trapper. He would catch coons and possums, minks. We went to his house and his wife was there. She said, "Muddy, he's in the woods pickin' up his traps." He was seeing about the traps he had baited to catch the game. We waited for him and he come back, wearing those hip boots. He had a gang of possums and threw them in the corner. His wife fixed supper for us, and me and Joe Williams and him played that night at his house. The next night Muddy had a job playing for a country dance and we all three played together there.

Me and Joe and Big Walter got together one time and joined a medicine show run by a guy named String Bean. String Bean was from Silas Green's Medicine Show, and he quit and started his own show, going around to all the little towns. He took all of us around in his old Studebaker, all piled in there with his big old tent. We was all the time laughing. String Bean set up his tent in all them little towns and the three of us played for him while he told jokes and lies and sold that medicine.

I played all different kinds of music. We'd all play anything to make that nickel—I'd holler my ass off about that nickel! Sometimes white folks would hire me from off the streets to play at country dances. They liked "St. Louis Blues," "Bring It on Down," "Corinna." They'd dance all over the floor to "Corinna," them white folks. I'd play for the whites in clubs, and serenade them in their neighborhoods. For a while I played on the riverboats with a saxophone player, a boy from Clarksdale called Willie. Willie had been to school and he taught me my keys and started me playing songs I hadn't played before. He'd blow on his horn and say, "This is B flat. Now you play it. Play in C." He taught me "Out in the Cold Again," "Sophisticated Lady," "Isle of Capri," "Shine on, Harvest Moon." He played lead and I run the chords behind him.

The black folks at the jukes liked the country blues, the shuffle blues, the low-down-and-dirty blues. I'd play slow, drag stuff for them to dance to. That was something to see them folks do the Shimmy, shaking all around the floor. They'd dance the Charleston and Ball the Jack. And the Butterfly, opening and closing their legs like a butterfly do his wings.

I listened to all them musicians and tried different things. All of them had a different way of making it, all of them had their own style. I was still working out my style then, copying other people. I used to play in Spanish, like Joe Williams, and with a capo on my guitar like him, too. When I first started to playing music in them different towns I'd even use Joe's name, I played so much like him. I was dead on his style, I patterned behind Joe and that's how I learned. But I started meeting so many musicians playing in natural key that I found when I played with them that I was lost. I changed over to natural key, tried different tunings and learned to play good with that slide. I was learning to make my own way, get my own style. I was learning that for me to do my best, to make some headway for myself, I had to learn my own style and hold to that. I think that's the most important thing you can get to. I started to come into my own sound.

Chapter Twelve

Daddy, you can be my lemon squeezer!

You could get in a lot of trouble messing around with women. That's why Robert Johnson died so young. I was lucky and finally I learned to leave that alone. When I was young, though, I had women everywhere.

When I was a boy, parents would watch their daughters all the time. But I'd find a chance to talk with them on the porch and say, "Meet me tonight in the cornfield." When they get through eating, that girl would slip on out to meet me. I'd be out waiting for her and here she come, creaking and rustling through the corn.

When I got older and was running everywhere, I always had a girl-friend to lay up with, someone to give me a place to stay. I was pretty lucky. I run up on a woman everywhere I'd go. I would always make a woman who was working for the white folks, nursing or cooking, making three or four dollars and bringing the food home. Sometimes she'd stay in the servant's house out in the back. I didn't have to pay no rent, didn't have to buy no food. Any nickels and dimes I'd make, I could keep. If a woman didn't have a stove in her house, I didn't talk to her! I'd lay up in the house all day listening to the radio and when she come home we'd go out walking, drink a little, and come home and fool around all night long.

I had all kinds of girlfriends in Greenwood. And in Tupelo, in a little part of town called Shakerag, I was going with so many women I wore myself out. The first time I was in Tupelo, I was in front of the courthouse right in the middle of town, playing my harp and guitar on a Saturday evening. A woman come across the courtyard. She was a brownskin, heavy. She stopped to listen to me playing the blues and I started to talking to her. Her name was Viola, and she said, "Come home with me." I went to her house and I stayed from April to near about June.

While I was staying there I met another gal called Dotty, and Audrey, I was going with her, too. Then I met Jean, she was tall and dark. She was going with me and this other guy, his name was Coot. Coot had a wife. I'd hook up with him once in a while because he played guitar. I'd even see him at Jean's house, but he didn't know I was going with her. She'd tell me, "Coot ain't comin' here tonight. Come stay with me." That gal was crazy about me. But one day somebody told him. Coot come to me and said, "Hey man, let me tell you somethin': Leave my old lady alone." I said, "Alright." But I didn't leave her alone! There was a big church down a gravel road and Jean would meet me out there in the graveyard! When we'd go back to town, she'd go one way and I'd go another.

I had another old gal in Tupelo called Pat. She was half albino, had a big ass. If you could play guitar and harp, you could have any woman you wanted. If you could blow a whistle, you could get a woman! Sometimes when I was playing I'd have a woman ask me, "Will you go home with me?" I'd say, "Yes," and then another would come in that I'd like better and we'd make the same setup. I didn't know which way to turn sometimes. I got mine. I'd play that "Lemon Squeezer," that was my main blues to make the women jump up. When I started to playing that song those women would holler, "Yes, daddy, you can be my lemon squeezer whilst you're here!" I sure likened that when I was young.

But that's how a lot of musicians used to get hurt. Women would come to where you're playing at, even with their husbands with them, and flirt with the musicians. Well, no man likes that. Sometimes when those women would come up and say, "Play me so-and-so," smiling and rubbing against me, I'd say, "Look, I'll play your request but go right back over there where your man is at." Because you take some ordinary man that's working hard, he's not a musician, and he's got a good-looking woman, he don't want to lose her. Because he figures he won't find another one like her, he'll kill you about her. He'd rather be dead than lose her. So I leave that woman alone. When I got older I learned that wasn't nothing but trouble and death. I learned to leave that alone.

That's how I got hurt in Tupelo. I was coming out of a tavern and a man hit me across the face with a brick, Charlie Pfeiffer. We had had no words. He just caught me unawares when I was walking out of a tavern. He said, "Little old nigger, you think you're somethin' because you play a freckled guitar," and hit me across the face. I had to go to the hospital there. I had tubes up my nose and a stopper to stop from bleeding. That man was really jealous of me and I had hooked up with one of his girlfriends. When you don't know who they got, that's when you get in trouble.

I learned to stay away from any woman going with a white man, too. My cousin Man Son was going with a pretty girl out of Shaw and a white man was coming to see her, too. This peckerwood was crazy about that old gal, and one night Man Son was coming to see her and that man was out on her porch with a damn rifle. He was sitting there and his little boy, about eleven years old, was with him. He pointed his gun at Man Son and that child said, "Daddy, don't shoot that nigger!" That old man was married but he was screwing that gal. Man Son said to him, "Don't shoot me, boss man!" Man Son laughs about it now. "Don't shoot me this time. I won't do that no more!"

That's how it was down south. If I'm a black man and a white man is going with my wife, I couldn't do nothing about it. And if I look at his wife, he'd want to hang me.

The white man always has wanted the black woman. We had some good-looking black women, some brown, some black, some yellow, some half white—we had all kinds. Prettiest people in the world, near about. And the white man was crazy about them. The black woman was scared of him, and if he want her, she going to let him have her. Then after he start to going with your wife, he don't want you to have her. He don't want to go behind no nigger. He'd come up with his mouth all twisted and say, "I hear you're doin' some bad things on my farm. God damn it, you've got to leave." He's got my woman then and he goes to town, gets her a little set of furniture, a refrigerator, and every day his pickup truck's sitting in her yard.

The white man would get the black man out on the job four or five miles from home and go back and have the black man's wife. And she come up pregnant and have a half-white kid. Wasn't nothing we could do about it. Wasn't nothing the white woman could do about it either. The white man do what he want to do. The children would stay with their mamas, go to a black school. It's all mixed up down there, been mixed up a long time.

They didn't marry any black women, though. Except there was one white man, Tilmon Branch, he was a bad man and all the white folks was scared of him. He had a whiskey store on 61 Highway and a black gal for a wife. A young black boy killed him one day, and the white folks was so glad Tilmon Branch got killed they helped that black boy get away from there.

One of my cousins, she had a half-white daughter. She was nursing a white man's baby. Him and his wife had a restaurant and they would be there every night. My cousin, she'd nurse their baby and at night when they come in at one or two o'clock in the morning that man would take her back home. On the way, they'd stop beside the highway and fool around. She got that baby and she said when she got pregnant she was so scared she didn't know what to do. It was raining all over the world. She told her father what the white man done to her while bringing her home and her father said, "Well, we can't do nothin' about it. That's a white man."

I wasn't going to settle down noway back then. I was young and good-looking, had a mouthful of gold. I had all gold teeth put in the front; I did that for attention and style. That's how the girls would describe me, "That boy with all the gold in his mouth." I could have any woman I wanted to have. There was one woman, though, who I thought about for a long time. I met her playing on the streets in Ruleville. Her name was Emma. She was little and chunky, had great big eyes. I was messing around with her for a while and I liked her, but she wanted to marry me

Honeyboy with a fan at the 1991 Chicago Blues Festival.

and I wouldn't do that. She tore me up though. When I left there I took a picture of her with me, and I scraped a little square off my guitar and placed her picture in there. I didn't see that girl no more for two years. Then one day I got to thinking about Ruleville and about her and went back. When I saw her she said, "Honey, I done married." She looked at me and said, "You wouldn't marry me." I felt real bad; I felt that in my heart. But I couldn't have married her. Baby Peaches married another boy, too. She said to me, "I'm married now, Honey." And all I said to her was, "Yeah? Y'all married?" I wasn't going to give up music and go back to farming. There's a whole lot of things I missed by the way I lived, but I didn't want to get hooked up to a plow to feed a woman.

Sometimes I'd stay with a girl just for convenience. I'd fool around with her just to stay at her home. I'd go with her a while and cut out and come back and go with her again. Be gone three or four months and go right on back to her bed. She might say, "Honey, you ain't no God damn good," but she'd let me stay. And then where I'd find them, that's where I'd leave them. Ain't nobody following me nowhere. I was young and wild—I didn't want to marry anybody. I had so many women, they was like flowers to me. I'd just pick them and leave them go. I didn't stay with them none, except for Minnie.

I met her when I was playing at my auntie's place in Coahoma. My Aunt Irene, Uncle Sylvester's wife, run a little restaurant along the railroad tracks there. I met Minnie one Saturday night when I was playing. That was 1941. I met her and went on home with her that same night. She was quiet but I started talking to her, buying drinks for her, and I went home with her that night. She lived about two miles from town and we walked down the dirt road together back to her home. I stayed with Minnie off and on for two years.

Minnie was older than me. I had her when was I was twenty-six, twenty-seven years old. She had a son, Jack, and me and Jack was the same age. Jack was funny. Me and him used to drink and gamble together, and he'd always say, "Honey, he got my mama for a old lady." Minnie was kicking forty. She was a good-looking woman, with coal black eyebrows that almost met in the middle. She had dark, smooth skin, dark lips, she was tall and heavy. Minnie was the prettiest black woman you ever seen, nice-made, nice smile. And she was good to me, she give me good, kind treatment.

She and her auntie sharecropped on a farm for a white man. Minnie was born around there, Minnie never traveled anywhere till she met me. She took me in and I stayed on that plantation, in and out. I had my own work; I never farmed on that plantation. I'd get tired of sleeping on the road and come stay with her. I lived with her but I was playing everywhere, in the little towns all around there. Minnie would clean and press my clothes, keep my shirts starched. I made enough money and Minnie fed me and took care of me.

I never did get hooked up with no plantation bosses, always kept myself free from bosses like that so he didn't have nothing for me to do. That way it was easy to get off the plantation. My old lady was good with her boss. She just said, "Honey is my boyfriend. He's a musician. He come out and help me sometimes, but he don't want to be hooked up with no crop." And he said, "That's alright, Minnie." The boss man, he never said nothing to me. He treated me nice. I worked now and then by the day for him. Sometimes when the truck would come down to pick up the workers in the morning, I'd say, "Do you need another hand?" and go out in the field and make a day chopping cotton. But no more than that. That way when I want to go, I take my guitar and go; he wouldn't be standing around rolling his eyes about "You owe me for stayin' here." I didn't get obligated to him.

One time Homesick James told me he was staying out at this plantation in Arkansas and playing the blues all night and keeping people up dancing and drinking all night long. Messing them up! People couldn't go to work the next day. The boss man doesn't like that. When the white man sees you with that guitar he thinks, "You got that machine so I know you ain't goin' to do no work." One Saturday afternoon, he had his guitar on his shoulder, and the boss man sees him and walks up to him. The boss man shot his arm out and grabbed Homesick, held him, and said, "Hey, boy!" "Yes, sir." "You out on my plantation down there, boy, keepin' my niggers up all night long. I want you to leave my plantation." Homesick said, "Yes sir." The man looked him in the eye and said, "I mean now—Right now!" They didn't always like musicians hanging around on them plantations. But me and Minnie's boss, we didn't have any problem. He didn't mess with me.

In '42, after Christmas, we left there. She settled up with her boss that fall. He sold her cotton and gave her the money for her share of the crop. She carried her little money out of there and told the man she wasn't going to work the crop no more. She wanted to get out of there, do something different. So we left, and the little money she had made out of farming, the money she had cleared, with the money I made playing and picking a little cotton, we put that up for wintertime. In the winter, after Christmas, we moved to Rosedale and stayed with some friends of hers. Then in April of '43, a man come through in a truck, picking up workers to go down to Louisiana to pick strawberries, and me and Minnie went with him. There wasn't nothing to do in the Delta so we went on down to Independence, Louisiana, and picked those berries. We'd pick them and crate them up and carry them in and put them on ice. Them you didn't pick that day, they'd be laying out there just plump the next morning. We'd make that five dollars a day and then everybody go to a tavern and drink whiskey and mess around till the next morning. On the weekend I would find a little joint to play in.

After, we come back to Rosedale for the fall and picked cotton by the hundred. And then one day I was a country boy. I got in a skin game and lost all my money. I lost every quarter I had playing skin. That ain't my game. The cotton fields was all picked by then and I had lost all my money. I didn't have nothing and the winter was just starting. Minnie had a little money but I didn't want to ride on her. So what I done, I told her, "Minnie, I'll be back," and I went to town. I saw a grocery truck there unloading groceries at a store. I unloaded the groceries with that man and asked him "Where you goin' from here?" He said, "I'm headin' to Greenwood." So I asked him for a ride and went with him to Greenwood.

I felt bad about leaving her, but I didn't know what to do. We worked all that fall picking cotton and then I got in that big skin game and lost everything I had. I was in such a state that I didn't give a damn about nothing. I lost all my money and I knew I couldn't get back to where I was before. I guess something had to happen like that.

So that truck driver took me with him to Greenwood, and when I got there I stayed at that good-timing house on Avenue F, Lula Spencer's. Lula was a half-white woman. She had a great big house, almost like a hotel, and five or six girls working for her. A lot of soldiers was stationed over in Grenada, and they would catch a bus from Grenada over to Greenwood to come and get with the women. Lula had a great big sitting room with couches in it where the soldiers would drink whiskey and talk to the women and I'd sit out and play. Then they take them gals to the rooms upstairs. I'd holler the blues and them soldiers would drink all night and carry on and come twelve o'clock they'd have to go back on that last bus to Grenada.

I slept and ate there at Lula Spencer's; I stayed there three or four months. She fed me and gave me a place to stay and a couple of dollars to play every night. The soldiers would give me quarters and dimes, too, so by the end of the evening I'd have a few dollars in my pocket! I had it made there, eat free, drink free. Lula sold whiskey, too. She'd get whiskey by the thirty gallons and pay the polices off. They'd come by now and then and she pay them off, grinning in their faces. She kept her stash out in the garage and bring it in a couple gallons at a time, set it in the kitchen sink. If somebody come in who seemed funny to her, she'd pull the drain and let it drain right down the sink.

Late at night, after the soldiers went back to camp, the women, Daisy, Carrie, Sister, Melissa, they would get together then and clean up everything and then we'd lay back and enjoy ourselves. Lula would take her cut and pay the girls off. Daisy got to be my girlfriend. I didn't care what she did. Daisy liked me and I liked Daisy and we had ourselves a good time. Daisy was a good-looking gal, too, a little yellow gal with short skirts on, always laughing and drinking.

I've had some of the prettiest women you ever looked at, some of them I thought was too pretty for me! Pretty, I mean beautiful, Lord have mercy, I had them. Clara, in Itta Bena, she was dark brown-skinned and shaped like a Coca-Cola bottle. Had a little gap in her front teeth and big, dreamy eyes. Lennie Dee, she was dark and had a mouthful of gold. Her husband worked at a compress, and I'd go out in the cotton fields and fool around with her. Eveline, she was big and tall, when I kissed her I'd close my eyes and hold my head up to hers like a baby bird reaching to get food from his mama. I've had my fun!

Chapter Thirteen

I didn't give a damn about nothing.

I liked to go south in the winter when it was cold and bad up in the Delta. I spent the winter of '37 in New Orleans and I was heading back up to the Delta and stopped a while in Vicksburg. At that time, Vicksburg was dry; there wasn't no whiskey there. There was a boat on the Louisiana side of the Mississippi River that was like a big house, had a bar and dance hall. The boat sat on the Louisiana side because it was wet over there; they sold whiskey over there. You could get a tugboat to take you there from Vicksburg.

I went across the river one night and that turned out to be a bad night for me. I was young and foolish. We would get beer out of big old kegs and pour it in buckets. Then four or five of us would drink out of the bucket, pass the bucket around. So a bunch of us was drinking, passing the bucket around, and it got back to me and I drank all the beer that was left in it. It wasn't that much. There was this guy, Caesar, I didn't know him much but we was drinking together. And Caesar said to me, "God damn. You drank all the beer! What'd you drink all the God damn beer for?" I said, "We all bought beer together. Some of it belongs to me, too!" We got to arguing. And he wanted to cut me. He had a knife.

Caesar was a big guy, and a lot older than me. He must have been about forty-five or older. I got a cane-bottom chair and put it in front of me. Every time he tried to cut me I fought him off with that chair. After a while things cooled down.

A couple of hours later, I come on back across the river to Vicksburg with a partner of mine, Robert. We was standing on the levee, talking. I had forgot about everything that had happened, wasn't thinking about Caesar or nothing like that. But when we walked up the hill by Levee Street, Robert looked and said, "That looks like that nigger who was tryin' to cut you just a little while ago." And that was Caesar standing on the top of that hill. He was waiting for me.

He was still mad. He was wanting to kill me. My friend Robert was a big, stout boy, and strong. He said, "You, nigger, what you tryin' to do? What you hangin' around here for?" And Robert run after him. Caesar broke and run. When he broke and run, by the dew being on the grass on that hill, he slipped and fell. Robert got up to him and hit him a lick. I run up there and kicked him on side of the head. I was drunk, and mad, too.

We left him laying there and went up to my girl's house on Levee Street, Carolina. Somebody saw us and told the police where we was and they come knocking on the door. "Who is it?" "Police. And if you don't open this door we're goin' to tear it down." When the police come in there, I had my guitar under my arm and was trying to talk trash to them. One police grabbed my guitar out of my arms and took it by the neck and started to throw it in the fireplace grate. The other police told him not to do that, so he threw the guitar on the bed and said, "Y'all beat up a man down there."

They carried us to jail. Because we both hit Caesar, that's what sent us to jail. Because it wasn't just a fight. They said we was double-teaming him. That was two days before Christmas. They gave us each thirty days. On Christmas day they gave all the prisoners a little drink of whiskey in a glass, and when Robert stuck his hand out through his cell door to get his, that big iron door closed and cut his thumb off. They turned him loose right then. They said, "You can go."

After my thirty days they turned me loose. And the day after I got loose, Caesar died from his wounds. Carolina told me. She said, "Honey, you know Caesar died this mornin'." They could've charged me for manslaughter because he died from that fight. I wasn't trying to do nothing like that, but he died from his wounds. He was gone.

While I was doing that thirty days, Joe Williams come through there and told my friends he'd take my guitar, that I wouldn't want nobody to have it but him. He left there with two guitars, mine and his! I never got that guitar back again.

I left Vicksburg right away after that. I was scared after Caesar died that they'd pick me up for manslaughter and put me back in jail. If I'd hung around they might have dug it back up and picked me up for manslaughter. I stayed away from Vicksburg for a long time after that. I didn't want to go to Parchman.

Parchman Penitentiary, that was for the bad offenders. You do something like murder anywhere in the state of Mississippi, they send you to Parchman. Son House was in Parchman, and Bukka White. Floyd Jones been to the penitentiary in Arkansas. Floyd killed a man when he was young. Some guy tore up his whiskey still and Floyd killed him. I think he did five years at Little Rock Penitentiary. Joe Williams, he had a cousin who was in the penitentiary; he was crazy, just like Joe. He had got to drinking and fighting and they put him in the penitentiary. And Joe told me one day his cousin just couldn't stand it anymore. He was out in the field working and he told the driver, "I'm leavin' this mornin'. You can do what you want to do." And he turned his back and started to walking away and the driver shot him. He walked away and they killed him. Back at that time if you went in the pentitentiary you was lucky to come home.

Except for that time in Vicksburg I only served for small offenses, like for vagrancy. I done a couple of months in Memphis for vagrancy. I was sitting in a bar with a friend of mine, Jesse, and a police come in. He walked down to the end of the bar and took a long drink of whiskey. He looked at us and we knew he was going to mess with us then! He said, "What's your name, boy? What is your name?" I told him my name and that I was in town visiting my sister. And just getting ready to leave. "Mmmhmm. And you?" he looked at Jesse. Jesse give him some answer out of the side of his mouth, and he pulled Jesse off his stool and took him out to the police car. Jesse told me the other police out there said,

"How many birds are left in there?" The first police said, "One more." "Well, get him, too." So he come back and got me. They give us sixty days for doing nothing.

In Coahoma, where I met Minnie, that's where I got this scar on my forehead. That was a rough town, a little cowboy town. I was playing at my auntie's one night and I laid down my guitar for a break, got up from the corner, and walked across to the counter to get a Coke to go with my whiskey. The Seabird jukebox was playing and my cousin, Annie, she was dancing. She stepped on this boy Will's foot. He said, "Annie, you stepped on my foot!" She told him, "Yeah, well, put your God damn foot in your pocket, man!" I wouldn't have been hurt if she'd kept her mouth shut.

Will, he went outside and picked up a rock and chunked it in through the door, trying to hit her. And I was walking across the floor and heard somebody say, "Look out, Honey!" I looked back and got hit right above the eye. Someone took me to the doctor in town and and he said, "This is bad. We got to send you to the hospital in Greenville." There wasn't no train coming through Coahoma till three o'clock that morning. I waited alongside the tracks and got on that train and took it the sixty miles to Greenville—Coahoma, Clarksdale, Lula, Shaw, into Greenville, sixty miles, and my head was hurting so bad. When I got to the hospital the doctor pulled and poked and stitched my head. I hollered louder than a freight train then! I hollered so much the nurse run out of the room saying, "I can't stand it. I can't stand it no more!"

When I got better I went on back to Coahoma and bought a pistol. I was going to kill that boy that hit me. I knew he didn't mean to hit me, but I had on my mind at the time to kill him. I was angry. But I never saw him no more. He lived close, he stayed on the Roosevelt Jones Plantation betwixt Coahoma and Lula. But he never come to Coahoma on a Saturday night to drink and have fun no more. I didn't give a damn about going to jail then—I figured I'd get out sooner or later. I didn't care about anything. But he never did come back to Coahoma no more.

I wasn't scared of nothing. I was really like some of the boys you see on the streets now, I didn't care about nothing. The boys now are selling dope and cocaine, and that's the life they're living in this generation. They got the same mind I had then but what they're doing is different. I

Passing Parchman's Farm–Mississippi State Penitentiary, 1992.

was gambling and fighting and they're doing cocaine. I was the same. I was crazy. I didn't think about my life then. I was in my twenties, just young and wild, and I didn't think about getting any older.

One time I got into it with this guy, Cotton, he was about fifty-five years old. Him and me got to fighting and I had a knife and I cut him. I was crazy, because Cotton had a pistol and was holding it right in my stomach! Men was standing all around us saying, "Cotton, don't you shoot that boy!" If them old men hadn't been begging him, he would have shot me!

Another time I was up in Charleston, Illinois, playing in the streets, and a hustling woman, Thelma, she was throwing me nickels and dimes and pouring whiskey down my throat. A man come up to me and said, "I'm John Wood and that's my woman." He pulled his knife out to cut me and I swung around to hit him with my guitar. I busted my guitar on a tree and then broke and run, and that man cut me as I was running. And the funniest thing, when I went to the doctor to get it sewed up that doctor knew who done it just by looking at me. He said, "I bet it was one of them Woods brothers. They'll cut you!"

I should have been dead fifty years ago. God just wasn't ready for me. Because I used to be a hell of a guy, raise hell and drink, I sure did. One time I got in a fight with Joe Morris, the harp player. We was playing down in Shreveport together and got in a fight about money. We got to arguing and he cut me and I cut him. I was crazy! Another time I was gambling at a big picnic up in Middleton, Tennessee, on the Fourth of July. Some guys got to fighting right at the crap table, started shooting them pistols at each other. And me, instead of trying to dodge and run, I saw all that money laying there and was trying to scoop it all up! I could've got killed but all I was thinking about was that money. I was just trying to survive. I wasn't scared of nothing, didn't have no sense.

There was one time I was really scared, it was up there in Tennessee, too. I was playing out in Ripley, staying with a friend of mine who owned a store in town. One Saturday evening I was playing in the back of this big old grocery with a old man who played the violin. People was standing around, listening to us play, and when we played a few pieces this old man starts passing the hat around. He held it in front of this big white guy, Bud, and asked him, "Give us a little somethin'." Bud didn't want to put nothing in the hat but the old man said to him, "You put somethin' in the hat, too." Bud got mad then and they got to arguing and Bud hit him. That old man hit him back and knocked him down and then run out with his violin, left me standing right there! Bud run out, too. A man there told me, "Boy, look here. Go to my house and don't come out because Bud went to get his friends and his gun, and he'll kill you."

I stayed inside that man's house a while then when it got dark out I started out walking. The moon was shining on that road and I was walking fast trying to get to my friend's house. I was walking down the road when they come, three cars full of white men! They had shotguns, pistols, and everything! One of them hung his head out the window and said to me, "Hey! Who hit Bud?" I said, "I don't know nothin' about it. I didn't even know that old man." They made me get in the car with them and I was scared, I didn't know what they was going to do with me. But they took me where I said I was going, to my friend's house, and when we got there they asked him did he know me. He said, "Yeah, he stays here with me. He's a good boy. He wouldn't cause no trouble." If it wasn't for him, they would have killed me, beat me to death. I was lucky.

One other thing I was scared of, that was the war. I didn't want to go in the army. It was around that time when I got hit in the head by Will that the Japanese bombed Pearl Harbor. World War II come up. I got a draft notice in Coahoma at my auntie's. The government sent me a call card, and I was Class number A. That means I was eligible for the draft and "Be ready to go." I had to report in to the draft board at Friars Point. Then they sent me back home, saying, "You stay there. You're liable to get called any time." I had to stay around Coahoma then. They said if I went anywhere they'd pick me up and shove me straight in the army.

My friends and me would listen to the news about the war on the radio stations. We was shook up, worried all the time. We would even think about how we fly over there and drop a bomb, we thought somebody could come over here with a small plane and throw one. It wasn't impossible. People was just scared.

Then I was called to go to the army camp in Jackson for a couple of weeks. They give me about twenty shots of different kinds of medicine. And then I had to show up for my physical. I did everything to stay out of the army. I took soap pills, little balled-up pieces of brown soap, to make my heart beat fast. I had to walk past about fifteen doctors all sitting in a row. I passed all them son of a bitches and all of them said I was fine till I got to the last one. I got to that last one and he saw that scar on my forehead, from Will chunking that brick at me, and that's what finally kept me out of the war. The doctor said, "That's a bad scar." He said, "Do that ever bother you?" If I'd said one word, no, it don't bother me, I would have been shot right through. But I said, "Yeah, I have fits. I fall down." Man, I didn't want to go. That was a bad war. Mussolini and Hitler, they was shooting people down like flies!

So first I was Class 1-A. Then they gave me 4-F—they were through with me then. With that 4-F that said I wasn't fit for nothing! I hit the road again.

Chapter Fourteen

I had to go back to Coahoma before I got found.

After I stayed all that time in Coahoma, I wanted some air. I left and kept going, looking for someplace where I could make it. I took my harp and my guitar and hit the road, would make good someplace for a while, and then jump up and go to another place. I was roaming further from the Delta. Things was changing in those little towns in the South. When the Depression really eased off was 1940, when the war started. Defense jobs started to open up, shipyards opened up. People was moving, people could see the way out then.

There was a time in the South you couldn't walk the streets in them little towns, there would be so many people. They'd be all at the train stations, sitting around eating and drinking whiskey. But then people started moving north, going north to get them jobs. The farmers wouldn't give the black folks no work, and if you stayed there you'd starve. The farmers run the black folks away when they got them mechanicals in the fields, those machines to pick cotton. One man could get on it and run it, pick all the cotton by himself. The only cotton to be picked by hand was at the ends of the rows where the machine couldn't reach it. No good cotton picker could make money off that. People said, "Well, hell. Damn this stuff. I'll go where I can get me a job." That's why the people left there. Some of those people could pick two or three hundred pounds of cotton a day, and after those mechanicals come in, there wasn't no cotton to pick. Just had to throw that sack away. The cotton they grow now, it's too nasty for a dog to lay on. When we picked by hand, it was beautiful, cotton white as snow.

After the people left, some of those houses, the little shacks sharecroppers lived in, just broke down out in the fields. People used to live out in the country, all spread out. One house here and ten acres over another. You don't see those houses out in the country no more, they either tore them down or let them fall. Some of the better ones, they moved into town and sold them. The shacks they tore down because they had no use for them. Or they'd store cotton in them. And those little country towns, they're just ghost towns now.

All the work was up in Chicago, in them factories. Those folks so busy working up there, it was just like putting out fires all day long. Some people come back south from Chicago for a visit, come back all dressed up, and said, "Man, I'm doin' good up there. Why don't you come up?" People get to talking and then they start to leaving there. "I'm goin' to Chicago." "I'm goin' to Detroit." "I'm goin' to California." People got ideas to go somewhere where they could do better.

I was wanting something better for myself, too, but I didn't know how to find it. I went to Dallas at that time; I thought I'd go see what Texas was all about. I hung around Deep Ellum, that was something like a slum neighborhood in Dallas. The trains run through Deep Ellum and it's all taverns along the street that curves around the railroad tracks, like a crescent moon. All the prostitutes would hang out there where all the taverns was facing the railroad track, sit outside and catch the sunshine, turn tricks. All the hustlers hung out in Deep Ellum. There was gambling, hustling, craphouses, piano houses. It was just like Memphis, with musicians standing on the corners playing.

I stayed there for a while and then made my way up to St. Louis. I got broke around that time. Some guy stole my guitar. I set my guitar in a corner to shoot some dice, and I turned around and some rogue had stole it. I had nothing to do. I didn't have no hustle. He had got my meal ticket. And I said, "What am I going to do now?"

I heard about a labor agent out on Eighteenth Street. He was shipping people out to work as gandy dancers on the railroads in Portland, Oregon. I went over there and signed up for six months' work. He said, "Can you ship this evenin'?" So I did. I didn't have a quarter. But they would give you a sandwich on the train and a apple, a orange. So I went out to Denver, Colorado, and we changed trains at Denver and went out through Boise, Idaho, and Pocatello. Then after we went through Pocatello we went through Pendleton, Oregon, to Portland.

When I got to Portland, I met a boy I knew from Helena, Eddie Murray. I said, "How long you been here?" He said, "I made a payday. I get paid today, man." We was good friends. He said, "You need some money? I'll give you some." So when he got off work, I got thirty dollars from him and got a game going with some guys, started shooting dice. It was summertime and we laid a blanket down in the pine trees where it was shady and cool, and rolled dice. And in a couple days I had made $1,300! All them guys was drunk, trying to hustle them Indian gals out there. They didn't know what they was doing! Shoot, I was just taking their money. Them guys was plumb fools, but they knew after they lost their money they could go back to the camp and eat. They wouldn't go hungry. They'd be back out there lining them tracks the next day.

After I won that money I worked one week. I wasn't going to work on no God damn railroad! That's hard work, too. Them big heavy trains run over the tracks and knock them out of line. You get a bar and knock them tracks back in line. A man stands way down the track sighting it for you, then you spike it. I thought, "I ain't going to work for this dollar and fifty cents a day lining tracks in the hot sun. I got all this God damn money!"

That Saturday I went to the office and got paid. I said, "I'm goin' to leave. I'm jackin' up to go." The boss said, "You know, we don't pay your fare back to St. Louis unless you work your six months. You know that, don't you?" I said, "I know that. I don't need your fare. I just want my pay now."

I left there riding a cushion. I had that $1,300 tied around my waist. We come back through the same way we went, through Pocatello, Cheyenne, Wyoming, and from Cheyenne back into Denver. I had my hands full of money and all I wanted was an electric guitar. I got one in

Denver at a pawn shop, it was a little old cheap guitar called the Singing String, and I bought a small amplifier, had about three tubes in it.
But it was pretty loud at the time. We got back on the train and come
back to St. Louis. I gave a lot of that money to my cousin Annie, who
lived in St. Louis. And I went to the stores and bought myself some nice
clothes. I got me a suit and some Florsheim shoes, and I went to a
tavern wearing my new pants and swinging a watch chain and I made a
girlfriend there. I said, "Y'all want to have a beer on me?" She said,
"Yeah, I'd like a beer." Then when I pulled out that big bankroll her
eyes got wide and she said, "I never did like beer too much. I'll have a
whiskey." It was about a week before I played guitar. I just set it back and
had a good time.

It was around then that I hooked up with Jay, Blind Jim Brewer. He
was only about eighteen years old. He just come from Brookhaven,
Mississippi, playing on the streets for nickels and dimes. He had a lot of
nerve, traveling around like that blind. Me and him hooked up together
and he played his steel guitar and I played electric. You could hear him
with that National real good. He stayed with a woman called Ophelia,
a big dark woman. Ophelia likened Jay but she was a player. Jay was her
meal ticket. Me and him would walk into the saloon to have a drink
before we head out to play and make money, and Ophelia would be
sitting way in the back with some niggers drinking. She'd wave at me. I
wouldn't tell him nothing on her. He was blind and couldn't see her
and I wasn't going to tell him and upset him. "Come on, Jim, let's go."

All that money I made went as fast as it come, and pretty soon I was
back out there hustling. I went on to Memphis after that, and got put in
jail on that vagrancy charge for sixty days. They gave me a job tending
to the cows, so instead of being in the penitentiary all day I worked with
a young white man, taking care of them cows. He'd carry me to his
house, and at dinnertime he'd eat with his family and I'd sleep in his
truck. So I didn't work very hard when I was locked up that time—I was
lucky. That slowed me down a little while, but as soon as they let me
loose I was on the road again.

I usually hoboed by myself but sometimes I'd carry someone with
me. My brother Mack used to try to play harp and he got pretty good. I
carried him with me for a while, but he didn't like the road. We ran

around to different towns around the Delta then we stopped by our uncle's house in Shaw. Our auntie was cooking all them big pots of food, and when Mack saw them pots his eyes got wide and he said, "I ain't goin' nowhere no more!"

Big Walter traveled with me a lot back then. One time we went all through Arkansas and into Oklahoma. The railroad dick put us off the train outside of Hope, Arkansas, where Bill Clinton was raised. We rented a little room there from some people and started practicing in our room, and two gals from the room next door heard us and come over with some whiskey and beer! We caught a train the next day to Idabelle, Oklahoma. It was hotter than a son of a bitch there. We just laid under the shade trees, drinking homebrew beer with them Indian gals. I had every kind of women but a blue one! I laugh, thinking about the things we used to do, me and Big Walter. We was in Monroe, Louisiana, one time and we started playing the blues in a barbershop there. It got so crowded the man couldn't cut hair. But he didn't mind. He said, "Boys, you ain't got no further to go. You found a home." We played the blues and drank white whiskey and made two gals that night, too.

I went to New Orleans almost every year in the winter. Many times I played in the Mardi Gras parades, riding down the streets on the back of a truck, playing the guitar. I was in New Orleans when Fats Domino made his first little recording, "Call Me the Fat Man." I was there when Ivory Joe Hunter made "When I Lost My Baby." I used to play in Westwego, over across the river, every Friday and Saturday night for a Creole woman, Miss Rebecca. New Orleans is a jazz town, and they'd hear blues on jukeboxes but they didn't see too many blues players around there. So I was something different to them. I did alright in New Orleans.

I would go in and out of Helena, too. It was a wide-open little town! There was two or three little sawmills in Helena, but mostly Helena was a river town. The boats would tie up there on the river bank and all them roustabouts would walk off the levee and into the juke houses, come into town and get little rooms. Sometimes they'd stay there a couple of weeks. And when they come in, when the river paid off, there'd be money up in the city. They'd have a pocket of money and the gambling and crap tables and whores was just waiting there for them! When the boats came in, the women put on their tight dresses and come out to meet them. It was a hot little town, a sporting town! Sonny Boy had his thing going there, and Nighthawk, Robert Junior. All kinds of musicians was in Helena at that time.

A lot of them little towns in Arkansas was just like the Mississippi Delta, and I would go up and down the highways there, too. Once I was in Blytheville, Arkansas, playing on the streets there and I had a big crowd around me. A police stopped me and cleared them folks away. "Get off the streets now." Then that next day, he come to the house where I was staying—he come looking for me. I told the woman I was with to tell him I wasn't in because I was scared to be picked up for vagrancy. He said, "Well, I don't want to do nothin' to him. We're givin' a party and we want him to play for us." My woman said, "Well, come back in thirty minutes and he'll be here!"

They was giving a stag party at the police station and I played for them that night! It was nothing but police, white men, all of them drunker than hell and buck dancing! They made me drunk, too, and every one of them give me a dollar apiece. I had a pot full of quarters and dollars. Blytheville, Arkansas. I used to run into some pretty good things, playing around. The world don't owe me nothing.

In Blytheville was where I teamed up with this white boy, Harmonica Frank Floyd. We teamed up and played together on the streets for a few weeks, booked up, and left there together and run all around Tennessee. Frank was a good harp player, a good blues player, and he'd tell a lot of jokes and clown, too. He was short, kind of chunky, sandy hair, sandy colored. He come out of the hill country in Mississippi, playing the blues. He acted just like a nigger; he knew how to make a living on the streets. Musicians was just musicians back then, it didn't have nothing to do with black or white. We was all glad just to see each other. We made music together.

A little north from Blytheville in Missouri is a place called New Madrid. One day I was hitchhiking there on 61 Highway, back when it was still a gravel road, and who picked me up but the high sheriff of New Madrid. He was driving a Ford with a red spotlight on. I got in with my guitar and he asked me, "Boy, do you know who I am?" I knew he was somebody but I said, "No, sir." He said, "I'm Mr. Stanton. I'm the sheriff here. Play me something on that guitar." I played him a number and he carried me to the jail and gave me a room there, said, "You got a place here as long as you want to stay in New Madrid. All you got to do is get up in the mornin' and make a fire in the stove for the cook. Then you can play on the streets and make your money and come back here to stay." Then he carried me downtown to a tavern and had me play and told everybody in there, "Give this boy some money." And here I thought he was going to arrest me! I stayed there a month, near about, had my own room in the little brick jail.

I went north from there, made that Mason-Dixon line, played in Cairo, that was another hot little river town. I went over Charleston, Illinois. That's a farming country out there, all vine watermelons and cucumbers. All them people would break and run out of the fields to hear me play. I went to Paducah, Kentucky, and sat down in front of the jailhouse and played for the prisoners there. I played and they chunked money at me from the window. They was lonesome for the blues. I went to St. Louis and Memphis again. I was running like Big Joe, just like a loose dog. But with all that running around I had to go back to Coahoma before I got found. It was in Coahoma that Alan Lomax come to record me.

When I was young and my daddy was out in Itta Bena I used to go to Ralph Lembo's store and push the broom around. Ralph Lembo had a furniture store, like H. C. Speir, and he used to record musicians, too. I got tired of waiting for him, though, and quit going there. Then I missed that record boom in '39, missed it because I was running too fast. But then I finally recorded in 1942.

Alan Lomax was going around the South recording folks for the Library of Congress. I saw him one time in Clarksdale and then when I was playing in the streets in Friars Point one Saturday evening, drunk, cap turned back on my head and hollering. He walked up after I got done playing and told me who he was, how he was recording different musicians. We talked for a while and he said he'd like to do a interview and a recording with me. I told him where I lived, but I thought he was just some honky talking out of the side of his mouth.

Then I played in Jonestown for that bootlegger Son Collins on a Saturday night, and the next morning I was laying up in my woman's bed and woke up out of a dead sleep. I heard a car pull up in the yard. I heard the car door slam and then a white man's voice, talking low, talking to my gal's auntie. It was Alan Lomax.

Auntie—back then old colored folks was scared of white people—she didn't know what to do. He stood out there and said, "Is David Edwards, Honey, here?" She said, "I don't know. He come by here sometimes." He said, "Well, my name is Alan Lomax and I'm from Washington, D.C. I'm from the Library of Congress. I just want to record him, that's all." He seen that she was scared, backwoods. When she told me this man from Washington wanted to record me, I said, "Tell him yes, I'll see him!" and I got up and put some clothes on.

I recorded for him that day in 1942, it was the twentieth of July. He had just come from recording Son House and Willie Brown. Alan Lomax drove up in the yard in a brand-new Hudson, 1942 super-six, dark green. I got my guitar, put my harp in my pocket, and got in the car with him. He took me to Clarksdale. He got me a room in a little Delta tollhouse, like a tourist camp. He got a room for himself and one for me and then he bought me dinner. He was really nice to me. Then we went to a great big school, a Rosenwald School. Rosenwald Schools was put up at that time all over the South for blacks, so they could have nice schools to go to. Rosenwald Schools was nice schools with ten or twelve rooms to them, painted brown with white windows.

So we went out there and he rented a space at this school for the recording. He wanted someplace quiet to record, and a place that had electricity. He set his machine up and I played "Water Coast Blues" for him. And "The Army Blues": "Uncle Sam ain't no woman, but he sure can take your man." I played "Spoonful" and "Spread My Raincoat Down" and "Worried Life Blues." I did seventeen numbers for him! I could think faster than a monkey, and just like that I done seventeen numbers in about an hour and a half.

In the middle of the session, there come a bad storm, a tornado. It hailed and rained; the sky got dark. It got so bad we had to quit recording, and Alan Lomax cut all the equipment off. We sat in that dark school for about a hour while it was lightning and thunder. It was a rough storm, but when it was over and the clouds started to raising up and it got bright again, we started back to recording. We recorded more

Stormy day in Greenwood, Mississippi, 1993.

back at the tourist camp. And after he gave me twenty dollars. That twenty kicked like a hundred dollars in my pocket then. That was my first recording and I felt good! I felt all right with twenty dollars in my pocket, too; I appreciated that. He brought me back home and then he went further down the Delta. He was recording everybody. He was going down then, on the way down to Rolling Fork to record Muddy Waters. Doing that recording for the Library of Congress felt real good to me. It got me a few little jobs here and there, telling people this man from the Library of Congress had come looking for me.

Chapter Fifteen

He didn't know how good he was.

I wanted somebody to play harp with me, so I went looking for Little Walter Jacobs. I first saw him in Helena. He come there to be where all the musicians was, but by him being so young they didn't pay him much attention. But I knew he was a good harp player and I wanted to hook up with him. I was like Big Joe, always scouting for something new. I went over to Helena and found out he was up in Marianna, Arkansas, staying with a woman, Pearl. She was a lot older than he was. Pearl worked for some white people and Walter was staying with her. I went to Marianna and found him. He was laying up in Pearl's bed with a quart of milk. Walter always did drink milk. Walter was just a little hobo then, a young boy running around with raggedy old tennis shoes. He didn't have no education; Walter could hardly write his name. He was real young, just about eighteen, and already a real good harp player. He was good but he didn't know what was in him.

He was glad to meet me and I was glad to meet him. He said, "I've been looking for somebody like you." He said to Pearl, "I'll be back tonight," and we took off, left there and come to Memphis and hung around Beale Street Park. And Little Walter met Big Walter and we all worked together. Little Walter got a whole lot of stuff from Big Walter, too. We played in the park, the two harps and guitar. Sometimes we'd hook up with Little Buddy Doyle.

Little Walter come from Marksville, Louisiana. He was a Frenchman. He'd start talking that old funny talk and I wouldn't understand a thing. I couldn't always talk to him but I sure did laugh with him. He left from there when he was young. He run away from home when he was about twelve years old.

Because he grew up in Louisiana, Walter played harmonica in the Cajun style. That's why it sounds so different than other harmonica players. He had that Cajun sound. He had the sound like those Louisiana boys playing accordion—he had that with the harmonica. Nobody could match him. A lot of them could play like him but nobody could master it like him.

For the next few years we was together almost all the time. Not just for music, it was always just me and him. Me and Walter hoboed around. We'd do anything and didn't want to stay nowhere. We didn't really care where we was going or when we get there—we just felt lucky to be going. Walter, at that time, he was like me with Big Joe. He didn't have no man-sense, wanted to play all the time, chunk balls, and kick up his heels. I was older than Walter, but we was just alike, wild, and liked to run around.

We stayed that summer of '43 in Memphis with Big Walter, and one day Little Walter said, "Honey, I'm going to St. Louis." I hung around Memphis with Big Walter for a while and then cut on out for St. Louis myself. When I got there, I was on Jefferson Street, playing on the street, and playing that guitar so loud it sounded like a turkey hawk! Some man said to me, "I heard a harp player, a little boy. I wish you could meet him. That son of a bitch can play harp and you'd sound so good together. He works at the lounge right up the street." So I went right over there and I'm hanging around and here comes Little Walter, walking down the street swinging his arms. That was the harp player! Walter said, "Motherfucker, where'd you come from?"

Walter was working at the lounge and at a laundry. Every day at that laundry he'd take a shirt and put it on underneath his shirt, come home with something new every night. We didn't have no clothes and all them nice shirts was there!

We hoboed over to Ruleville and signed up with a man to make a crop for him on his plantation. We signed up in the winter, borrowed a hundred dollars from him and told him we was going to stay and farm. We stayed, got groceries, and then the first time the weather broke, when it quit raining and snowing, we got away from there. They farm in March, but me and Walter, we marched in March! Nobody going to hook us up all summer in that hot sun, no, Lordy. Get someone else for that.

One time we was down in New Orleans, playing outside the Union Hall down on Rampart. We was finished playing and I started walking down the street, Walter stayed behind talking to somebody. I was walking up Rampart and a police shined his light on me. "Come here, boy. What's your name?" I told him. "Where you from?" I told him. And here come Walter, running up. He was a crazy old boy. He said, "What's going on, man?" The police say, "Who want to know?" "Me!" "You?" "Me! That's my partner!" The police said, "Both of you, get in the car!" He drove for around three blocks trying to think of some reason to arrest us and then he stopped and said, "Get the hell out!"

Walter, he was like that. We got so close that if I stayed someplace one night and Walter stayed somewhere else, we'd get up in the morning and first thing go looking for each other. "Y'all seen Honey?" "Y'all seen Walter?" I never did get close to nobody in my life like Little Walter. He was my partner.

In '44, in Carruthersville, Missouri, we was playing on the streets one day. Me and Walter was playing and who walks right up but Sunnyland. He said, "Hey, man, I ain't seen you in a long time!" and told us he was playing down around the sea wall that night. The sea wall means the concrete built around the levee, that's called the sea wall. It's put there to keep the water out of the city. He said, "Why don't you join me?" So we went down there and played with Sunnyland.

Sunnyland was playing there for a guy called Juke. Juke was a half-white guy. He was sharp. His white daddy had given him money to set him up and he had a big piano joint and craphouse that sold whiskey.

Sunnyland was going with a gal at that time, a woman called Enid. She was a good-looking dark gal, tall and heavy, built like a stallion. Hair all puffed up on her head. She come in that night and damn if she didn't fall for Walter. Fell for him! And Walter starts slipping around with her. Sunnyland gets mad, but hell, ain't no man going to turn down no woman. Sunnyland got mad, and me and Walter had to go back to playing on the street corners.

About two or three weeks go by. Me and Walter was playing at a little restaurant in town, and Sunnyland walked in and stood in the crowd for a long time, watching us play. Finally he come up and said, "Hey, man, come on out to where I'm playin' at." He said, "I'm not goin' to fall out with you about no God damn woman. If that woman wants you, she wants you. She ain't nothin' to me. She ain't nothin' but a God damned whore anyway! So come on back and let's get together." So we went back down there and Sunnyland and Walter made it up. Sunnyland liked her but he let that go.

Walter, he went with Enid clean until we left town, and Sunnyland, he left her alone after that. We stuck together, had a good time. We'd drink and laugh—we stuck together. No fighting or nothing like that, nothing but good times. Walter went with that Enid as long as we was in town. We wouldn't carry nobody with us when we left, though!

In '45, me and Walter come to Chicago. We had heard all about Maxwell Street—they called it Jewtown, too—and we wanted to go there because that was where the happening was. Musicians come to Chicago from everywhere then just to play on Maxwell Street. Because they could make a living there. We was in St. Louis when we decided to go. We hitchhiked from East St. Louis to Decatur, Illinois. We had only a few dollars; we didn't have enough to get to Chicago. So we hit the streets in Decatur, and found a little whiskey house and played a while there. Then we walked on over to the train station. We played at that train station, Walter playing that harp loud. I had my guitar and little amplifier. The trains would come in and people coming in to the depot stopped to listen. And we made enough at that station to buy tickets to ride to Chicago. We rode the cushions!

We got in to Chicago about eleven o'clock that night. We got off that train and come straight down Halsted and over to Maxwell Street. Max-

Passenger train coming into Chicago, 1995.

well Street was all the time wide open and really crowded. At that time all the steel mills and slaughterhouses, packing houses was wide open. Everybody was working two or three shifts, people was working the graveyard shifts. There was always people out on the streets, the street was full of people of all kinds, blacks, whites, Mexicans, Jews. Lots of people had come up from the South to get a job in Chicago.

There wasn't room for all the people back then. In the rooming houses, two or three people would rent the same bed in shifts. Like, if you go to work this morning at seven o'clock and I get off at seven in the morning, the landlady takes that linen off there and I come in there and sleep all day. And when you come in, you sleep at night in that bed.

We met a boy there who knew we was new and he said, "Y'all just got into town, didn't you? Y'all can come to my house and lay down there."

People sure was nice then. I said, "I'm goin' over there, Walter. I want to sleep." Walter, though, he was like a flea: he was hopping.

I went on and laid down. And about seven o'clock in the morning I heard all these musicians playing in the streets. Floyd Jones was out there, Jimmy Rogers, all them was playing in the streets. Jimmy Rogers had a girl with a little baby, he had just come out of the army. He was wearing a suit and a high straw top hat. Snooky Pryor was there. And Tampa Red, not the original Tampa Red, another guy called Tampa Red, tall, yellow, walked kind of bowlegged. Had a real heavy voice and played in Vastopol. And old Stovepipe who used to play the harp. Stovepipe was a old-time minstrel show musicianer; he played ragtime stuff. Pork Chop, playing the washtub bass in the street; One-Leg Sam Norwood playing guitar, who used to play with Tommy Johnson; John Henry Barbee was out there trying to throw tricks; a fellow playing banjo called Fat—they was all playing on the corners. Some of them was down by the hot dog stands, some of them be way down about Newberry, some across Fourteenth Street. Just strung out all hooked up to different peoples' houses. Musicians would give the people in the houses two dollars to plug their instruments up in their houses. And there was so many people in Jewtown you couldn't walk the streets.

A lot of hustling was going on there in Jewtown. Those country boys from Mississippi heard talk of this town, Chicago, and sat on them stumps, whittling sticks and thinking how to beat these niggers in Chicago when they got here. They come up to the city looking crazy and foolish and get in them gambling games and walk away with all the money in their arms. There was gambling and hustling going on all over Maxwell Street. You had to have your eyes wide open.

Walter come to me and said, "Get up, man, get up!" I said, "What you want?" "Get up, boy! Let's get out here and make some of this God damn money!" I said, "I ain't got no shirt." "Well," Walter said, "Give me a dime." I give him a dime and he went out and got me a clean shirt. We went out in the street together and made more money than we ever made before. We made about twenty dollars apiece. We emptied our cigar box about four or five times. Every time we get a boxful of change, we'd go into a saloon and the man would take all the change and give us greenbacks for it. It was a big saloon, a big whiskey store with hus-tling women hanging around.

We had the biggest crowd around us, with people chunking quarters and dollars at us. Money was floating then. On Maxwell Street, who could play the best, that's what got the best crowd. And the best sound, that's what got the best crowd. They would stop by, but if it wasn't sound-ing good they would go to the next.

Walter was playing his song "Hey, baby, don't you want a man like me." That boy could play a harp. He was like Big Walter but had a better style, a sound and a style. Now, Big Walter could play more harp than Little Walter but Little Walter had a cooked, solid sound. Big Walter could get more notes, he knew more flashy notes, he knew more keys, but Little Walter had the best sound because he had a dead sound. Just a little something can make a big difference in harp playing.

Little Walter started playing and this woman walked up with a tablet in her hand, wrote her address and phone number down there, and threw it in the kitty. It said, "Come out and visit me." And she was a church woman, too! She was about forty years old and good-looking. She had a sanctified Jesus Christ church up on North Avenue some-where. The woman was making money. So Walter looked at that letter and said, "Man, I'm going to see what this old broad is talking about." He went out there and stayed Tuesday, Wednesday. He come back down on Maxwell Street on Thursday. He had a blue suit on with cable stitch going up the side, a dark fedora all crimped up on his head. She carried him downtown, got him all dressed up! I saw him and said, "Man, who is you?"

After we'd been in Chicago a while Walter made another girlfriend. He was making it with a girl called Marie living over on Newberry. And Marie's man, Willie, got over to it. We went to Marie's house one morn-ing and Willie showed up. Walter and Willie only exchanged about two words before they was fighting. Walter had a old hawk-billed knife, and he cut Willie in the mouth with it. Walter was mean, quick-tempered. He never got mean with me. And he never got mean for no reason, but he was quick-tempered if somebody started something. So Walter cut Willie and we went downtown then and caught a train to Milwaukee. We thought Walter would go to jail for cutting that boy, so we left town.

We found a place to play in Milwaukee, with the house band, an upright bass and a drummer. We stayed a month playing just about every night and then come back to Chicago.

Walter was crazy. When we come back to Chicago we went back to playing at our old spot on Maxwell Street. And Walter had bought himself a .25 automatic and hid it in his amplifier. I never will forget that. We was playing on the street one Sunday morning and Willie come up there. The crowd was all around us. Willie kept looking at Walter. Walter jumped up, got that .25 out, and said, "What the hell you looking at me like that? Get on now!" He shot at him. Willie got away and went and told the police. The police come but we said, "Ain't nobody got a gun." And all the people around there told them the same thing. Walter was crazy. That's how he got killed. And I sure hated that.

I stayed with Walter in Chicago till the last of August. I was scared of the cold then. I said, "Walter, I'm going back south." He said, "Honey, I ain't going back down there. I'm sticking around to freeze with these niggers here." Walter had got the hang of Chicago. I went on back down south, blinded a passenger from Chicago to St. Louis.

When I left Walter in Chicago he spent that winter sleeping in them Salvation Army boxes where people donate their clothes. He come back south after Christmas and come to Helena. We played around Helena for most of that year, and broadcast every day on the KFFA station. Sonny Boy wasn't broadcasting on KFFA by then. We had Dudlow on the piano, old Five by Five. He was so fat, he couldn't hardly walk, but he could rock a piano. And we had James Peck Curtis on drums. Some nights, we played at the Hole in the Wall, Arthur Crawford's place. And that's where I met my wife at. That's when I got Bessie. After I hooked up with Bessie, Walter went back north and made Chicago his home.

Next thing I know, I heard Little Walter on a record with Muddy Waters. He was playing on the jukeboxes. I said, "God damn, that's Walter! He cut! He done cut!" It made me hungry to do something.

After Walter recorded with Muddy Waters's band for Chess, they toured and was playing and traveling all through the South. They was together a little while. It was after Walter had recorded this song "Juke," and that song was hot as fire. They just finished a gig in Memphis and the band was driving down the highway somewhere around Hayti, Missouri. And Walter and Muddy got to arguing, fighting about money. Muddy pulled off the road and Walter got out of the car. Walter was mad, and he said, "I ain't gonna ride with you. Go on." They drove on without him and he started walking down the highway. Hip Linkchain, he was in the car, and he said later they felt bad and went back to get him and Walter wouldn't get back in. He said he'd rather walk to Chicago. "Come on, you come on and get back in the car." Walter said, "No, I don't want to ride with you." And Walter hoboed all the way back to Chicago.

When Walter come back to Chicago, he didn't go down to the studio. Leonard Chess sent for him to start back to playing for Muddy Waters. Chess knew Walter was good; he knew Walter was an artist. But Walter said, "No, I refuse to play with Muddy anymore because he didn't treat me right." Chess tried to sway him to go back to Muddy. "Why don't you go back? You're doin' so good." Walter said to Chess, "I'd rather get a job!" That's what he told me. He was mad.

Walter was staying with a gal down on Indiana Avenue somewhere. He always had a lot of girlfriends, always had a good place to stay. Chess sent for him again and said, "What about if I put you with Louis and Dave Myers and Freddy Below?" Chess put them together as The Four Aces and recorded them. Next time Walter saw Muddy he told him, "I don't need you no more." He didn't need him neither. Chess bought Walter his first Cadillac and put him on the road behind "Juke." That shows you how people can come up. Sometimes things go overnight for you.

Little Walter had the best sound of any harmonica player. He could take one key and kill them dead with that key. Big Walter Horton, he was the best harmonica player there ever was. He could play any kind of harp in any style. But Little Walter had the best sound—a sound and a style like no one before or since.

After Little Walter made it with "Juke," he played with different bands, on the road everywhere. He started to make it, make him some money. But me and him never changed. Shortly after he made "Juke," I was down in Alexandria, Louisiana. Me and my wife drove down there in a old '40 Buick. I was hustling through there, playing at a club and driving a tractor on a farm. I was walking down the street one day and Little

Walter come driving up in his Cadillac. It was my luck to be on the street that day, and Little Walter drove up and said, "God damn, man, what the hell are you doing here?" I said, "Walter!" He got out of his car and said, "Oh, man!" and he grabbed me and we talked.

He was going to Marksville, his hometown. He had just come from Chicago and his record was swinging then, keeping the jukeboxes hot as fire. He was driving home to his people in a black 1951 Cadillac. He said, "I'm goin' to Marksville, my home. I'm goin' to put on a dance. You come work with me." He went down, got acquainted with this man, and got something set up at a club for a Friday night. Then he drove around and put placards up all up and down Louisiana. Man, and that night when we played, you couldn't get in the joint. He got a local drummer and me, and we packed that house. I made one hundred dollars that night. By being Little Walter he packed that joint. His record was playing on the jukeboxes and people come to see him from fifty, sixty miles away. He left back to Chicago after that and I had enough money to hit the road. He said, "You comin' to Chicago?" And I said, "Well, I'll be up there probably after the winter's over with."

Little Walter, he was smooth—he was a player. Nice-looking, he wore good clothes and always had a smile on, all the time laughing and talking. He acted like nothing ever worried him. He was a woman-player; he had a lot of girlfriends. And he'd give me anything, he'd give me the clothes right off his back.

Chapter Sixteen

We did so good together, I kept her.

I stayed single a long time, till I was about thirty-two years old. I didn't want no woman to take care of. I couldn't make enough with my guitar to take care of me and a wife, and I didn't want to put my guitar down. I'd stay with one woman one week, go on to another the next week. Sometimes I hated to go. And I had some women crazy about me, I've had a couple girls beg me to marry them. But I wouldn't marry them because I wouldn't get no job, go out to the field and be tied down because I got a wife. And that's what I'd have to do. I didn't want to stake my life with a woman, but after I got Bessie we did so good together, everywhere I go, I kept her.

I met Bessie at the Hole in the Wall, a juke house in Helena. Me and Walter was playing there with our band, Dudlow and Peck Curtis. The place was crowded with people, and Bessie come in with another girl. She was around twenty-six years old, nice-looking. She had a big mouth but she was good-looking! She had smooth brown skin, coal black eyebrows. She come in the door, and I was high, drinking, and I see her walk in. I said to her, "Hey, girl, come here! What's your name? I sure like you." I was laughing and joking with her. I said, "I'd sure like you to get to be my girlfriend." She said, "I don't know. I'll tell you later." I said, "When?" And she said, "When I come back another time." Then she left and she was only gone about ten minutes before she come back! She wanted me as bad as I wanted her.

She had a man she was living with, Jake, and he found out I was going with her. In a small town like that, everybody telling your business. Robert Nighthawk's band was in Helena at that same time, and Jake thought I was playing with Nighthawk. One night Bessie was sitting in the tavern eating and Jake come in the tavern and stood up over her, behind her while she was eating. I walked in. I had on a dark green overcoat, and a green derby hat. I was looking good. When I walked in, Jake said, "That's the son of a bitch right there." She said, "No, that ain't the one, Jake. You wrong." She was trying to throw him off the track like a woman do. I acted like I didn't hear him. I walked on by and said, "Give me a drink, Joe." Jake said, "That's one of them damn Nighthawks."

Jake, he was working out of town, across the river in Mississippi, driving a log truck. He would take his truck over the river on the ferry every day and haul logs in Tunica, Mississippi, about fifteen miles from Helena. But one night he took his truck over to that other side of the river like he was going to work and then slipped back over on the ferry to Helena. He was supposed to be gone. But instead of going, he went and hid behind the Helena Grocery near the Hole in the Wall, and he was back there with a big, long knife, waiting for me and Bessie.

We walked down Cherry Street after the club closed, about one o'clock in the morning, and walked behind the Helena Grocery Company on the way to my cousin's house. We was walking along, talking, laughing. Knew he was gone. We turned that corner together and he broke on out at us with his knife. "Oh, yeah, I caught you now!" He was trying to get to me with his knife to cut me and she grabbed him, saying, "Jake, you got the wrong man! You wrong!" He said, "You God damn liar, that's that son of a bitch." And while she was fighting with him like that I got away. He probably would've killed me! But she blocked him. She done that so I could get away. I turned the fan on then! I run so fast my feet didn't touch the ground!

**Honeyboy's wife Bessie (left) and a friend at Clark's tavern
on Chicago's South Side, 1962.**

I went on to my cousin's house, and about five o'clock that morning, Bessie come knocking on the door. She said, "Jake done put me out and I ain't got nowhere to go." They fought all night long. They raised so much sand that night. I felt like she lost her husband on account of me, and I thought it was my place to take it up. That was in my heart, if he put her out about me, I thought I was supposed to take up the tote. God done that; God was in the plan. I really didn't want a wife then but I got her, and after I got her, I was glad.

Things got kind of slow in Helena then. It was wintertime, and there was so much snow that people out in the country couldn't come to town. And the people in Helena, they got their support from those country folks coming out of the backwoods to gamble and spend their money. But nobody was in town, and that last night when we played at the Hole in the Wall, the boss come up with the kitty and said, "Boys, you know I didn't make no money. Here's what I cut off." He had about nine dollars. He said, "Y'all can have the whole thing."

I called my sister Hermalie the next day and she said, "Come on to Memphis. Come up here." Hermalie and her husband had moved to Memphis by that time. There used to be a train out of Helena called the Eagle that went to Memphis, and I got on that Eagle. I said to Bessie, "I'll send you a ticket tomorrow." Her people said, "You crazy about that guitar player and now he's leavin'. He's goin' to put you down. Your husband don't want you and that nigger with that speckled guitar, he's goin' away." I fooled all of them. I sent her a ticket. I sent her a ticket and Bessie come where I was, at my sister's house in Memphis there on Jackson Street.

I got a job in the iron yard on Union Street in Memphis for seventy-five cents an hour. I worked a little while there. And Bessie worked on Jackson Street at Al's Restaurant, as a carhopper. She wore a little white cap turned up on her head. People drive up in the car, she go out, they order what they want, and she carry it out and hang it on the window. I'd come pick her up every evening, and she'd have my supper there waiting for me. That was 1947. I worked there all the winter. Spring come up and I went to Morris's Pawnshop at Second and Beale and bought a amplifier. And me and Bessie left out of there and went to New Orleans. Bessie got pregnant that year in New Orleans and we went back to Shaw, amongst my kin peoples.

Bessie and me worked picking cotton by the day there in Shaw that fall, and Bessie hurt herself. Our baby was born dead because Bessie got hurt while picking. We named him James. He was born in October of '48 in Shaw, amongst our kin peoples, where Mack was living. He was stillborn when the midwife caught him—my first baby by Bessie.

Bessie had been married before. She come from Radshaw, Arkansas, and had been married to another man before Jake. Dollie McGinister was Bessie's daughter by him. We call her T-Baby. She was Bessie's first child, born in 1940. T-Baby and her brother Jake Junior and two babies, Joanna and Mary, stayed with their grandmother, Miss Dollie, in Arkansas. In later years T-Baby come to us in Chicago.

We started to traveling together, all around, to Texas, Louisiana, Florida. Bessie and me was all the time traveling. Bessie was a smart woman, and she always liked to work. She got jobs in taverns, restaurants, hotels. She always was smart. And she had that nice big mouth and big eyes, smooth skin and pretty smile. She talked a whole lot to people all the time; she would bullshit with them. People liked her right away. She helped me, and I tried to help her. Every once in a while I'd get a little old job, but I always played. I always had somewhere to holler on the weekend to make some money. I'd hustle, get different little jobs, and we lived alright.

We rode the bus to different places, or we'd hitchhike on the highway. Bessie would put on her blue jeans and be right with me. She was a tomboy. I even tried to teach her to play music. Bessie loved music, she was a music-head. She used to try to sing. She had a hell of a mouth on her, but she couldn't get control of her voice. She could spit it out, but she couldn't control it. And I got her a cheap set of drums, and she'd beat the hell out of those things. We played together down in Florida for many months. I was studying ways to keep out of those fields.

Bessie saved my life twice: once with Jake and another time down in Texarkana, Texas. We was staying in a little hotel and another guy was staying there, Horace. He went with me to a skin game. I broke everybody that night—I won all the money. Horace, the guy with me, he couldn't win no money. He just couldn't win. So he got kind of mad. He rode back to Texarkana with me, and after we got back, he had hell on his mind.

When I got to my room, I put my guitar up, had a good washup, put my watch on the post, and told Bessie, "I'm goin' downstairs to get me a half a pint." She said, "OK, Honey." I went out, and before I could get back he had come in. He went in the kitchen, pulled out a butcher's knife. Sharpened it. And Bessie said, "What you goin' to do with that knife, Horace?" He said, "I'm going fishin' in the mornin'." I come to the door then. Bessie hollered out at me, "Get back, Honey! Horace in here with a knife!" Horace come at me with the knife, and Bessie grabbed his arm and said, "Horace, you drop that knife, you sombitch!" Bessie was strong and young, and she tussled with him and knocked it out of his hand. He grabbed a hammer that was sitting on the counter then, and hit me, right on the forehead. I was bleeding all over. The ambulance come and took me to the hospital. I still have the scar from that, right here next to my eye. Horace took off and never showed up again. He had a woman there but he never even come back to get her.

We used to pull a lot of shit, me and Bessie. I ain't joking. She was with me and I was with her. Don't care which way, up or down, we was together. I had to make it. I wasn't going to work for nobody. It was nobody but me and Bessie. Everywhere I played at, they give her a job, too. We went dressed up all the time; we went presentable. She had that big smile all the time. When I get a job at a club, they'd say, "That's your wife?" I'd say, "Yeah." "Well, I can use her. She can work in the bar here." "Yeah, if she want to. That's up to her." So we work in the same joint. When they get funny, I'd say to Bessie, "Let's go." She'd say, "OK, Honey."

We was a team. One time we went to New Iberia, Louisiana. That's when I worked for this guy Chapman who run a little tavern. He gave me the crap table to work. I played and would draw a crowd of people in there, help get the crowd in there, and then start to cutting the dice. I was supposed to get a cut from the crap table but Chapman didn't know how much I was winning so I was making some money. Bessie was selling beer and sandwiches. She'd sell one sandwich and give the dime to Chapman and sell another and put the dime in her pocket! He was stuck on her. He was crazy about my wife. He'd give her anything she want. Bessie'd say to me, "God damn sombitch is crazy about me." I said, "I know it." The last Saturday night I played there, running the game, I had made about thirty-five dollars natural money. I went up to my room to count the nickels and dimes up, what I cut off. Bessie counted the money what she cut off the sandwiches onto the bed. I told Bessie, "Let's pack our clothes tonight." We packed our suitcases and come downstairs with our luggage. Chapman said, "Where y'all goin'?" I said, "Man, I'm goin' to Houston." He said, "You ain't told me nothin' about it!" "I didn't have to tell you!" He said to Bessie, "You goin'?" Bessie said, "Well, I come with him, didn't I?" I never will forget it! She said, "Damn right! I come here with him, didn't I?"

Many men was crazy about my wife. But she didn't go nowhere—she was for me and I was for her. But she always knew what was going on. She was a hustler. She couldn't talk good, she talked tie-tongued. Bessie would say, "I got this sombitch, le's go!" She'd get them, too. I ain't joking!

Site of the once–popular Chicago blues club Teresa's, 1994.

Once in Montgomery, Alabama, we got broke and was stuck in town for two weeks, near about. Bessie and me was staying in a room above a tavern and we didn't have enough money to pay the landlord and leave. One Friday evening this fellow, this one-armed guy, come to the tavern. He come to town with two cows, his grandmother's cows, to sell. And he sold them to the market there; I think he got two hundred dollars for them. Bessie kept pouring that man drinks until he couldn't barely see straight, and then when the tavern closed up I got him up to my room and got him into a game. And I beat that guy out of every quarter he had. I needed that money bad. I couldn't get any work and I couldn't leave town. He was shaking. He said, "Please give me some of that back." I said, "The best thing I can do for you, partner, I can give you twenty dollars. You can walk with that." Then I woke Bessie up and said, "Let's go, baby. Let's go to Memphis." If Bessie was living today, she'd tell you, I gambled for many a dollar to feed her.

One time I met a labor hustler in Carruthersville, Missouri. He was pulling people into buses and trucks, bringing them to Michigan to pick fruit. He said, "I'd like to take y'all up to Michigan with me. Give you a shack to stay in, pick fruit, and make some money." I said, "Well, yeah!" and we pulled out and come up to Michigan. We had a place to stay, and he got food to feed the people.

I broke him gambling the first night, I did. We was shooting dice and Bessie was in the back room, laying down. I was playing like I had never played in my life. Bessie was chewing gum back there and everytime I hit one she went "bam!" with that gum. I'd shoot, and Bessie'd "bam!"— eleven! The man said, "If that God damn woman would quit chewing that gum, I could win!" I beat that man out of $250, all the money he had for bringing the people up there. Bessie got pregnant that same night.

We got up the next morning and he said to me, "You going to pick?" I said, "Hell no, I picked last night!" I went to the nearest town, to a big car lot, and bought a '37 Studebaker, straight-eight with the cylinder straight down the block. It would run eighty miles an hour, best car I ever had. I went back up to the campground, got my clothes, and the boss said, "That son of a bitch bought him a damn car!"

We went through Chicago then and stayed with Sunnyland. Sunnyland had moved to Chicago by then and was running a gambling joint on the South Side. He had a wife named Bessie back then, too, Black Bessie. Me and my Bessie stayed there two or three months with them. We had them two Bessies cooking sandwiches, fish, and hamburgers for the people, and we'd gamble and play music and drink whiskey. Then we hit the road again.

Oh, yeah, me and Bessie, when I got her I just run around like I was running around by myself. She liked to travel and she liked to be with me, and when I started going, she liked to go. We went to New Orleans, stayed in New Orleans a while, left there and went to Gulfport, Mississippi, stayed there a while on the coast. And we left there, come back to Greenwood, left Greenwood for Tallulah, Louisiana, and from Tallulah to Shreveport, and from there back over to Houston and from Houston back to Orange, Texas. We rented a trailer house there from a woman who had a trailer house parked right beside her home. Bessie got a job there on the highway at a barbecue place and I played inside. One night we got drunk at work and when we got home we got to fighting. The landlord called the police. Bessie was beating the hell out of me, and the police come and arrested me! I said, "God damn, she got the best of me! What did y'all arrest me for?" That's the truth! They carried me to jail and left her! And she was on top of me in that fight! I got seven days.

Bessie kept her job and every evening she'd come and bring me dinner. After I got out of there, I got my guitar and started back to playing. Then we stayed there another week and we pulled up and went to Houston.

Me and Bessie stayed together about six or seven years before we married. We married in Houston in 1952. She was already married to one man in Arkansas so she couldn't marry in Arkansas. So I got her in Texas.

With Bessie working and me playing we'd get by. We'd go up and down the road, she right with me, and when we made a good hit I'd buy me a suit and she'd buy her a suit and we get on the buses. "Bessie, get your things," and she'd say all tie-tongued, "OK, Honey." I'd be toting the amplifier, and she'd carry my guitar. She'd be with me. We'd get a place and go out and make a hustle.

Chapter Seventeen

The blues is something that keeps you moving.

I had Bessie but the way I lived didn't change. The blues kept me on the road, it was always leading me somewhere. That's what the blues is, it's a leading thing, something on your mind that keeps you moving. My son David was born in Memphis in 1952. We give him to my sister Hermalie. Hermalie had never got pregnant and she wanted David, so we give him to her and she raised him.

We went in and out of Memphis all the time. Memphis was a different scene by then, by the late forties and fifties. Not so many musicians played in the Beale Street Park at that time. And different musicians was in town. Howlin' Wolf, B. B. King, Bukka White was all there. Wolf was playing at different places in Memphis and out in the country. He got pretty popular at that time because he was broadcasting on the radio from KWEM in West Memphis, and that helped him a whole lot in the farming areas through there. They advertised feed and seed and farm implements, stuff like that. In Mississippi and across West Memphis, Arkansas, around Little Rock and Franklin and Marianna, the people would hear him on the radio, and the folks that had them country jukes, the bootleggers, they would get him to play. He had Willie Nix on drums, little Willie Johnson on guitar, and sometimes he had a second guitar player, Pat Hare.

Wolf went in the army in '45 and when he come out two years later he made a couple of little numbers for Sam Phillips at Sun Records. And when he come out of the army he got that G.I. loan and bought him a couple of old tractors and forty acres. Then luck come to him out of the deep blue sky. The two years following, that was the best crop years since back in the twenties and Howlin' Wolf made money. In '48 he drove the blues away then! He made a whole lot of money in '48, and he bought a brand-new DeSoto station wagon. Wolf always wanted to play music, so he quit that farming and left for Chicago. Willie Johnson went with him. When Wolf come to Chicago he made it with that harp. He cut a right-of-way with that!

Howlin' Wolf was a kind of quiet type; he didn't raise no lot of hell. He always just played his music and paid his boys alright, but he could be kind of mean if you make him mean. He didn't take too much shit. One time him and Willie Johnson got to arguing, and Willie went after Wolf with a knife. Little old Willie run him all around the room and then outside and down Sixteenth Street in the dark. Wolf was running down the street, then all of a sudden he stopped and turned. He had a pistol in his hand and he pointed it at Willie and said in that big old voice of his, "Willie, I done got tired now."

B.B. had quit singing with the choir and come into Memphis then. He was playing in the Beale Street Park and a disk jockey, Nat D. Williams, heard him play and carried him to the radio station. He gave B.B. his name, "Beale Street Blues Boy." Every day B.B. would broadcast over WDIA for Pepticon, the medicine company. That's when he got his little old band together. He had a 1948 Mercury Ford, yellow, club coupe. Him and his band went everywhere, playing Arkansas, Missouri, all the cotton patch countries. He played lead, and he had a drummer and a bass guitar player—that's all he had. Later, he made that first little old record about "Miss Martha King."

When me and Bessie come to Memphis we would stay with my sister, and every Friday and Saturday evening we'd go where B. B. King played out on Sixteenth Street. B.B. had one suit, a blue serge suit. B.B. had one suit! We didn't make no money back in that time. He was singing as good as he do now, but he wasn't making no money; B.B. didn't have a quarter.

Roscoe Gordon was pretty popular around then, playing a lot of little gigs. Bobby Bland, he was down there too, and this other boy, Junior Parker.

I saw all these guys starting to make it. My friends was recording, getting a little something on wax out there, and I wanted that, too. I wanted to get good and to where I could start making money. And I figured whatever you do, you got to keep up with it, keep trying, put yourself into it. And I was still thinking in order to make it I had to hustle from town to town, play in different places, get to know different people. No telling who you run into if you keep trying, so I was still running everywhere. Me and Bessie would get a old car and go from town to town, playing in different places.

If we wasn't in Memphis, we was all the time traveling. We'd go to Independence, Louisiana, to play and pick strawberries. We spent a lot of time in Louisiana—I used to be on the bayou all the time. We went to Lafayette and we was the only folks speaking English there. I played the blues for those Frenchmen and they really enjoyed it.

In 1950, I played with another medicine show, with Chief Thunder Cloud. We had a fellow called Bow Tie and one called Ham, two comedians. They dressed in black-face and always acted like they was fighting. We went all around Missouri with that show, went into Cairo, southern Illinois. In Cairo we run up on Kansas City Red and Earl Hooker. Matt Murphy was there, too, he had a little band, playing about three nights a week at the time.

Bessie and me went to Pompano Beach, Florida, after that and spent a long time there. We played at Pompano and in Belgrave, too. There was a whole lot of harvests in Florida, and people there picking them string beans and corn and tomatoes. Me and Bessie spent a lot of time in Florida, working in taverns. Then, in '51, we hit Houston.

I heard so much talk of Lightnin' Hopkins and T-Bone Walker, Gatemouth, I said, "I believe I'll go out to Texas. Maybe I'll do a little better out there." I always wanted to be where the musicians I liked was at.

That was the first time I went to Houston. Me and Bessie went there on the Greyhound bus. When I got off the bus I had eighty cents in my pocket, eighty cents and my guitar and a suitcase. I got off the bus in the Fifth Ward and before I did anything I called old man Bill Quinn from Gold Star Records. I heard Lightnin' and them had recorded for him. He said, "Yes, sir, I heard of you. You just in town?" I said, "Yeah." He said, "Well, catch the bus and come on out here." He was a widow man, stayed all alone. He had some great big old German police dogs. He recorded musicians and done his own pressing, made his own masters. I went out there and he said, "You're broke, ain't you?" I said, "Sure is." That old man knew how musicians was. I done two sides for him and he give me about thirty-five dollars. That set me free right then. He said, "Take this and go on and get yourself straightened out." I come back out to the Fifth Ward and got a room for me and Bessie. And I started getting acquainted with people and playing little joints, started to make me a little money.

I got a job playing in a joint over in the Fourth Ward. And on Friday nights I would drive twenty miles over to Pearland, I found a little job out there every Friday. My wife would play with me there, sing and play drums a little. And every Saturday Lightnin' Hopkins played at the same place. We had a night apiece. It was a lively little town; a lot of people lived out there, worked at a big lumber mill out there. And it was a good time. I'd listen to Lightnin' play the blues and I felt good. Didn't nobody have a sound like Lightnin' Hopkins. He had that Texas road blues, real country, way-down-in-the-country blues. He played a lot different from Mississippi blues players. When I listened to Lightnin' play the blues and when I played, sometimes I stopped thinking about where the blues would take me. We wasn't making no money then or anything, but just listening to Lightnin' made me feel good, and I felt good playing.

I met all kinds of musicians in Texas. I met Candy Harris and Lowell Fulson and Big Mama Thornton. She was big then, too, good-sized. The first time I saw her she was just walking down the street in the Fourth Ward, wearing big blue jeans and a man's hat cocked on the side of her head. I got to know her then, her song "Hound Dog" was playing all over at that time. She was a damn good harp player, Big Mama was—she was hell with that harp. Before she got started she played on the streets and in the juke joints just like a man. She sounded good and

A street scene in Houston, Texas, 1994.

made something for herself. After the fifties in Texas I didn't see her again until many years later, when we had a gig together at Carnegie Hall in New York City.

Me and Bessie drifted to Arkansas and then come back to Houston in '52. We come in to Houston that time on a Sunday morning. I was driving a yellow 1942 Ford. We drove around and got to the Fifth Ward and I stopped there that morning. I was tired from driving, and dusty. There was a tavern on the corner there, Clint's Tavern, that opened up at noon. I didn't change my clothes or anything; I just went in there when they opened up, went in there with my guitar. I got me a drink and started talking to Clint, the man who owned the place. He said to me, "Why don't you go on and play?" I hooked up and started to play and people come running in that tavern like horses to a trough.

Clint called a friend of his, Miss Lola Anne Collum, to have her come over and meet me. Clint said to her, "I got a boy here, a damn good guitar player. Come over and listen at him." Miss Collum was handling Artist Recording Company and she come and listened to me play and grabbed me and signed me up.

Miss Collum hooked me up with a band. I had Thunder Smith on the piano, I had a old half-Mexican boy on tenor sax, and a drummer named Shorty. Thunder Smith, Wilson Smith, he got to be a good friend of mine. We called him Smiley. Miss Collum gave him that name Thunder to go with Lightnin' Hopkins because he was Lightnin's piano player for a while. We'd rehearse over at his house. Thunder was short, kind of light brown skin. He couldn't talk too plain; he was like Bessie, tie-tongued. He was a nice guy, a smooth-sailing kind of guy. And a smooth piano player. Him and Lightnin' had fell out and wasn't working together at all. Thunder was doing a little day work then.

We recorded "Who May Your Regular Be" and "Build Myself a Cave" for Miss Lola Anne Collum. I was rocking then. She recorded me and had my picture taken and had big placards made for me. Miss Collum would put them 45s and placards in her Cadillac and we started to driving through them little country towns. We'd stop at them little clubs, sit down, have a few beers. She'd say to the club owners, "Y'all have bands play here?" "Yes." "Well, this is one of my bands, right here. David Honeyboy Edwards." I didn't have nothing out there—I was running the streets—but she fixed it up for me. She'd say, "I'm going to let you listen at him. Go over to the jukebox and put that on there." They'd listen and say, "Is that him?" "That's him!" "Yeah, I want him!" She was a slick old gal, too. "It'll take two hundred dollars to get him." She'd get that money, too; she'd get a deposit. "Well, OK." They'd sign a contract and we'd go on, eat a big dinner, and drink and celebrate.

That "Build Myself a Cave," I recorded that for Miss Collum and that's my number. But I heard it first in Helena. Willie Love sung that on "King Biscuit Time" on KFFA, sung it over the air, but they never done nothing with it except sing it over the air. I went and recorded it—I beat them to the recording. That song was about wartime. I never heard of nobody else recording it. Everybody used to take everybody else's numbers and do something with them. That's where the songs come from. You sit down, get one verse out of one number, one verse out of another. That's the only thing that make it new! Or take two or three verses and play a different tune with it. You got to do that, and you got to take them lyrics and study them and memorize them like you got them laying down in front of you. I played "Build Myself a Cave" in Spanish, and for "Who May Your Regular Be" I jumped back into natural key. And I sure liked having those numbers out there.

But I was a fool. Miss Collum liked me. She was a big old Creole woman, weighed about two hundred pounds. Had a big old bust, hair like black silk on her head. That's the woman I should have made time with, she could do something for me. Her husband was a doctor. She had a oil well in her backyard—the woman had money. She was the one that made Amos Milburn. She made Amos Milburn! And she was the one who found Lightin' Hopkins, who gave him his name. But I didn't think about her in that way; I wasn't even looking at her. After, I knew I was a fool! That woman had everything, a big Cadillac, a home, a husband out of town. Now I messed up with that!

Me and Miss Collum used to ride two or three days at a time all through Texas. We'd go to Beaumont, Port Arthur, Texarkana. Bessie would stay in Houston. Bessie, she didn't get in my way for nothing. Me and Bessie were partners; Bessie didn't slow me down none.

After I made that recording, Miss Collum booked me on a gig with Charles Brown. Charles Brown was big then! He was with his band, The Three Blazers. We played on a revolving bandstand and I made the news, my picture was in the paper. I sent my brother Mack the paper. "There's Honey on the bandstand with Charles Brown!"

Bessie and me got married in Houston that year. Bessie became my wife in 1952. Then one day I woke up and said to her, "I'm tired of this, let's change cities and go somewhere." Bessie said, "OK, Honey, le's go." And we hit the road. We left there, went over to Galveston. I played about a month in Galveston. Went to Lafayette, Louisiana, and stayed there for a while. And kept running.

I was so fast, I went too fast to catch any root anywhere. I don't know why I was like that. I was always wanting to pull up and leave, go somewhere else. I kept with that little band in Texas a year, near about. I didn't have to leave for money because I was making money, but I just didn't want to stay nowhere long. I thought, "I'm tired of this place. I'm gone." I couldn't stay nowhere. I made it pretty good around Texas with Miss Collum, sure did. She didn't do nothing to me but get me work, and I was a son of a bitch and left her. I just picked up and left and left my chance of making it there. I was so hardheaded and I just couldn't stay nowhere too long.

Chapter Eighteen

It don't always matter
how good you play.

M e and Bessie jumped in the car and come to Shreveport, Louisi- ana. And I was playing in the quarters in Shreveport, in the black neighborhood. The house was full of people, and this boy come up to me. He said, "Man, you good." I laughed and said, "Yeah!" He said, "Who are you?" and I told him, "I'm just a drifter." He said, "You good. I tell you, why don't you talk to my boss? I work for Stan Lewis at Jewel Recording Company. Up on Texas Avenue. I'm goin' to tell him about you. You come down there to see him on Monday mornin'."

So I went to Jewel on Monday morning, and me and Stan Lewis talked. I played a few numbers for him, he cut a few tapes and listened at it. He said, "Well, I like your style but we're not doin' any blues." He was handling all gospel then. "But I'm goin' to send you to my cousin, Chess." He called Leonard Chess, and Chess said to send me up to Chicago.

That was the first of the year, 1953. I left my wife in Shreveport and I got right on a bus and went to Chicago. When I got off at the bus station I met a guy. He saw my amplifier and guitar and asked me about it. He was a music-head guy; he was into music. I hung around with him all

175

that evening. I was supposed to be at the studio first thing that next day. So this guy and me come to Jewtown, and he paid for my room, bought me some whiskey, and followed me to the studio when I recorded the next day! He called in sick, said, "I can't come to work." Honest to God, he followed me to the studio!

We got to Chess studio and there was Muddy Waters. Muddy was there and Willie Nix and Jimmy Rogers. Jimmy was playing with Muddy at that time. And my friend Big Walter Horton was there. He was playing for Muddy, too. They was all at the studio. Now, I had met Muddy only twice before. I met him that once in 1939 when me and Joe Williams had come to his house. And I run up on him in '43. I was in Blytheville, Arkansas, playing on the street and Muddy walked up. Muddy said, "Hey, man, I met you a few years ago. How you doin'?" We talked, had a little drink together and he took my guitar and played a couple numbers on the street, too. He was headed for Chicago at that time.

Somehow, Muddy, he come into Chicago and got a job driving a truck. Leonard Chess had a junkyard and Muddy was driving a truck for him. Chess had these other companies, and probably Chess never even mentioned to Muddy that he had a music studio. And he had probably never met anybody played the guitar like Muddy either. Here Muddy was just driving his truck! And what happened, Sunnyland Slim was recording for Chess and he knew Muddy Waters. Sunnyland told Chess, "Man, you got as good a guitar player as you want to find out there drivin' your truck!" Chess said, "Bring him on here. Let's see what he can do." And Muddy come in and turned out to be his best artist. I heard that Chess told him, "I'm going to make you." He made him, too; he made Muddy Waters. Took him out of that truck, put the guitar in his hands, and recorded him.

So, when I got in there, Chess asked Muddy about me, "Do you know him, Muddy?" And I heard Muddy say, "Oh, yeah, that's Honey. I know him." But I hadn't really spent much time with Muddy. I played for Chess and played maybe too much in Muddy's style with the slide. I used slide good, better than I use it now. My voice was more stronger then, too. I could tell Chess liked what he was hearing. But then him and Muddy started to fighting.

We recorded "Drop Down Mama" that day. Piano Bo Jenkins was on that record with me. He was from Alabama, passing through Chicago on his way to California. I was playing so good on that slide, and every time I used it old Jimmy Rogers would laugh and point at Muddy. Big Walter, he'd look at me and then cut his eyes over to Muddy and look at him. And Muddy got all puffed up and mad. Muddy and Chess stood in the back of the room and they started fighting and arguing. Muddy said, "You know I recorded somethin' like that already." And Chess said, "Man, he don't even sing like you. He don't sound anything like you." But Muddy didn't care for me because I was too close to his style. Didn't want anyone to slow him down. He had everything going for him but he didn't want no competition. Muddy had recorded for Chess and made a couple of hits for him already, and Chess didn't want to hurt Muddy. Because Muddy was making money for him. So I could understand that.

I never run into Muddy much over the years after that, but when he finally come to talking to me again was when we played at the Palladium Club in New York City. That was in the eighties. We was playing there with John Lee Hooker and Johnny Winter and Eddie Kirkland. Kansas City Red was there, too, Sunnyland, Clifton Chenier. It was a big thing. And he started to see people being nice to me and he loosened up. Muddy was losing his hair by then. He come up to me and said, "Look here. This guy's got all his hair and I'm bald-headed now!" And we started to talking and laughing. I guess he had finally got over it. A lot of musicians are jealous. And Muddy didn't want no competition; he wanted to hold the line himself. Until then he never looked too friendly on me but I thought of him as a friend. Except he had recorded and made all that money, and he didn't want no one to make that money but him!

Chess cut me a check for one hundred dollars, and I left Chicago right away after that day and went back to Shreveport, to Bessie. We got back in the car then and headed to Dallas. Bessie was pregnant with Betty then. I was looking for Chess to put a 45 out with my song but he never did. "Drop Down Mama" didn't come out until 1970. It's out now, on a album, and my song is the title song on that album, *Drop Down Mama.* I'm not a fool, just because I play music. I understand how business works. If it hadn't been for Muddy, Chess would have put my song out on a 45.

Things just didn't go right for me then. My recording for Chess come to nothing. I done some recording around that same time for Sun Records in Memphis, in '52. I done "Sweet Home Chicago," for Sam Phillips at Sun. I got word that he was recording so I went there one day. I recorded "Sweet Home Chicago" and then Sam went and put somebody else's name on it, sold that number under somebody else's name. Here I was trying to get my little name out there, trying to get to the point where I could make me some money without hustling too hard. You get a name and you get a little following. If you ain't got no name, I don't care how good you play, it's hard. He released that number under the name Albert Joiner. But it's my voice and my changes, my playing. There wasn't nothing I could do about it. If you can't help yourself, you can't help yourself.

It wasn't always somebody else's fault, though. I wanted to make it, but sometimes I hurt my chances, like when I left Miss Collum. I was wild and crazy, and wouldn't stay no where much. And sometimes I was just too hardheaded. I had a chance to record for the Peacock label in Houston a long time ago, with Don Robey of Peacock, but I was fractious, I was quick-tempered. He had Clarence Gatemouth Brown and Willie Mae Thornton at the time. I was out there playing and he wanted me to be one of his artists.

Robey, he was black. His daddy was a Jew and his mama a black woman. He used to be a peddler all through Texas, selling clothes on his back. He used to be something like a gypsy. He made a little money and opened up a studio, and Clarence Gatemouth and a few artists got him started.

I cut a dub for him with a band. And I was half drunk. Don Robey played it and he said, "Let me listen at it. Yeah, I like that style. I like that lick." But by me being high playing, some of the verses I was singing wasn't clear. He couldn't understand what I was saying. He said, "You got a good sound, but I don't know what you're saying." And I tried to tell him what I was saying. He said, "You know what you're saying, but you didn't make it clear. Cut it over, make the words more plainer. Take your time and make the words more plainer." And the man was

Honeyboy at his home in Chicago, 1995.

right. But I got mad. I said, "Fuck you" and walked on out, jumped up and went to another place. I don't know what even come of that tape. I told him to go to hell, so what's the point of him working with me then? You can take somebody can't even play and make something out of him. You don't have to be stone good to make that money.

A lot of people can't play but they made it big. Doesn't fool this son of a bitch here; I've heard music so many different ways, I listen to it and I can tell. The sound of it, the beat of it. I've played all my life just about. But sometimes what matters is just getting along and I was too hard-headed. You ain't always got to do no hell of a lot of playing to make something for yourself. It takes more than that.

I run around a lot on my own trying to get some work out there. I knew if I ever got something cut I could make some money. I could play and I figured I had a pretty good little sound. A lot of guys not as good was doing alright. But I was quick-tempered back then and wouldn't do what the people told me. I thought I knew everything and sometimes you don't know everything just because you can play. Sometimes you got to get along with people, don't care how good you is. I had to find that out.

When Bessie was ready to have her baby I brought her right back to John Gaston Hospital in Memphis where they knew about her. Betty was born on the eleventh of October, 1953, one year behind David. Bessie had such a hard time with Betty that I didn't let her have no more kids. When she got on empty we hit the road again.

When Betty was born she traveled with us; we carried her everywhere we went. Betty's been to New Orleans, Houston, all over the South. We'd make a bed for her right there in the back of the car. We let my sister have David, and we couldn't do that again. We couldn't let her go.

We spent about a year in New Orleans at that time. We got a little apartment on Rampart Street. I hooked up with Dave Bartholomew. I played with him and he wanted me to stay with his band. But he was too much on the jazz side and that wasn't my sound.

We went to Terrell, Texas, and stayed a while there, went to Texarkana and Shreveport and Lake Charles. We stayed with Son Stuckey the whole winter of '54. He was farming out in Morgan City. Son, he used to play with Skip James. He'd play that song, "Cherry Ball" all day and all night. He played it so much Bessie would say, "God damn, don't you know nothin' but that song?" He'd play it and get it good, then play it so much he'd get bad again! After we left him, we stayed with Bessie's brother in Little Rock for a while and we'd go see my people in Memphis and in the Delta.

Me and Bessie ended up back in Houston in '55, and it was there that my brother wrote to me, sent me a letter from Chicago. Mack come to Chicago in '49. His wife's father was a foreman on a construction job up there and he give Mack a job. My sister Altie and her husband come to Chicago, too. Mack wrote to me and said, "Honey, why don't you come up? You been running up and down the roads a long time. Make your home here. If there's anything for you, you'll find it right here in Chicago. You ain't never been around your family much and you need to come around us now." That stuck in my mind. We left Houston in the winter of '55 and went to New Orleans. Then we left New Orleans in August and went to Shaw, went back to my hometown for a while. In the winter of '56 I come to Chicago to my brother's home.

Chapter Nineteen

Chicago used to be a music town.

At one time Chicago wasn't nothing but piano dives. Chicago had Red-Eye Jesse Bell, Speckled Red, Sunnyland, all the old piano players like Roosevelt Sykes and Memphis Slim. In later years Eddie Boyd and Otis Spann come in. The guitars started to come in, Scrapper Blackwell, Big Bill Broonzy. They broke the houses down, breaking them down with them strings! Chicago used to be a music town.

Me and Bessie settled in Chicago in 1956, in the winter. I had tore up my car, my old Hudson, down in Shaw and I sold it to a boy for thirty-five dollars. That got me and Bessie and Betty to Memphis, and I left them there with my older sister, Hermalie. I didn't have enough money for us all to catch the bus to Chicago. I come to Chicago by myself with what was left of the money.

I took the bus to Chicago and got on a streetcar from the bus station right to Forty-Seventh and Wentworth where my brother was at. I had my amplifier and guitar. When I got off that streetcar a man walking by looked at me and said, "You're Mack's brother, ain't you?" Because Mack told him I play, and Mack and I looked every spit alike, except he was taller. I said, "Yeah!" He said, "Come on, Mack, he's right down the street." He carried me straight to Mack's house, sure did, and my sister-in-law Alice was there cooking.

I didn't have any money—I was broke. When Mack come home I said to him, "Man, look. My wife is with our sister in Memphis. I need some money to send back and get her." Mack gave me a twenty-dollar bill. I put that in a letter and put "special" on it and when Bessie got that she come up with Betty. Betty was about three years old then. I met them at the bus station and we stayed in Chicago ever since. We got a little place right near Mack's and Bessie got herself a job cleaning up at a grocery store.

I found Big Walter and he was glad to see me. He had quit playing with Muddy Waters by then. Big Walter could be kind of fractious, too; he wouldn't play with you if he got mad. He was playing at Turner's and we played there together for a while. We started playing on the weekends at Forty-Sixth and State, at the English Lounge, me and Big Walter and Big Johnny Young and Johnny Temple. It used to be so crowded in that club you couldn't walk in there. Jimmy Walker, he used to play with us too. A boy out of Atlanta, Georgia, owned that club. He was a big time gigolo, mouth full of gold, diamonds on his hands, long side-burns, always dressed up.

We'd play at the Sawdust Trail, too. That was cut down when they built the Dan Ryan Expressway in '63. We had a drummer called Big Dukes then and sometimes another boy, Dizzy, he could only see out of one eye. Sometimes we'd play four nights a week. Other musicians would come to where we was playing all the time. J. B. Hutto used to come in, Good Rocking Charles, Sunnyland. Big Walter, he sure could play, but he couldn't sing at all. He wasn't much of a vocalist. When Sunnyland come by and listened at us he'd tell him, "You'd do alright if you just keep your mouth shut!" Walter would say, "Damn you!" I sure miss that old boy.

Big Walter was married then; he had Anna Mae. Later, he got Fannie. Before Anna Mae he was staying with another woman named Irma. She used to buy him a lot of clothes and stuff but she was a jealous kind of woman. One time she come into the club and saw him on the band-stand and got jealous because he was talking to some other woman. She started fighting and carrying on. She said to him, "I bought you

From left to right, Honeyboy's brother Mack, Mack's wife Alice, Honeyboy's sister Altie, Alice's stepmother, and Alice's father in Chicago, 1959.

that suit you're wearing!" Walter got mad then. He said, "I don't need no woman to buy me nothin'!" He pulled that suit off right there on the bandstand, took it off right there and threw it at her!

Magic Sam played right on the corner of Forty-Seventh and Princeton, and I hooked up with him for a while on Friday and Saturday nights. Magic Sam was a friendly guy. I was playing a lot of Elmore James then, a lot of slide, and one Saturday night Sam said to me, "Man, me and my band like how you play. I'd like to get you to work in my place while I go out of town." Money was so scarce, he'd get booked and go places and play with the house bands that were there, leave his band at home holding down the fort at the regular job. Make more money that way. So I filled in for him with his band. Elmore James, he had some gigs and once in a while would get me and Big Walter working with him. I worked sometimes with Junior Wells and with Louis Myers. Kansas City Red was in Chicago, too. Everybody was in Chicago by then. But we was just country boys. Musicians, they used to be glad to see you coming in. You could sit in on everyone's job then, and they'd give you a little taste of money. Musicians would want to get together and see what you could do and how you do it. We would try to get together and show each other what we was doing, help each other out a little.

Little Walter was playing with his band, with Hip Linkchain and Below, and he told me, "Honey, anything you need, you can get it from me." Little Walter was like that. He had his success and he was trying to hook something up for me. We all worked together then; we wasn't trying to work against each other. We liked to see everybody make a little change.

Then I used to go out to Cadillac Baby's place over on Dearborn and Forty-Seventh to play with Morris Pejoe. Cadillac Baby was a big-timer. Every year he bought a new Cadillac and he was always dressed up. He had a lot of young women, had a little money, had a nice tavern. I played a lot at a mixed joint on Forty-Fifth and Wentworth, too, white and colored both used to come to that club. And on the end of Wells at a place called Virgil's. They closed that down when a couple of people got killed down there.

Chicago was wide open then—us musicians could work every day. We'd play Thursday, Friday, Saturday, Sunday, up all night long. Then sometimes start on Monday, have a Blue Monday. It was popping then. We had clubs, taverns, on Wentworth from Twenty-Sixth to Sixty-Third on both sides of the street. On State Street it was the same way, the Green Frog, the White Elephant, all of them had music. Around Thirty-First and State was a place called the Bucket of Blood. On Forty-Seventh was the White Owl. There was Moore's place, Kelly's, the Green Door. There wasn't nothing but clubs then.

Muddy and Wolf was working most nights. I used to see Howlin' Wolf at the Club 708 over on Forty-Seventh Street all the time, playing the blues. Before that time, that was the place where Memphis Minnie and Son Joe and Big Bill Broonzy used to play. That place was the head-quarters for musicians in Chicago for a long time. Tampa Red played there, Freddie King, Bobby Bland, Junior Parker. Muddy played there all the time, too. And Muddy would play at Smitty's Corner, at Thirty-Fifth and Indiana. We'd walk out of one job and into another. Them were flush times then. The club owner would say, "They don't want to pay you what you want over there? Come play for me. Bring your stuff on over here." It used to be good in Chicago.

**Honeyboy's sister Altie in a tavern on
Chicago's South Side, 1959.**

Sometimes the union steward would come looking for our cards, checking to see do you belong to the union. He'd say, "At least one of you has got to have a card!" I'd say, "I got mine!" and slip him five dollars. He'd take that five and hit the road. Come back the next night and I do the same thing. Slip him some money, have a pint of whiskey waiting for him. They'd pull you off the bandstand if you didn't slip them something, and you wouldn't get to holler then.

Sunnyland had that gambling joint in Chicago on South Prairie. He had a piano down in the basement and two crap tables. He was selling whiskey—he'd get it from the bootleggers out in Gary—and he'd sell sandwiches, too. Back at that time, the police was walking the beat. The policeman on the beat by Sunnyland's used to walk from Twenty-Sixth to Thirty-First Street, back from Thirty-First Street to Sunnyland's joint and then come in and get drunk and go to sleep with the pistol hanging right off of him! Wouldn't nobody bother him! He'd go in that joint and get drunk, go to sleep till he get ready to go back to the police station and punch the time clock. Sunnyland paid him off by keeping him drunk all the time, and there was plenty of women laying around there for him, too. So this policeman didn't let no other police even know where it was. Sunnyland was doing good at that place.

Sunnyland come to Chicago in the forties. He helped a lot of people out, got a lot of musicians their start here in Chicago. He helped people out in all kind of ways, feeding them, giving them money, bringing them in for recordings. Sunnyland got Big Time Sarah her start. He picked Big Time Sarah up on Sixty-Second and South Parkway when he was staying over there. Sarah was nursing a baby. Sunnyland had a little old place there where he fixed tires on cars, and he sold candy and cookies in the front for the schoolkids. He gave Big Time Sarah a job selling at his storefront. Then he found out she could sing and he recorded her.

Everybody hung out at Sunnyland's. Muddy used to go down there, Baby Face Leroy, Floyd Jones, Little Walter, we all used to go down to Sunnyland's to drink and gamble. Sometimes we'd hook up and start to playing music. We'd all holler and play, Sunnyland would play the piano, draw the people out off the streets and get a game going. Just like he used to down south. We had a good time. It was all the time lively, he never closed up. Sunnyland, he been a hustler ever since I known him.

That Sunnyland, he was the hardest working man. Later, in the sixties, he used to run up and down the alleys in a truck with a winch on the back, picking up motors and junk and selling them. He has always worked! Sunnyland would say, "Hell, I've got to have me some damn money." And he'd be out there by himself with that truck, putting that money in his pocket. Then he'd play on the weekend. Sunnyland was strong. Well into his eighties he'd still be getting in his old car to drive up to the north side to play the blues.

I met Carey Bell in '62, met him at the Sawdust Trail. Carey was just a young man. He come in there and listened to us and come up to talk to me on my break. Carey said, "I play harp." So I said, "Come on, play a couple numbers with us." Him and his wife, Sally, had come up from Meridian, Mississippi, and was staying with her people. Carey couldn't find no job so they threw him out. Carey come over and talked with me. I said, "Boy, stay with us. Me and Bessie ain't got nothin' too much but we cook a big pot of beans, cook some neck bones." "Well," he said,

"I love beans." "Well," I said, "I'll kill you on beans!" Carey stayed with us a long time. Me and Carey and Dizzy, that one-eyed drummer, we used to go down to Kankakee to play. We might not always get a lot of money but we always had fun, got some whiskey, had a good time. We'd drive over to Gary, too, and Benton Harbor, play at little clubs over there. He fooled around and got a little old job over on Sixteenth Street, out of Jewtown, trucking papers. He worked there about a year. He and his wife had decided to bust up. Carey said one day he was trucking that paper and he said to himself, "I ain't got no wife. I'm goin' to take this chromatic and make it. I'm goin' to take this harp and make it." He started playing, making money, got some woman to back him up, to take care of him when he didn't have nothing. He cut a little record and started to make it.

I remember when I took him over to Jewtown to meet Little Walter. Carey was just like a little boy when he met him, "Him? This is Little Walter?" He wanted to know everything from him. He'd follow Big Walter around, too, watch his mouth while he was playing. But Carey found his own style. Carey can play! Carey plays that down-in-the-basement kind of harp—he can sound almost like a saxophone sometimes. Carey has that big, wide sound. Carey was down on his luck when he come to Chicago but he made it. We all had to crawl before we could walk.

Carey and me, we'd carry our amplifiers down to Maxwell Street, walking through the alleys, and play there on the weekends. We'd hook up, some other musicians hooked up on the next corner, and in the middle all tables with the goods to sell. Maxwell Street was a big market. When they closed that up, that messed up a lot of local musicians. A lot of guys played on the streets out there. I was sorry to see it go. I remember when musicians walked from Memphis, Arkansas, and Mississippi with their guitars on their shoulders because they found out they could make some money on Maxwell Street!

For a time Big Joe Williams was in Chicago. He stayed in the back of a record shop on the north side. We used to go there and cook and eat. At nighttime we'd go out to the taverns and Joe would catch some woman. We used to have a lot of fun.

Joe Williams used to like to fight. People made him mad, he was quick-tempered all the time. When I met him, when I was young, he drank and got quick-tempered and would want to fight. He'd cuss women out and then get mad because they didn't want to go with him. He went to California for a while and he was going with some old woman out there. The woman, she was a prostitute but he didn't know it. He was playing the blues at a little old joint, and he started to shacking with her. When Joe caught on to what she was doing, he wanted to kill her. And he tried to cut her with a knife and she called the police. They give him a year in the Oakland prison—that cooled him off!

Sonny Boy was in Chicago at that time. Sonny Boy was kind of hard to get along with, too. The doctor told him to quit drinking and he went out and got a fifth of whiskey and poured it half full of castor oil. He used to come to the bandstand at Turner's and bring that whiskey with him. The last time I played with Sonny Boy was 1964. We had a big jam, sat in together all night and had a good time. That was the year before he went back to Helena and he died. Sonny Boy, he just killed himself drinking that whiskey. You can make a few years on your life if you take care of yourself. But that whiskey will kill you quicker than anything. That's a dead killer, steady drinking whiskey; it'll eat you up. Big Walter, in his later years, he drank all the time. We used to buy many a half pint of Kentucky Fly. He always liked whiskey.

But we all had a nice time back then. Back in them crowded clubs, people would pull their tables all together and talk and have a good time. Wasn't much fighting, just a nice time. Sunday evenings we'd start around two o'clock and play all night. People just lying and drinking and having fun, thinking about the music. On the evenings I'd play I'd go there early and set at the tables a couple of hours before we start to playing. Jive with the women and talk trash. Before I get to playing I'm higher than a Georgia pine!

There come a time, though, when I played but I wasn't trying to get too many jobs. Sometimes Big Walter would come to get me to play and I'd just tell him, "Y'all go on ahead." He'd come to get me many a night and I wouldn't go. I still liked playing but I didn't play regular. I slowed down from about '64 till '67. I got tired of running so fast just to make a living. I set the guitar aside for a while, till one day some guys come looking for me to record me.

Chapter Twenty

I never doubted myself.

In the sixties I was working and had slowed up playing for a while. When I went to work, I wanted to work, I was just that tired of the streets. I had been hustling all my life. And when I went to work I felt good. I thought I was doing something big! We put Betty Jean in school, and Bessie was working at the Palmer House Hotel. I was a lucky man — I didn't go to work till I was about forty years old. And I got good jobs, machine operator, lift truck operator, construction work.

I started to chilling off on music. I went to work on that job and come in on a Friday night and went to bed. I just had a feeling that I'd been through enough. I'd play now and then on the weekends at the clubs or at someone's house when they give a skin ball. Or I'd stay home and play my guitar for my daughter.

T-Baby, Bessie's daughter, come to stay with us in Chicago. She lived with her grandmother and then with Bessie's brother in Arkansas, and then she left her uncle and come to us. My brother was right down the street with his wife and family, and my sisters both in Chicago, too. Altie had married and had three boys. Hermalie and Smith, they come to Chicago with my son David. I was glad to be around my family.

When I was young I wouldn't see them but once every two or three years; that guitar kept me rolling. I was glad when I settled down and come to Chicago and we all was together.

I didn't see my friends so much at the clubs. I'd get out now and then, but mostly I was lying low. Things started to change in Chicago. Daley put that Dan Ryan Expressway through the South Side and tore up all them neighborhoods, and all those clubs we played at come down.

One day in 1962 I was down around Twenty-Second Street and Clark at a big junkyard. A lot of hoboes used to stay down there and they called it the Jungle. It was just a old flop camp. People used to go and carry junk there, and them people living out there would beg quarters and dimes from them and then haul up and buy themselves a bottle of wine. I went with some boys to sell some scrap iron and who do I see there but Tommy McClennan! Tommy was living out there in a truck trailer made into kind of a house. Tommy saw me and said, "Honey! Oh, I done found my partner." He was nothing but a winehead then. Ophelia, his wife, was in Chicago, but Tommy had left her and was staying down there with them wineheads.

I took Tommy home and tried to keep him with me. I was playing at Turner's on the weekend at the time and Tommy would go there with me. He even sang some nights. He wasn't able to do much playing but he always had that voice. He studied drinking all the time. He stayed with me and Bessie and every day he'd wake up and say, "Partner, I got to have a bottle of wine." I'd go out and get him a bottle. Two hours would go by and it was, "Partner, I got to have another bottle." I had to buy him wine all the time till finally I said, "Man, I just can't hang with this. I ain't got the money to buy wine for you all the time like this." And he asked me to take him back to the Jungle. I carried him back down there.

Later on I heard that he had taken sick, that he was in the hospital. I went there and asked about him. Tommy died in that hospital in 1962. Tommy had tuberculosis down south; he was born with that. Tommy was sick for a long time. Before he died, he wasn't no size and he wasn't able to talk or nothing. That alcohol was what Tommy was living for, but it ate him plumb up. I heard his son and daughter, Bubba and Carrie Mae, was up in Chicago. They buried him.

**1992 photograph of the site on Chicago's South Side where
Honeyboy returned Tommy McClennan to a hobo jungle.**

Just a couple of years ago, I was standing in line at a grocery store and this man kept a-looking at me and laughing. He said, "Ain't this Honey? You used to play with my daddy, didn't you?" It was Bubba, looking just like his daddy. And here I used to play with Bubba when he was just a child. We got lost track of Robert Petway. Robert moved to Blytheville, Arkansas, for a while, he was picking cotton there, then he come to Chicago and I heard he was living on the north side somewhere. I never did see him in Chicago, though, and nobody I know heard what become of him.

I used to be a pretty heavy alcohol drinker when I was young, but I found out how bad it was and I let it alone. I don't fool with it much now. When I'm playing a gig, I'll get me a double shot and about two beers and play all night. Somebody may bring me another beer to keep me kind of lively. I don't have to get where I get drunk on the bandstand and have to have someone pull me off.

Little Walter was using dope, but he didn't want me to know. I remember once he played a good gig and went out and bought himself a big, white 1956 Cadillac. He called me one day and said, "Come meet me in Jewtown." I got in his car and he said, "Well, I got a couple suits in the back seat that I'm going to give you." Walter was always thinking about me. They was suits he performed in and he got new ones. He stopped at a tavern on Fourteenth and Newberry and bought me a half pint of whiskey. And that's when I found out he was using drugs. When I opened that bottle in the car I said, "You want a drink?" and he said, "Man, I don't fool with stuff like that." I looked at him.

He went around the corner and found this guy and the man handed Walter a little bag. At that time, Walter was going with Memphis Slim's old lady. She lived in a house there in Jewtown. She would have a lot of people playing cards and gambling all night at her house, and Walter had his room there. We went there and Walter said, "Have a seat, Honey, sit down and drink your whiskey." And he cut out. Later, I went to the bathroom and when I opened the door he was in there. I opened the door and he was standing there with a needle in his arm. He said, "What'd you come in here for?" That's the only way I found out he was using. He didn't want to tell me. We was real close friends and he didn't tell me he was using dope. I felt real bad about that.

When Walter got broke he knew I kept money, and I'd give it to him when he needed it. He hung around at Turner's all day long. He used to go there every day and shoot pool. I'd lend him that money and he'd just stay there all day long, shooting pool.

Walter fooled around and got his own self killed. And I hated that. He was going with this no-good woman who had four or five kids. She lived at Fifty-Fourth and Indiana. She had a husband but they was separated. Walter used to go to her house every month when she got her check. She'd get four or five hundred dollars for all them kids and she'd give Walter $150 to put in his pocket. And Walter would get in his Cadillac and leave, and she wouldn't even buy her kids shoes and things. She'd give him money to buy cocaine with, give him money to put gas in the car, and them little kids be hungry all the month. This one particular day this girl got her check. And her husband come by her house because he heard that Walter was getting this money.

He had been drinking and Walter was full of dope, full of cocaine. And they got to arguing and started to fight. This man was mad because he knew Walter was getting this money from his kids' mouths. They got to fighting and tussling out there, hitting at each other, and this guy had a blackjack. A blackjack is something like a sandbag, it gives you a heavy blow but it don't cut you. He took that blackjack and knocked Walter out. Walter was unconscious. They took him to Michael Reese Hospital and he never gained consciousness, never come back no more. When I went to see him, he was out; he didn't know nothing. There wasn't no scar on him, wasn't no cut or bruise. After a few days, he died. That was in 1968.

Walter had got so unruly, messing with that dope so much, it just started to carry him down. He didn't try to do nothing for himself at that time. And this was a man who, before he started using that stuff, was dressed up every day, changed his suit two times a day. Always had a nice Cadillac to ride around in, was making good money, had three or four women working for him.

The last time I played with Little Walter was on his show, playing with his band. A big club used to sit at Eighteenth and Wabash; it's tore down now. The last time I played with him, he had been shooting up then. He was just as happy, laughing, coming off the bandstand with a long cord on his mike walking all around amongst the people. He was a great performer. He just lived too fast. And here when I first met him he was wearing those shoes with the bottom wore out of them and his hair all down his neck, hadn't had a haircut in so long. But he sure could play the harp. We stayed together a long time, in and out. When me and him stopped playing together, that took a lot out of me. I said, "I'll never get that close to a musician no more." That kind of friendship never will be no more for me. The closest one I was to was Little Walter. I miss that boy.

Blues started to be less popular. The black people stopped supporting us, that's what happened. The black folks started giving parties with spinning records and that run us musicians to the north side. We started playing for the whites. Musicians want to play for an audience, have people to talk and laugh with them.

Blues lost popularity with the blacks and then it come back again amongst the whites. After that, people started to come looking for me. One day a man drove up in a van and said, "I'm looking for Honeyboy Edwards." He was from a record label. He come looking for me to record me. Then other people started showing up, and I recorded for a few different labels.

I recorded with Fleetwood Mac back then, that was '67. Willie Dixon set that up. He come to my house and said, "I got a job for you." So me, Big Walter, Homesick James, J. T. Brown, the sax player, and Otis Spann, we recorded with them. Marshall Chess, the son, he recorded that session.

Because they're white, white musicians, when they play blues, they get the benefit of our music. They get more recognition for our music than we do. But then it makes blues more popular, too. I think a few different ways about it. But I was glad to do something with them, because if you ain't got nothing out there, you can't make no money. A lot of these white boys play the blues real good. Ain't but one thing about most of them though: most can't sing a thing.

One day I got a phone call all the way from Vienna, Austria. "Honeyboy Edwards? I'm hoping to bring you over." They sent me a contract for one week, $3,500. I was working as a security guard then, and I asked my boss if I could take some vacation time to go on this tour. He said, "Sure, you can work through your vacation." Then he took a look at the contract and said, "If you're making this much money, you don't need a job." I told him I'd call him when I got back. And I sure liked going there—that was alright. They sent me a airplane ticket and I flew across that ocean. But after I went overseas and come back I couldn't get my job back. I'd call my boss and he'd say, "Well, we don't need you now. Things are kind of slow." I just quit calling after a while. I started to make it with that guitar.

I played a long time and it looked like everywhere I turned, I got pushed back. I knew I could play. I didn't doubt myself. All that running around, all that hustling and then it finally come through. Then all these folks, these different recording companies, they found me, they just come. I worked hard and it finally paid off.

Since then I been to Sweden, I been to Belgium, Germany, Holland, Scotland, Ireland. I go to Europe two, three times a year. I went to South America, Argentina. I even went to Japan and come back with six thousand dollars. I did that and said to myself, "I never thought when I was playing on the streets for nickels and dimes, I never thought the guitar would bring me this much money."

Out of all that runaround, all that scuffling I done, all them states I been in to try to make a piece of bread or a hamburger and never getting the money till then. But then the guitar started to paying off. Money's not everything. But it's a damn good thing to have!

Chapter Twenty-One

I just got lucky when I got Bessie.

W hen me and my wife was on the road we never did fight too much. After we come to Chicago, after a time, we started to fighting a little bit. Most of the time when we did fight I would be the cause of it. Because I would come in drunk, jump on her sometimes. Which I had no business doing.

She'd cut on me! I'd be wanting to fight and she'd cut me up! She'd be right on me with that pocketknife. I got cuts all over me. Bessie was tough; she was bad with a razor blade. I remember one time when our daughter Betty Jean was only six or seven, there was a girl on the street bigger than her who would jump on her and beat her. Betty would come to Bessie crying. Finally, Bessie told the girl's mother to tell the girl to stop, that Betty was too small to be fighting. That woman started to arguing with Bessie and Bessie pulled a razor blade out of her pocket and cut that woman's dress right off her. When she got through cutting, that dress was hanging around that woman's legs! Bessie could hardly talk, she was so mad.

We had some bad fights sometimes. I remember once my brother told me, "If you don't leave Bessie alone, she's goin' to kill you one of these days." And I realized I was wrong. I cut out that drinking and fighting with her.

She started to running around with her women friends at the tavern. They'd sit down and drink, men come up and buy them drinks. But I never caught her with no man or nothing. I come in the tavern sometimes and Bessie be sitting down there drinking and she'd holler, "Come on, Honey. Come here!" And if a man was sitting with her she'd say to him, "This is my husband."

So, we never really got into it about no man. But I figure she was just like I was. I didn't really run around on her, not nothing serious. There was never a woman on the side I had to go see. She'd slip around a little bit; I slip around a little bit sometimes. But we never knowed nothing. Bessie loved me. I know she did. I didn't worry about it. Whatsoever, they wasn't nothing noway. She loved me even though I wasn't no good at the time. I liked a lot of women, I liked to play around. I come home to her every time, though. And I didn't mess up a whole lot with money—I always took it to her.

We stayed together till she passed. Bessie started to getting sick, and I really didn't know she was as sick as she was because she was a strong person. Bessie had diabetes and heart trouble. But she wouldn't let nothing get her down. She'd say, "Honey, you know I don't feel good," but she'd go to work every day. She never missed a day at that Harrison Hotel. She first started at the Palmer House. And she quit that and went over to the Harrison. When she passed, that was where she was employed.

One of Bessie's friends told me she was sick and it hit me, just like that. After that, when we got to arguing, I'd get in my car and go on down the street, stay away about an hour and come back. Then it would be, "Come on, Honey. Dinner's done!" I'd cut out of the house, come back, "Where you been? I done cooked!" We was together a long time. Any fighting we did, some of it was my fault. I'm drunk and she be cutting me everywhere out of nowhere. But I'm messing with her. I got nobody to worry with now. The women I got now don't mean nothing. Like Howlin' Wolf said, "You may look good but you don't mean a thing to me!"

Honeyboy in front of his home in Chicago, 1995.

My wife died in 1972. She was in the hospital. On Monday she said, "The doctor says I can come home Wednesday." When I got there the next day she had got sicker, fell back just that quick. I went there with T-Baby. Betty had just had a baby. Her baby was only four days old. Bessie was laying in the bed and I knew she wasn't going to make it. Bessie knew it, too. She told me, "Don't y'all worry about me." She must have made it up to God. I was standing right over her when she died. That was the twenty-eighth of March. She went with the season, went out with the spring.

And boy, when I lost my wife, I was so lonesome. I went to work at Around-the-Clock Security Company. I was so lonesome; I wanted something to do to keep from being at home because I'd be at the house and she wasn't there. Betty was married and out of the house and wasn't nobody there. When Bessie passed, I was just lost. I'd go to work in the morning at eight o'clock and my shift lasted till four-thirty in the evening. They'd ask me, "You want to work till twelve-thirty tonight?" and I'd say, "Yeah." I'd work to keep from being at the house. Work till midnight, one o'clock, get home and sleep a few hours, wake up, and go right back to my job. Or stop by the tavern, not to play—I didn't feel like playing the blues then. I'd just go to have company, sit around and drink and talk. That's how I stayed away from the house, till I got that off my mind.

My wife's the only somebody I worried about, and when she passed I had other women, white women, black women, but I never took to bury my soul in them. I liked them, liked them as long as they liked me. I know I'll never marry again. If I hadn't married Bessie I don't think I would have ever married anybody. I play around but I never will do nothing like that again. I take care of myself. I'm like a old mule! I got my place, and my friends and my kin peoples come in and sit and visit.

My daughter, Betty Jean, married Ronald Washington in '72. He was a real nice boy, easygoing, and I was glad she met him and turned out to be a good girl. They had three children. KinderLin, that's the oldest daughter, and her boys are Ronald and David. My great-granddaughter is Kayla. And that's all she got. Her husband passed and Betty say she don't want to marry no more. She's got a nice family. She's my daughter and I'm her father and if anything happen to me, Betty will be there in ten minutes. T-Baby, she's living on the South Side. She has two boys Jackie and Anthony. T-Baby thinks as much of me as Betty does. And my son David and his wife Jackie live in Chicago, too. I'm lucky to have them. I'm lucky to have the family I got.

Me and Bessie stayed together twenty-four years. I just got lucky when I got her and started getting children by her. She settled down with me. Bessie was crazy about me and I was crazy about her, too. Them big eyes, that big smile. I'd say, "Look at your big mouth," and she'd say, "Look at my cute little nose!" We'd laugh. I was with her twenty-four years before she died. I lived a good life; we had a good time. The world don't owe me nothing.

Chapter Twenty-Two

I stayed with the blues.

Jean moved in with me in '75, a couple years after my wife died. Jean was just twenty-three years old then. Jean's mother was Big Walter's wife, Fannie. She stays with me because she needed someplace to go, and she's good company for me. We don't fool around; we just live together. She cleans the house and gets up and cooks me breakfast and dinner. Jean can cook. She can cook beans, cook cornbread with buttermilk so light it's just like cake. Blackeyed peas, ham hocks, pinto beans, cabbage greens smothered down. She can burn! She looks after my things at home when I'm traveling. Fannie, her mama, she used to go with Sonny Boy before she married Walter. That was down in Helena. That song, about "Goin' down to Fannie Mae's house," that's who Sonny Boy was singing about, her mama. There's a few women who come in and out of my house, who stay here sometimes. After all those years I was running around letting those women take care of me, now here I am with all these women looking to me for a place to stay.

I've had my fun. Like St. Louis Jimmy says, "I've had my fun if I don't get well no more!" I had some good-looking women—I've had girls lining up for me! I've had a good time in my life. I've had a lot of things some people ain't had. I play around but I never will marry again. What do I want with a old woman? She can't do nothing for me. If I find a woman I want to be with, I carry her to the hotel.

Me and Jean raised a boy from the neighborhood, Charles. His mama left him with us when he was no more than three months old. He's going on five now, and he is smart! That child knows everything. I give him a little guitar and he plays it and throws his head back and sings about "My baby's gone." When I go out of town Jean tells me Charles will see a airplane in the sky and say, "There goes Honey." Charles will never forget me and Jean. We're in him like blood.

I been through a lot of things and the Lord still keeps me around, and I appreciate it.

I still got a mess of family around here, all of them come north to Chicago. Man Son, my first cousin, and his sister Iola are here. Iola had fifteen children and has lots of grandkids. They're my kin peoples. Altie's son, Maurice, is here. Her other boy, Nathan, got out of the Viet Nam War and moved to Hawaii. Her third son, James—we call him Ricky— he's in Chicago. Mack and Alice had eight children, Joann, Rachel, Jule, Anne, Darwatha, Little Mack, Curtis, and Levon. And I still got people down in Mississippi, too, my cousins T.C. and Willie Mae. Willie Mae was the one who went with Robert Johnson. Her and her mother, my Aunt Daughter, they was like sisters. They lived together till Aunt Daughter passed at age ninety-three. She was my mama's baby sister.

I believe the Lord keeps you around, even when you do against your health. When He get ready for you, He call you. I was the oldest one in my family and all of them gone but me. I was the first to come in the world and the last going out. I was seven years older than Mack. Hermalie died in the eighties and Altie and Mack followed right behind her. I miss them. God, so long to be here. That's the debt you got to pay. I say, "Lord, I know You're keepin' me here for somethin'."

After all I been through I don't care what nobody says, there is a God somewhere. God learned me music, He give me that gift. He looks down on me. Still today I'm going on: I go out and play my guitar, travel all over the world. There ain't no harm in playing blues, that's a gift God give me. I wouldn't know how to play if He didn't mean to give

Charles with a guitar Honeyboy gave him in Chicago, 1994.

that gift to me. God didn't give everybody that. We all got different gifts. Ballplayers, gamblers, He give us each a gift. That's how we learn.

It ain't but one God. People are Sanctified, Seventh-Day Adventist, Baptist, all that, but there's one God. The sun goes down and comes up every day, the weather changes, it rains and thunders and lightnings and clears off. Somebody's working that! There's a God somewhere. He made man with sense and knowledge enough to write the Bible. I believe that. And then if you live long, you got time to straighten up and talk to Him. And I believe that, too. I been through a whole lot of stuff, but I guess God was in the plan. He give me this life, He give me a gift, to be able to play music.

And the longer I live, the more I play, I learn more and more. When you play so long, there ain't too many things you can't do. I hear something once or twice and I can play it. Or if I set a while and think about some old song I used to play, it comes back to me. Music is a funny thing. Playing music is just like plowing in the field. It might be you haven't plowed in a long time, but you don't never forget how to hold them handles. And it's the same with music: you might lose a little something if you don't play it regular, but if you think about it, it comes right back.

Way back, all of us musicians wanted to get together and see what each other could do. We would try to get together and show each other different chords, different positions, how to play. Us musicians have had some fun together. We listened at different records and listened to each other.

And as the times changed, the blues has changed. I changed some since the forties, from the blues I was playing then. I learned new styles of playing in the city, but I bring them country blues with me still. Back in old times we played straight through, like a horse trotting all the way through a song. It was good, but in later years I listened at different kinds of music and that kind of opened my eyes up. I used to play a lot of different God damn songs back in the country. I'd try anything. In my later years I come into my own style. I found my own style, my own sound.

The blues might change but it's going to stay around. Young people now play a different style of blues, hard and fast, but it's still the blues. When I was a child coming up, it was mostly ragtime stuff. Then it grew, that big road blues, country blues, then the shuffle and the low-down-and-dirty blues. It just keeps on changing. The blues are always going to stand.

Things have got pretty rough in my neighborhood in Chicago. Sometimes it seems like half of Chicago is doing drugs. I been living in this same area ever since 1956. Me and my wife used to leave home, go to the tavern, and not even lock the door behind us. People would walk in our house and see we was gone and just shut the door back up. If you go out now, in five minutes they move you out of there! One time I come home from Turner's and I caught a boy coming out of my house with my daughter's stereo. I shot at him. I missed him but he dropped those components and moved!

Some of these folks here ain't got nothing at all and some of them are just getting along. Some live in the streets—so many of them can't get no jobs. And a lot of them are dangerous. The younger generation, they don't care about nothing. They'd do anything to get that cocaine and dope. If they want your money, you give it to them quick because they'll hurt you. I don't have much trouble, though. These boys in the neighborhood, they recognize me. They say, "I saw you on television," and most of them give me respect. But some of them know because I'm out playing and making some money, they want a piece of that. When I come in from out of town, I got sense enough to watch myself. You don't know what they got on their minds. When I come in and have money in my pocket, I got my gun in my hand when I get out of the car. I got it ready.

I got carjacked just last year; my car was stolen. I was filling up at a gas station and left the car running. I just finished putting gas in the car and locked up the gas tank and was walking to the driver's side when this boy run up behind me. He said, "Get out of the way, man! Get out of the way!" I said, "What you doin'?" "Get back! Get back, man!" He got around behind me and jumped in my car, got behind the wheel. I was trying to hold onto him, but when I see he was getting away I pulled my knife out of my pocket and cut him on his arm. I got a sharp knife, like a razor. I saw he wasn't going to turn my car loose so I cut him. But his partner jumped in the passenger side and they pulled away.

I called the police and gave them a description of my car, tan '82 Lincoln, got a convertible top and mag wheels and a spotlight on it. They found it right away. That boy, I cut him so bad he had to go to the hospital and get stitched up. And the police found my car. You got to take care of yourself out there. There's a lot of violence, lot of killing. These boys go through the neighborhood shooting at each other, shooting out of their cars. And some of them known each other since they was young boys together.

There was a man got killed right on my porch! This woman was living with a man in my building. But every morning, her old boyfriend would be out in the street in front of the building calling to her, saying "Come out, baby." And she would go down in the street and talk to him.

The man she was living with would get mad. One particular evening, this woman come to my house and sat down at my kitchen table. She just sat there quiet, didn't say nothing. I said, "What's wrong? You and your man got to arguin'?" She said, "Uh-huh." And then I look outside and this boy, her old boyfriend, was coming up to my house walking. And here come her new man walking up, too. They both got to my doorstep at the same time. I said to her, "Don't go out there. You might get hurt or somethin'." I couldn't see it, but the old boyfriend had a old piece of pistol by his side. And this woman jumped up and reached over my table and got a knife and run out the door. She run out and struck at her man with this knife, but she missed him. Then her old boyfriend come up and shot him right through the neck! They killed this man right on my doorstep! I called the police and they come and I'm the first son of a bitch they put handcuffs on!

But the man who shot him, he come over and said, "I shot him." He didn't lie. The police, they found a knife in the other guy's hand, too; he had a death hold on a knife. So the police called it self-defense and nobody went to jail.

So many people around here doing dope. I come around in hard times myself, but I never let nothing like that pull me down. A lot of musicians, when they got some money, it went to their heads and they started to using dope. That stuff will kill you quicker than anything. I even laid off drinking so much when I seen what that does.

I remember things, I had some hard times, but I don't let nothing worry me too much. If you let that worry lay on you, your mind will go wrong. I keep my mind moving—you got to do that. I seen some bad things but I made it. And I'm glad to tell people about it because it takes me way back. So many people don't stay here long enough to do that. I talk to some of these young boys about what happened in my time and you know what they say? "Oh man, you tellin' a damn lie." They don't believe me! It's changed so.

I go to the South and see how it's changed down there. Greenwood's all growed up, got hotels, black police. There's a black city councilman there now I knew when he was a boy on the plantation. And there he is now in the city hall! One time me and Kansas City Red was back in Mississippi, eating at a hotel on 61 Highway one Sunday morning. Two

Honeyboy and his family in 1994.

old white guys, farmers, was sitting there at a table next to us, about seventy, eighty years old. Red looked at them and said, "You know what, Honey? I bet them two beat many a nigger's ass down here in their time." Them white folks down there were a bitch years ago. Not till them niggers started dying for what they wanted did them folks sit up and stop that shit. It's all changed there now, white and black are going to school together, working together. They can't keep them young people apart no more.

I'm still traveling, playing the blues all over the world. I go to England a few times a year, go to Europe a couple times a year. And I go to all these festivals in this country. I play at the Chicago festival every year. I been to festivals in Canada, the East Coast, West Coast, that big festival in New Orleans.

I still like to listen to different musicians. I met a lot of musicians in my early years, and then when I started traveling around to all these festivals I met more. I played with Sam Chatmon at Wolftrap. That man was eighty-some years old and he could play that guitar. Every chord he hit was true, just as solid as a dollar. I met Elizabeth Cotten at a festival in Winnipeg, Canada, and we talked a whole lot. She said she run off from home with her guitar when she was a little girl, trying to play. Just like me. That old lady could play. I enjoyed hearing them older people.

I run up on some of my old friends at festivals and we laugh about the things we used to do. Roosevelt Sykes was playing at Wolftrap at that same time. That was something to see him again and think about them days in Memphis when he was playing at the Chicago House for a dollar a night. I played in Atlanta with Yank Rachell a few years ago and we had a good time, laughing and remembering Sleepy John and old times. I was with Robert Junior at a bar in Boston, we was both playing there one night, and some white guy come in with a pretty black gal and she started talking to me. I didn't notice she had a old man and I started rapping right back at her. Robert was looking at it all with them big eyes of his and he said, "Man, I don't see how you lived this long." We laughed about that.

Most of the musicians, my old friends, a lot of them are gone now. Big Walter, Little Walter, Sunnyland, they all passed. Sunnyland worked right up until he died. Sunnyland was a strong man. He lived a good, long life. Sunnyland was a funny guy. He told me once, "Man, when I was young I didn't give a damn about no money. I'd play for free if I could just get some whiskey and a woman to go home with." We had many good times together. I got a few old friends though, to sit around with and drink and talk. And a lot of young people come to see me, young folks who want to sit around and play some blues, hear about old times. I tell them. All my stories are true. I don't make up nothing because it don't make you no better. I went through a lot of stuff out there. Some people won't believe it but I remember. When I think about it now I laugh sometimes. How stupid I was—I done a lot of old stupid things. But you had to do that to live, sometimes.

I think about how funny that is, that I'm going to all these different God damn places. I'm still running, still hustling. I took that TGV train out of Paris, France, going to Toulouse one time. It runs two hundred miles an hour. You couldn't hardly hobo on that train! I like to see different parts of the world. Every country is different. Some of them people eat the damnedest food though. In Sweden, just a lot of old stuff all boiled in water. In Japan they give you raw fish cut so thin you can near about see through it. When I was there with Sunnyland, we left

Honeyboy performing at the 1993 Chicago Blues Festival.

our hotel and went down the street to a grocery store one day. Sunnyland said, "God damn, Honey, I need something to eat!" We bought hot dogs, pork chops, orange juice, and we went back to our room and cooked that stuff up! They're crazy about the blues over there. I like London best, and Edinburgh and Dublin. I like Belgium too; that sure is a pretty country. Some parts of it look just like the Mississippi Delta.

I always wanted something for myself. Out in the country when I was young, there wasn't no bright lights shining for me out there. I wanted them bright lights. I learned how to hustle so I could make it. My cousin Willie Mae tells people, "Honey been smart his whole life. When he was a little boy he had a whole lot of sense. I knew Honey was going to do somethin'."

I ran around a lot on my own, trying to get some work out there. I knew if I ever got something out there for people to hear, I could make it. I knew that. But it was hard. I made it harder because I was hard-headed and wouldn't do what people told me. I thought I knew everything. But you got to keep up with it, you got to keep at it, whatso-ever you do. I stayed with the blues.

Way back, I never thought the blues would be like it is now. How I felt about it at the time, I felt like playing because I had the blues my-self. The music comes to you. The blues comes to you from the feeling that you have. The blues is the feeling. If you get the right feeling, everything that you hit on the guitar neck is true. I listened to all them different musicians, Andrew Moore and Tommy Johnson, Big Joe and Robert Johnson and Lightnin' Hopkins, and their music thrilled me. And I felt good playing the blues. I felt good playing.

The blues is something that leads you, that lays on your mind. You got to go where it leads you. When I was young I'd sit around and play the blues, and sometimes it would put me in mind of someplace else. I'd always follow it. I'd get up and go wherever it took me. And every-where the blues took me was home.

Miscellany

The purpose of this appendix is to offer the reader some interesting background information on words and phrases, names of people (other than musicians), and place-names Honeyboy Edwards mentions. The material is listed here alphabetically, and not as mentioned in the text by Edwards.

Baptist Town: One of several neighborhoods in Greenwood, Mississippi, occupied exclusively by blacks. Baptist Town is on the east side; its name derives from the Baptist church there. Other black Greenwood neighborhoods during Honeyboy's time were Gritney, Ram-Cat Alley, G.P. Town, Buckeye Quarters, Burkhalter's Alley, and New Town.

Barrelhouse: A juke joint.

Barrelhousing: An improvised style of piano playing with a heavy beat. Also a word meaning to dance and carry on.

Beale Street Park: The city of Memphis built a park at the corner of Hernando and Beale in 1931 and dedicated it as Handy Park, in honor of W. C. Handy, the Memphis bandleader who popularized blues music by collecting and publishing songs. Honeyboy rarely refers to it as Handy Park, preferring the name Beale Street Park. The area around the park had been noted for music, gambling, and prostitution since the turn of the century.

Biddies: Young chickens.

Black cat bone: A voodoo good luck charm of the highest power obtained by boiling a black cat and passing its bones through one's mouth until a bitter-tasting bone is found.

Blackjack: The origin of this widely played card game is unknown. The object of the game is to get a higher count of cards than the dealer without exceeding a count of twenty-one.

Bootlegger: This term referring to the seller of illegal alcohol is an old one and may have its origins in the frontier custom of hiding bottles of liquor in boot tops.

Broadcloth: A woolen or worsted fabric with a smooth, glossy texture.

Buck dancing: A lively dance that was a precursor to tap.

Calaboose: A small jail. A Creole adaptation of the Spanish word *calabozo* (meaning "dungeon").

Canned heat: Sterno, which apparently is good for more than warming food. Not only was canned heat used as a source of alcohol, but some women in the South also used it to dress their hair.

Capo: Basically a clamp. Fastening this device across a given fret on the guitar will result in raising each string a corresponding half tone per fret.

Census: An investigation of the census for 1920 shows Honeyboy's father, Henry, aged 51, Henry's wife Pearl, the four girls, Honeyboy, and one of Henry's sons from a previous marriage, William, aged seventeen.

Chess, Leonard/Chess Records: Leonard and his brother Phil were the founders and owners of Chess Records, a company that was the driving force in Chicago blues for many years. The brothers were Polish immigrants who started a record label based on their experience as club owners. Their first label, Aristocrat, was followed by Chess and its subsidiaries, Checker and Cadet. Chess recorded many great musicians including Muddy Waters, Howlin' Wolf, Little Walter, and Elmore James. Leonard Chess died in 1969. *Chess Blues* (MCA-Chess) is an excellent four–compact disc boxed set offering of their recordings.

Chess, Marshall: Leonard Chess's son, at one time, the president of Chess Records.

Chinese/Italian immigrants: During the Reconstruction, Chinese were brought to the Delta by the plantation owners in the hope that they would eventually replace black laborers. Instead, they quickly turned to operating grocery stores. In the early part of this century, local planters encouraged the immigration of Italians to the Delta with the same hope. The Italians, also, found work in the towns more to their liking.

Chops and grind: Ground corn.

Class 1-A/4-F: Draft board classifications. 1-A classifies the draftee as healthy and available; 4-F status means he will never be eligible for the draft.

Collum, Lola Anne/Artist Recording Company: Collum hailed from Waimer, Texas. When she settled in Houston with her dentist husband, her love for the blues led her to pursue a career booking musicians. She discovered Sam Hopkins on the streets and christened him Lightnin'. She also discovered Amos Milburn and toured with him. In 1951 she started her own company, ARC. As Mr. Honey, Honeyboy recorded "Build Myself a Cave" and "Who May Your Regular Be" on this label with Wilson Thunder Smith.

Cooling board: A reference to the custom of laying the corpse on a board for viewing in the house. It is possible the word *cooling* is a reference to a one-time practice of packing the corpse in ice.

Cotch: A card game similar to poker and played with chips.

County farm: It was a practice in the state of Mississippi to use convicts to clear swamps and work cotton fields. In 1876, an act was passed that allowed the leasing of convict labor to planters for the monthly rate of little more than one dollar per convict. There was terrible abuse of the prisoners under this system. Convict leasing was brought to an end in 1906, when the state moved to work convicts only on prison farms, levees, and public lands. The establishment of these state and county farms where prisoners were housed and used as forced labor was not much of an improvement. Conditions on these farms, like the one Honeyboy describes, were often brutal.

Craps: A gambling game played with two dice.

Creek Indian: The Creek, of the Muskhogean family of Native Americans, at one time occupied most of Alabama and Georgia and parts of Florida. Small tribes of Creek also lived on the upper Yazoo River in Mississippi.

Crossroads: A reference to the belief that a supplicant standing at a crossroads at midnight would be approached by the devil, ready to bargain for a soul. This legend has its origins in the African Yoruban religion. The Yoruban god Legba is a trickster and associated with the devil. He is the god of crossroads, considered in this religion as the place where the physical and spiritual worlds meet. In his November 1936 recording session, Robert Johnson recorded "Crossroads Blues."

Deep Ellum: Once known as Central Tracks, this Dallas neighborhood was located along the railroad tracks on Elm Street. It was a lively place, full of clubs and cafés and frequented by many musicians. The local dialect of the black residents stretched the name Elm to Ellum.

Depression: The stock market crash of October 24, 1929 led to an economic decline that lasted for many years. At its worst, thirty percent of the U.S. workforce was unemployed, wages for those who had jobs were low, and businesses failed by the thousands. Shanty towns and hobo jungles appeared throughout the United States as people took to the road in search of work.

Dockery's: This large plantation, Dockery Farms, was established by an early settler of the Delta, Will Dockery, in 1895. It is still a working operation. Among the many musicians who lived on and frequented

Dockery's plantation were Charlie Patton and his mentor, Henry Sloan; a young Howlin' Wolf; and Roebuck Staples.

Doodlebug: This is a common nickname used by railroad men in reference to the rail motor cars used for section men and linemen.

Driver: See Gunman/driver below.

Dropsy: A common term for edema, an abnormal accumulation of fluid in connective tissue or in body cavities.

Dry/wet counties: National prohibition was from 1919 to 1933, but Mississippi voted to stay dry even after it was repealed. In fact, Mississippi retained statewide prohibition until 1966, but liquor was sold openly in many counties. Whether counties would be dry or wet was determined by local opinion.

Gandy dancer: Railroad track laborers were referred to as gandy dancers, a name derived from the Old Gandy Manufacturing Company, maker of the spikes, picks, and shovels they used.

Gig: A pronged spear for catching fish.

Good-timing house: Whorehouse.

Gramophone: The trademark name for a phonograph that first came out in 1902.

Greenhorn: An inexperienced, unsophisticated person.

Gunman/driver: Paid employees of the county farm or penitentiary. They oversaw the convicts in the fields and at the barracks at night.

Handy Park: See Beale Street Park above.

High water: In the spring of 1927, after months of rain, the Mississippi River became dangerously high, eventually breaking through the levees and flooding the land. More than sixteen million acres were flooded in seven states, with Mississippi, Arkansas, and Louisiana suffering the most damage. More than one hundred million dollars in crops were destroyed along with 41,000 buildings and 162,000 homes. In the Delta, an area one hundred miles long and thirty miles wide was covered with water four to fifteen feet in depth. A million people were made homeless along the length of the river and more than 325,000 were cared for in Red Cross camps such as the one Honeyboy describes.

Hoboing: During the Depression it is estimated that from two to four million Americans were vagrants. Approximately one-fourth of them were adolescents and many were black.

Hobo jungles: The jungle, or hobo encampment, in Effingham was just one of many scattered around the country during the Depression. These shanty towns made from wooden boxes and cardboard served as temporary homes for the many transients on the road at that time.

Hog law: See Vagrancy law below.

Jump contract: Most sharecroppers signed up with plantation owners in January for an entire year of work. Workers "jumping a contract" left before they fulfilled that commitment.

Jump-up songs: A song made up on the spur of the moment.

KFFA: The Helena, Arkansas, radio station famous for broadcasting the "King Biscuit Flour Time" show, a live fifteen-minute blues program sponsored by the makers of King Biscuit flour. In 1941, Sonny Boy Williamson 2 and Robert Jr. Lockwood were featured daily at noon, along with Peck Curtis on drums and, alternately, Dudlow Taylor, Pinetop Perkins, and Willie Love on piano. Guitar player Houston Stackhouse joined them also, and in later years Little Walter Jacobs and Honeyboy performed on this very popular show. Sonny Boy Williamson 2 played regularly for three years, returning only periodically after 1944, but his image is still printed on bags of King Biscuit flour. Original staff member Sonny Payne still broadcasts "King Biscuit Time" daily around noon from Helena.

KWEM: The West Memphis, Arkansas, radio station that broadcast performances by Sonny Boy Williamson 2, Howlin' Wolf, B. B. King, and others.

Lembo, Ralph: Ralph Lembo (or Limbo) was an Italian immigrant who established a furniture store in Itta Bena, Mississippi. Eventually he began selling records and acted as a talent scout for various recording companies.

Levee: When settlers first established themselves along the Mississippi River, they fought the river's cycle of springtime floods by building embankments to prevent flooding. Over time, a continuous ridge of earth was built along the river. The task of building the series of levees ever higher and controlling the water fell to the Army Corps of Engineers when the Flood Control Act was passed in 1928. The camps Honeyboy refers to housed the workers who built the levees.

Lewis, Stan/Jewel Recording Company: At one time a top disc jockey in Shreveport, Louisiana, known as Stan the Record Man, Lewis became a record distributor, jukebox supplier, and owner of a record shop and studio on Texas Avenue. His labels other than Jewel include White, Ronn, and Paula. These labels recorded many blues and gospel greats and are still in operation.

Lomax, Alan/Library of Congress: Alan Lomax and his father, John Lomax, archived thousands of American folk songs for the Library of Congress folk collection. In the Delta in 1942 Lomax was conducting a project run jointly by the Library of Congress and Fisk University to record blues and other black folk songs as part of an investigation into black folk culture. In addition to Lomax's work for the Library of Congress, he is the author of *The Land Where the Blues Began*, *The Folk Songs of North America*, and *Mister Jelly Roll*, among others. He has served as director of folk music for Decca Records, as editor of the World Library of Folk and Primitive Music, and as a professor at Columbia University.

Maxwell Street/Jewtown: An open-air market that was located on the near west side of Chicago, Maxwell Street Market was established by Jewish street peddlers shortly after the Great Chicago Fire of 1872. At one time the market was a mile in length. Anything could be purchased on Maxwell Street, from furniture to tires, clothing, fruit— in later years, even birth control pills! The crowds attracted musicians who played on the streets for tips, and Maxwell Street came to be known for the blues. The market was relocated by the city to nearby Canal Street in 1994.

Mechanicals: The mechanical cotton picker drove thousands of blacks from the Delta to the northern cities, to Chicago and Detroit, seeking work. Between 1940 and 1950 the black populations of twenty-nine northern and western cities more than doubled. In Chicago there was an eighty percent increase in the black population during that decade. The migrants were both driven from conditions of want and pulled by the lure of wartime jobs. The introduction of the cotton picking machine to the Delta brought an end to the sharecropping system that had held sway since the Reconstruction.

Medicine show: Medicine shows were important employers of musicians in the generations previous to Honeyboy's. These traveling shows developed after the Civil War and featured musicians and other entertainers who would bring in an audience and warm them up for the "doctor's" pitch. It was a popular form of entertainment in the small towns. Because malaria was a severe problem in the Delta, this region was worked continuously by patent medicine manufacturers and salesmen.

Melrose, Lester: A producer and talent scout who had his first success with Tampa Red and Paramount. He later worked with the RCA-Bluebird label and Columbia Records. Melrose recorded many prewar blues artists including Big Bill Broonzy, Lonnie Johnson, Big Boy Crudup, John Lee "Sonny Boy" Williamson, Yank Rachell, Robert Nighthawk, and Big Joe Williams. Melrose was born in 1891 and died in 1968.

Memphis hotels: The Peabody Hotel was originally built in 1869; the building Honeyboy frequented was built in 1925. Serenading guests in the lobby of the Peabody and the other luxury hotels Honeyboy mentioned was a common practice of the local musicians. The lobby of the Peabody offers additional entertainment in the form of a family of mallard ducks, who are escorted daily from their penthouse apartment down the elevator and along their very own red carpet to spend the day in the lobby's fountain.

Mississippi Delta: The northwest region of the state of Mississippi is a flat land covered with alluvial deposits left by the Mississippi River during its frequent floods. The Delta extends from near Memphis on the north to Vicksburg, Mississippi, on the south and from the banks of the Mississippi River on the west to the hills of central Mississippi on the east. Its rich soil was perfect for the production of cotton, and the hardships of Delta plantation life contributed to the region's other yield, Delta blues.

Mojo: A voodoo magic charm, often associated with fertility but sometimes kept just for plain good luck, generally a small assortment of substances enclosed in a little bag.

Mollyglasper: Meaning a descendant of the Malagasy, a tribe from Madagascar (an island off the southeast coast of Africa).

Mourner's bench: The bench in a black Southern Baptist congregation of the early twentieth century generally located in front of the pulpit at revivals and designated seating for those seeking redemption. Its name is derived from the biblical reference "He hath sent me to comfort those who mourn."

Natural key: Standard guitar tuning, with strings tuned to EADGBE.

Open key: See Spanish/Vastopol below.

Parchman: Parchman Penitentiary is a twenty-thousand-acre prison that began operation in 1904. Until the seventies, Parchman was a working cotton plantation. The inmates labored in the fields guarded by shotgun-carrying trusties who threatened them with whippings. The almost entirely black prison population suffered terrible abuse and suffering. Prison reform came to Mississippi in the 1970s, but the name of Parchman is still legend. In the thirties, nearly two thousand prisoners were at the infamous penitentiary. Guitarist Bukka White did time at Parchman and in 1940 recorded a song about his experiences there, "Parchman Farm."

Phillips, Sam/Sun Records: Phillips started his career in the music business as a disc jockey and went on to open the Memphis Recording Service in 1950. He acted as a talent scout for the Modern and Chess labels until he started his own record company, Sun Records, in 1952. Sun began as a blues label, recording B. B. King, Little Milton, and Junior Parker, among others, but Phillips turned to country and rockabilly after Elvis Presley entered the studio in 1954. Phillips sold Sun in 1969. Phillips was born in January 1923 near Florence, Alabama. Collected recordings are available on *Blue Flames: A Sun Blues Collection* on Charly.

Potter's Field: A common name for a public burial place for paupers, unknown persons, and criminals.

Prisoner cage: The barracks that housed inmates on the county farms and at Parchman Penitentiary.

Pullet (or biddy): A young chicken.

Quinn, Bill/Gold Star Records: Quinn opened his studio in 1942 and started his Gold Star record label in 1946, originally as a hillbilly label and later as a blues label. He went out of business in 1951, but at one time many of the recordings made in Houston were at the Quinn studio on Telephone Road, including some by Lightnin' Hopkins.

Railroad dicks: Detectives (also referred to as "cinder dicks") hired by the railroad companies to keep the cars clear of vagrants. It was a full-time job: in 1932, the Southern Pacific Railroad threw 683,000 people off their freight trains, and authorities in Kansas City estimated that 700 hoboes passed through their town every day.

Record boom: The recording industry boomed in the twenties, but with the Depression came a rapid decline in sales. In the late thirties, record companies again found a large market for blues in the black communities, and the industry rebounded. This rebound was aided by the introduction of the jukebox.

Revenuers: Federal agents from the Commission of Internal Revenue who sought out those illegally making spirits. This task came under the jurisdiction of this department because the makers of illegal whiskey were depriving the government of excise taxes.

Revivals: These highly emotional prayer meetings traveled the country, with stays extending over days and weeks at each stop. They included fervent preaching, shouts, dances, and trances.

Ride the cushions/ride the blinds/ride the rods/ride the reefer: To "ride the cushions" means to ride a train as a paying passenger. The "blinds" are baggage cars on passenger trains that have no side doors. Hoboes would ride at the front end of these cars. It was a cold, dangerous, and sometimes fatal ride. The "rods" are the brake rods that run beneath the freight cars. A tramp would place a board across them and slip onto it. This also was a very hazardous ride: dozing off or a moment's inattention could lead to slipping and rolling under the wheels of the train. The "reefer" was a car cooled with ice to keep perishable goods cold. When the car was empty it was an ideal spot to hide because you could close the door from the inside and no one could get at you from the outside.

Robey, Don/Peacock: In addition to his Peacock label, this Houston club owner also owned the Duke, Back Beat, and Songbird labels. Artists associated with Robey included Clarence Gatemouth Brown, The Five Blind Boys of Mississippi, Roscoe Gordon, Bobby Blue Bland, Junior Parker, and Big Mama Thornton. Robey died in June 1975. The Duke/Peacock labels are now owned by MCA Records.

Rosenwald schools: Black schools were vastly underfunded in the Delta, and the only source of money for building schools before the Roosevelt adminstration came from the Rosenwald Foundation. The Foundation was established by Julius Rosenwald, president of Sears Roebuck from 1909 to 1924. A great percentage of Sears's business came from catalog sales in the southern states, and Rosenwald saw that some of this money came back to southern blacks in the form of education funds and medical services.

Roustabout: Originally the name for flatboat or keelboat men, "roustabout" came to refer to the deck crew on steamboats. Such workers carried freight, usually cotton and cattle, on and off the boats, manned pumps, and handled mooring lines. They slept on deck and lived on the leftovers from passengers' meals.

Seabird: In the Delta, the Seeburg-manufactured jukebox was commonly known as the Seabird.

Section houses: Small houses built alongside railroad tracks originally used to house railroad workers or section gangs.

Settle up: In the fall of the year after the cotton crop was harvested and sold, the plantation owner would meet with family heads, confirm their purchases and credit over the past year, subtract that amount from their share, and pay them the remainder.

Shakerag: A black neighborhood in Tupelo, Mississippi, located near Park Lake.

Sharecrop: The sharecropping system developed after the Civil War, when cash-strapped plantation owners made arrangements with the newly freed black population to exchange their labor for housing, food, seed, and a share of the cotton harvest at year's end. While not all plantation owners took advantage of their laborers, the system was rife with corruption, and many unscrupulous farm operators made their profits off the backs of their generally illiterate black tenants. The system included three classes: renters, who hired land for a fixed amount, payable in crop or cash; share-tenants, who furnished their own animals and tools and paid a fixed percentage of the crop as rental; and sharecroppers. The majority of farm laborers in Honeyboy's time were sharecroppers.

Shimmy/Charleston/Ball the Jack/Butterfly: These were typical dances in the black juke joints of Honeyboy's youth. The Shimmy, with its snake-hips action, was a popular dance in the twenties. The Charleston was introduced in the 1923 musical *Runnin' Wild*, and Ballin' the Jack became popular after a 1913 Harlem production known as *The Darktown Follies*.

Shoat: A young, weaned pig.

Shotgun houses: The cabins typically inhabited by sharecroppers in the Delta. Small and boxey with frame side walls, they had an entrance at front and rear connected by a straight hallway. "Shotgun" is a reference to this hallway—a bullet shot through the front door would go out the rear.

Silas Green's Medicine Show: "Silas Green from New Orleans" was one of the most famous medicine shows of its time. It visited small towns throughout the South into the fifties. It was an all-black show managed by Green, the only black circus owner in America. Its stars included Bessie Smith and Muddy Waters.

Skin game: A fast-paced gambling game played with cards and similar to the game of Ziginette, from which it possibly derived its name. The object of the game is to win a bet that the dealer's or another player's card will be matched from a card pulled from the top of the deck before your own is matched.

Southern cross the Dog: A famous railroad crossing in Delta blues. The Southern Line, as it passes through Moorhead, Mississippi, crosses the Yazoo and Mississippi Valley Railroad, popularly known as the Yellow Dog. There are a few theories on the origin of this name. One is that the train was named after a dog in Rome, Mississippi, that barked at the passing trains. Honeyboy tells us the term "dog line" is a slightly derogatory name for the short railroad lines that ran between small towns in the South and mentions a Black Dog line also. Additionally, the railroad phrase "walk the dog" means to run a freight so fast that its cars sway from side to side.

Spanish/Vastopol: Respectively, open G and open D tunings, named after two traditional guitar pieces, "Spanish Fandango" and "Sevastopol." Vastopol is also known as "cross-natural." Both tunings are commonly used for bottleneck-style play. In open G, the guitar is tuned to a G chord, DGDGBD. In open D tuning, the guitar is tuned to a D chord, DADF#AD.

Speir, H. C.: The Jackson furniture store owner, record dealer, and talent scout who discovered Son House, Skip James, Tommy Johnson, and Charlie Patton, among others. Though it may seem odd that a dealer in furniture would expand into the recording industry, at the time record companies actively sought out local representatives such as furniture dealers and drugstore owners in small communities who could both sell race records and survey the local talent for the record company.

Sun Records: See Sam Phillips/Sun Records above.

Syndicate Plantation: This thirty-eight-thousand-acre plantation was owned by a syndicate of British mill owners under the name of the Delta and Pine Land Company. In 1936, the syndicate had total assets of approximately five million dollars. Three thousand three hundred black sharecroppers labored there, and the tenant families received an average of $525 yearly. The plantation had its own school, church, and hospital for its tenants.

TGV train: A high-speed luxury train (Train á Grande Vitesse) built in France in 1989. The TGV travels at approximately 180 miles per hour.

Trusty: Generally, inmate guards, prisoners acting as unpaid security for the prison or farm. They carried guns and guarded against escapes. At Parchman Penitentiary, a trusty who killed an escaping prisoner was eligible for a pardon. Honeyboy uses the term here in a different sense, meaning he worked as an unpaid employee for the county farm, but he did not carry a gun or act as a guard.

Vagrancy law: A crime bill passed in Mississippi in 1876 redefined grand larceny (acts punishable by up to five years in prison) to include petty theft. This would include the common practice of theft of farm animals (hence its nickname "hog law"). Another law passed at this time required blacks to contract with a plantation owner by the first of the year or be subject to arrest. These laws greatly increased arrests. The increased prison population was desirable to planters, who, under the Convict Lease laws, were able to borrow prisoners from the state to clear land and work the cotton fields. When convict leasing was brought to an end, a local practice developed in which farmers requiring labor provided bail for prisoners who then had to work out their debt. When an insufficient number of prisoners was available, sheriffs made blanket arrests of all vagrants in order to satisfy the labor needs of the local farmers. Sometimes the farmers themselves would just pick blacks up off the streets and truck them out to the fields.

Vastopol: See Spanish/Vastopol above.

Wet counties: See Dry/wet counties above.

Williams, Nat D./WDIA: Memphis radio station WDIA began broadcasting programming for blacks in 1949. Williams was the disc jockey on WDIA's "Tan Town Jamboree" show. He was also a professor of history, teacher at Booker T. Washington High School, columnist for the black newspaper in Memphis, and emcee at the popular amateur nights at the Palace Theater. B. B. King was a contestant at the amateur nights and eventually came to play regular segments on

WDIA, on a show sponsored by Pepticon tonic. This show gave King his start in music, and Williams became King's patron and manager. Williams died in October 1983 in Memphis.

Musicians

W e've listed musicians alphabetically by last name or, if Honeyboy refers to them only by nickname, alphabetically by that name. We have listed only artists Honeyboy mentions in the text and only offer the barest of biographical references. For comprehensive biographies of these and other blues artists, we recommend the excellent reference guides *Blues Who's Who* by Sheldon Harris, *The Encyclopedia of the Blues* by Gerard Herzhaft, and *The Big Book of Blues* by Robert Santelli. Recommended recordings are offered; obviously there are many other fine recordings by these artists.

Alexander, Texas: Born Alger Alexander sometime between 1880 and 1900 in Leona, Texas, this vocalist based his sound on the work songs and field hollers common in his region. He was an itinerant musician, moving from town to town and performing with guitarists including Funny Papa Smith and Lightnin' Hopkins. He recorded with Lonnie Johnson, King Oliver, and The Mississippi Sheiks before his death in Houston around 1955. His work is collected on *Texas Alexander: Complete Recorded Works 1927–1950* on Matchbox.

Arnold, Kokomo: Arnold came to the Delta from Lovejoy, Georgia, where he was born James Arnold in February 1901. Arnold was known for his strong left-handed bottleneck style. His 1934 recording "Old Original Kokomo Blues" gave him his nickname. He made more than one hundred recordings (including "Milkcow Blues," later made famous by Elvis Presley) before drifting out of the music scene. He died in Chicago in November 1968. Document's *Kokomo Arnold: 1930–1938* is recommended listening.

Baby Face Leroy: Born Leroy Foster in February 1923 in Algoma, Mississippi, Baby Face Leroy came to Chicago in the forties. He played both drums and guitar and performed with Little Walter Jacobs, Sunnyland Slim, Muddy Waters, and others. He was a mainstay in Chicago's South Side clubs, playing with a number of bands, and a popular performer into the fifties. He died in May 1958. He can be heard on *The Blues World of Little Walter* on Delmark. *Baby Face Leroy and Floyd Jones* on Flyright is also recommended.

Barbee, John Henry: His real name was William Tucker, and he took the name John Henry Barbee after a shooting incident. Born in Henning, Tennessee, in November 1905, he traveled around the South with John Lee "Sonny Boy" Williamson and played with Sunnyland Slim in Delta juke joints in the thirties. He moved to Chicago where he played guitar with Moody Jones's Maxwell Street Band. Barbee died in 1964, shortly after a European tour with the American Folk Blues Festival. He is featured on Storyville's *John Henry Barbee*.

Bartholomew, Dave: Born in Edgar, Louisiana, in December 1920, Bartholomew was a trumpet player who headed a popular band in New Orleans in the forties. He had a hit with his 1949 recording "Country Boy," but had greater success as a producer, composer, and talent scout. Some of the musicians he worked with were Fats Domino, Roy Brown, and Earl King. Bartholomew was a major influence on New Orleans R & B, as can be heard on *Spirit of New Orleans: The Genius of Dave Bartholomew* on EMI-Imperial.

Bear: This percussionist attached woodblocks to his hands and wrists and beat them rhythmically.

Bell, Carey: Born Carey Bell Harrington in November 1936 in the hill country of Mississippi, Bell is a native of Macon and Meridian. He came to Chicago in the fifties and made his mark playing harp in bands with Muddy Waters, Honeyboy, Lovie Lee, and others. Bell now heads his own band and tours constantly. He appears on Honeyboy's *Delta Bluesman* on Earwig, and *Deep Down* on Alligator is also highly recommended.

Bell, Red-Eye Jesse: There is little information available on this blues piano player, who greatly influenced Roosevelt Sykes during his early years in Helena, Arkansas. Sykes adopted Bell's "West Helena Blues," a song Honeyboy plays frequently.

Below, Freddy: Drummer Freddy Below was born in Chicago in September 1926 and left his first love, jazz, for the blues. He was a member of The Aces with Little Walter Jacobs and the Myers brothers and came to be the house drummer at Chess Studios, where he recorded with other musicians throughout the fifties and sixties. His celebrated beat can be heard on the *Best of Little Walter* volumes from Chess. Below died in Chicago in August 1988.

Big Dukes: No information is available about this Chicago-based drummer.

Big-Eyed Willie B.: Big-Eyed Willie Borum played guitar and harmonica and was a vocalist with The South Memphis Jug Band in the twenties. He was born in Memphis in November 1911. In addition to his affiliation with The South Memphis Jug Band, he traveled and performed with Sonny Boy Williamson 2 and Frank Stokes. In the late forties he occasionally broadcast on the "King Biscuit Time" radio show in Helena, Arkansas. Look for Prestige's Bluesville recording *Introducing Memphis Willie B.* Big-Eyed Willie B. died sometime in the seventies.

Big Time Sarah: Sarah Streeter was born in January 1953 and came to Chicago from Coldwater, Mississippi, in 1960. She first used her powerful singing voice in church and came to the blues as a teenager. She performed with The Aces and with her mentor Sunnyland Slim and became a staple of the Chicago blues scene. She performs regularly and can be heard on Delmark's *Lay It on 'Em, Girls*.

Blackwell, Scrapper: Blackwell and his partner, piano player Leroy Carr, were an immensely popular duo in the early thirties. Blackwell, born in February 1903 in Syracuse, South Carolina, was a bootlegger who played guitar as a sideline. His introduction to Carr in 1928 resulted in a seven-year partnership and approximately one hundred titles, including their hit "How Long How Long Blues." Blackwell also recorded with a number of other musicians, including Georgia Tom Dorsey and Bertha Chippie Hill. He left music for decades after Carr's death in 1935. He began recording again in 1959, but this career revival was brought short by his death in October 1962. *Blues before Sunrise* on Portrait features the duo, and *The Virtuoso Guitar of Scrapper Blackwell* on Yazoo is also recommended.

Bland, Bobby: Born in Rosemark, Tennessee, in January 1930, soul singer Bobby Blue Bland began as a gospel singer in Memphis. He was a member of The Beale Streeters with Roscoe Gordon and Junior Parker in the fifties. His "Farther up the Road" was a number-one R & B hit in 1957. A later release, "That's the Way Love Is," was also a big hit. He toured with Junior Parker for a number of years and still tours today with his own bands. His recording career spans four decades. Some of his recordings can be heard on MCA's *The Duke Recordings* volumes 1 and 2.

Blue Coat: Blue Coat Tom Nelson was a singer and violinist who performed frequently in Vicksburg, Mississippi, in the thirties. Honeyboy last saw him in Helena, Arkansas, in 1941, writing policy (also called "numbers," a form of lottery). Look for *Country Blues Collector's Items: 1924–1928* on Document for a sampling of his sound.

Boyd, Eddie: A popular singer and piano player in Chicago after World War II, Boyd eventually left the states to settle in Helsinki, Finland. It was a long way from his home near Clarksdale, Mississippi, where he was born in November 1914. He left there for Memphis in the thirties, coming further north in 1941. In 1952 he recorded his hit song "Five Long Years." After touring Europe as part of a folk blues act in the sixties he decided to make Finland his home; he lived there until his death in 1996. Boyd can be heard on *Five Long Years* on Evidence.

Brewer, Jim: Guitarist Blind Jim Brewer was a well-known figure on Maxwell Street in Chicago from the mid-forties until his death and had also played the streets and clubs of St. Louis and of Brookhaven, Mississippi, where he was born in October 1920. He played both blues and religious music. Earwig's *Tough Luck* showcases his blues repertoire. Brewer died in Chicago in June 1988.

Broonzy, Big Bill: William Lee Conley Broonzy was *the* popular Chicago blues guitarist of the thirties. Born in Scott, Mississippi, in June 1893, Broonzy came to Chicago as a young man in the twenties, where he quickly became one of the city's leading musicians. Broonzy made more than three hundred recordings. He was a mentor to many musicians and often performed and recorded with a number of them, including Lil Green, Jazz Gillum, Lonnie Johnson, John Lee "Sonny Boy" Williamson, Georgia Tom, Washboard Sam, and Memphis Minnie. To get an idea of his early and later sound, try *Good Time Tonight* on Columbia and *Treat Me Right* on Tradition. Broonzy died in August 1958.

Brown, Charles: Born in Texas City, Texas, in September 1922, Brown earned a degree in chemistry and was a teacher and a chemist before he gained fame as a pianist and singer. He settled in San Francisco, playing local clubs while attending the University of California. He was one of a trio, The Three Blazers, when that band recorded his song "Drifting Blues" in 1945. It was an enormous hit. Brown started his own trio for a very successful run of recordings through the fifties. For the next two decades he performed and occasionally recorded. New audiences have been introduced to Charles Brown in recent years thanks to Bonnie Raitt's association with him. *Honeydripper* on Verve is recommended, along with *The Complete Aladdin Recordings* on Mosaic.

Brown, J. T.: Sax player J. T. Brown was a popular sideman who recorded and performed with many musicians in Chicago including Muddy Waters, Howlin' Wolf, Roosevelt Sykes, and Elmore James. As a young musician he traveled with a minstrel show throughout the South. This native Mississippian was born in April 1918. He died in Chicago in November 1969. A compilation of his recordings is on the Pearl label's *J. T. Brown: Windy City Boogie*.

Brown, Willie: A guitarist and singer, Brown was born in Clarksdale, Mississippi, in August 1900 and died in December 1952 in Tunica, Mississippi. He played the Delta juke joints from the twenties through the forties, often with Son House and Charlie Patton. He can be heard on *Son House and the Great Delta Blues Singers: 1928–1930* on Document.

Chatmon, Sam: Born January 1897 in Bolton, Mississippi, Chatmon performed ragtime and popular music in addition to blues with his family's string band, The Mississippi Sheiks. They enjoyed tremendous popularity with their 1930 recording, "Sitting on Top of the World." Chatmon played guitar, mandolin, banjo, bass, and harmonica. He left music for a number of years and was brought back on the scene during the sixties, when he played at many folk festivals, performing until his death in February 1983 in Hollandale, Mississippi. *Stop and Listen: The Mississippi Sheiks* on Yazoo is recommended as are the Document recordings *Mississippi Sheiks* volumes 1, 2, and 3.

Chenier, Clifton: The Zydeco King, Chenier was born in Opelousas, Louisiana, in June 1925 and learned accordion from his father. With his brother Cleveland on washboard, he played throughout Louisiana and Texas. It wasn't until the sixties that he began to attract a national audience. Chenier was responsible for popularizing zydeco before his death in December 1987. You can hear Clifton Chenier on the great recordings on *Zydeco Dynamite: The Clifton Chenier Anthology* on Rhino.

Corley, Dewey: Born in June 1898 in Halley, Arkansas, Corley left home and hoboed around the country, settling in Memphis in 1916. He played harmonica, piano, kazoo, and washtub bass and blew jug with The Memphis Jug Band and The South Memphis Jug Band. He also played jug and bull fiddle with Sleepy John Estes and Frank Stokes. He died in Memphis in April 1974. See The Memphis Jug Band below.

Cotten, Elizabeth: A singer and guitarist from Chapel Hill, North Carolina, Cotten played her blend of blues left handed on a right-handed guitar played upside down. As Honeyboy mentions, she left home and played from a tender age, but she did not make a vocation out of her music until the fifties. She had a thriving music career during the sixties' folk revival and performed widely and recorded from that time well into the eighties. Cotten was born in January 1895 and died in June 1987 in Syracuse, New York. Arhoolie's *Elizabeth Cotten Live!* and *Negro Folk Songs and Tunes* on Folkways are recommended listening.

Cotton, Reverend: Reverend Frank Cotton, from Baird, Mississippi, recorded for Paramount Records in 1928.

Curtis, James Peck: The drummer and vocalist on Sonny Boy Williamson 2's "King Biscuit Time" show, Curtis was born in March 1912 in Benoit, Mississippi. In addition to drums, he played washboard and jug and was also a tap dancer. He performed with jug bands in Memphis before joining Sonny Boy Williamson 2 in Helena, Arkansas. He is featured on the Arhoolie recording *King Biscuit Time*. Curtis died in Helena, Arkansas, in November 1970.

Darby, Blind: Blind Blues Darby was a singer and banjo player who also could play guitar and piano. He was born in Henderson, Kentucky, in March 1906 and moved to St. Louis in the twenties. There he became a popular local figure, playing at clubs and parties through the twenties and thirties. He recorded with a few labels in the thirties before he left music. Look for the Document recording *Blind Teddy Darby: 1929–1931*. His date of death is unknown.

Davis, Walter: Born in Grenada, Mississippi, in March 1912, Davis moved to St. Louis in the twenties, where he became a popular pianist and singer. He recorded approximately 150 numbers, accompanied on some by guitarists Henry Townsend and Big Joe Williams. He left music to become a preacher, dying in October 1963 in St. Louis. His work can be heard on *Walter Davis*, volumes 1–7 (1933–1952), on Document.

Dixon, Willie: Born July 1915 near Vicksburg, Mississippi, Dixon's background included a couple of stays on prison farms and a short career as a boxer. His first musical undertaking was as a bass vocalist in a gospel quartet. He settled in Chicago in 1936 and took up the bass, playing with The Five Breezes and The Big Three Trio. He became a very important figure in Chicago blues and a fixture at the Chess studios, where he acted as session musician, talent scout, songwriter, and producer. Many of his songs became hits for Muddy Waters, Howlin' Wolf, Little Walter Jacobs, and others. Dixon died in January 1992. His work with Chess is highlighted in *The Original Wang Dang Doodle: The Chess Recordings and More* from MCA-Chess.

Dizzy: No information is available on this percussionist.

Domino, Fats: R & B singer and piano player Antoine Domino, nick-named Fats, was born in February 1928 in New Orleans. He played in local honky-tonks for tips from a very young age. In 1949 he recorded "The Fat Man" and had a huge hit with it, selling more than a million copies. Other popular songs of his include "Blueberry Hill" and "Ain't That a Shame." Fats Domino is still playing and based in New Orleans. He can be heard on *They Call Me the Fat Man: The Legendary Imperial Recordings* on EMI-Capitol.

Doyle, Buddy and wife Hedda: Honeyboy remembers Charlie Buddy Doyle well, but there is not much information about him in blues literature. He recorded for Vocalion and played with Sunnyland Slim and Big Walter Horton. Some of his recordings are available on *Memphis Harp and Jug Blowers (1927–1930)* on Document.

Dudlow: Perhaps because he was a reticent man, little is known about Robert Dudlow Taylor. His birthdate and birthplace are not known, though he may have been from Louisiana. Dudlow Joe or Dudlow Picker was a common nickname for boogie-woogie piano players. A big man, also known as Mr. Five by Five, Taylor was one of the original band members playing with Sonny Boy Williamson 2 on "King Biscuit Time." *The Fifties: Juke Joint Blues* on Flair-Virgin includes some of his work. He was still a "King Biscuit Time" entertainer when Sonny Boy Williamson 2 died in 1965. Taylor passed away around 1968.

Estes, Sleepy John: A guitarist and singer, Estes's birthdate is variously listed as January 1904 and January 1899. From Ripley, Tennessee, and nicknamed Sleepy John for his frequent naps (a result of a physical disorder), Estes was frequently accompanied by Yank Rachell on mandolin. In the twenties, they teamed up as a jug band with harmonica and jug player Hammie Nixon. Estes recorded around fifty titles between 1929 and 1941. His career was revived in the early sixties when he played at numerous folk festivals. He died in Brownsville, Tennessee, in June 1977. Try *Someday Baby* on Indigo or the Delmark recording *Brownsville Blues*.

Fat: No information is available on this banjo player.

Fleetwood Mac: This rock band formed in 1967 as a blues revival group. They were led by Peter Green, formerly a guitarist in John Mayall's band, and named for the bassist, John McVie, and the drummer, Mick Fleetwood. Their 1975 album *Fleetwood Mac*, was a hit; their 1977 recording *Rumours*, sold fifteen million copies worldwide.

Floyd, Frank: Born October 1908 in Toccopola, Mississippi, Harmonica Frank Floyd left home as a teenager to work in carnivals, in medicine shows, and on the streets as a comedian and harp player. In addition to harmonica (which he played by placing the instrument in his mouth like a cigar), he played guitar, kazoo, and footdrums, sometimes performing as a one-man band. Floyd traveled and played for many years, periodically made appearances on radio shows in Arkansas and Memphis, and then found work outside music in the sixties. He returned to the music scene to play at colleges and festivals in the seventies. Floyd died in 1984. His song "Goin' Away Walkin'" can be heard on the Blues Classics album *Memphis and the Delta: The 1950s*.

Fulson, Lowell: Guitarist and singer Lowell Fulson represents the West Coast blues though he was born in Tulsa, Oklahoma, in March 1921 and began his career in Texas. Fulson played with Texas Alexander until his musical career was interrupted by World War II. After leaving the navy, he made his home in California, where he recorded "Everyday I Have the Blues," an R & B hit. Fulson enjoyed several hits in the sixties and continues to be active, touring Europe and playing at festivals throughout the United States. *Hold On* on Bullseye showcases this artist.

Gatemouth: The influential Texas bluesman, guitarist Clarence Gatemouth Brown learned early to play fiddle, guitar, mandolin, bass, drums, and harmonica. He played with a number of bands in Houston, where Don Robey created the Peacock label in order to record him. Brown cut more than fifty numbers for Peacock but had no great commercial success until the seventies. It was then that he began touring regularly, reaching a large overseas audience. Brown's performances are a musical gumbo of blues, jazz, country and western, and Cajun-zydeco. He has recorded several highly acclaimed albums, among them the Grammy winner *Alright Again!* on Rounder. Brown was born in April 1924 in Vinton, Louisiana, and is still performing today.

Good Rockin' Charles: Harmonica player Charles Edwards (no relation to Honeyboy) was born in March 1933, possibly in Pratts, Alabama. He moved to Chicago in 1949 where he played on Maxwell Street and in the clubs with Johnny Young, Louis Myers, Jimmy Rogers, and others.

Gordon, Roscoe: This blues pianist, whose first name is sometimes spelled Rosco, got his start in Memphis in the forties and fifties playing with The Beale Streeters, a band that included Bobby Blue Bland and Johnny Ace. He recorded "Booted" for Sam Phillips in 1951 and "No More Doggin'," which was a hit in 1952. He had a few more hits before moving to New York in the sixties. Gordon was born in Memphis in 1934 and still performs. Charly's *Let's Get High* is recommended.

Graves, Blind Roosevelt: Guitarist Graves played both blues and gospel and recorded in the late twenties and early thirties. Look for *Blind Roosevelt Graves* on Wolf. He and his brother Uaroy, a tambourine player, formed The Mississippi Jook Band in the thirties. No birth or death dates are available for Graves.

Handy, W. C.: This Memphis bandleader was an early promoter of blues music, publishing such classics as "St. Louis Blues," "Beale Street Blues," and many others. He was born in Florence, Alabama, in November 1873. Handy played cornet with traveling shows in the South, eventually becoming a bandleader. He died in March 1958 in New York City.

Haines, Frank: A guitarist, possibly never recorded, who associated with Tommy Johnson. Haines was born in Canton, Mississippi, and moved to Jackson, Mississippi.

Hare, Pat: Guitarist Pat Hare was part of Howlin' Wolf's band in Memphis, where he was a session musician at the Sun studios. He moved to Houston for a short time with Junior Parker, and then moved to Chicago and played with Muddy Waters's band. In 1964, Hare was imprisoned for life for murder. Born in Cherry Valley, Arkansas, in December 1930, he died in St. Paul, Minnesota, in September 1980. He can be heard on *A Sun Blues Collection* on Charly.

Harney, Hacksaw: Richard Harney, also known as Can, of the guitar duo Pet and Can. His birthdate is listed variously as June 1898 and July 1902. From Money, Mississippi, Harney traveled throughout the Delta playing music and tuning pianos. He spent time in Memphis and was on a recording with The Memphis Jug Band in 1934. He and his brother recorded with accordion player Walter Rhodes for Columbia in 1947. Harney also briefly ran a music shop in Clarksdale, Mississippi, in the mid-forties and made guitars. A recommended recording is *Sweet Man* on Adelphi. Harney died in December 1973.

Harris, Candy: Honeyboy calls him Candy, but he is more commonly known as Peppermint Harris, and his real name is Harrison Nelson. Born in July 1925 in Texarkana, Texas, guitarist Harris played in Houston clubs after graduating from college, eventually recording a hit for Bill Quinn's Gold Star label, "Rainin' in My Heart." Harris toured with artists including Ray Charles and Amos Milburn, wrote for a number of musicians, and now records and performs only occasionally. A recommended recording is *I Got Loaded* on the Route 66 label.

Homesick James: Singer and guitarist Homesick James Williamson left his home in Somerville, Tennessee, at an early age and hoboed around the South, where he played with bluesmen Sleepy John Estes and Yank Rachell. He recorded in Memphis in the thirties with a band, The Dusters, and with Buddy Doyle. In the fifties, he played with Elmore James in Chicago. Born in May 1910, Williamson still performs and records and can be heard on *Goin' Back in the Times* on Earwig and *Blues on the South Side* from Prestige-Bluesville.

Hooker, Earl: Born in January 1930 in Clarksdale, Mississippi, Hooker moved to Chicago where he attended the Lyon and Healy Music School. There he learned to play drums, piano, banjo, and mandolin, but in his performing career he distinguished himself as a slide guitarist. In 1949 he moved to Memphis and began touring with Ike Turner's band. Back in Chicago in the mid-fifties, he played regularly in the clubs with his own band and with Junior Wells. The Black Top recording *Play Your Guitar Mr. Hooker!* is recommended listening, as is *Blue Guitar* from Paula. Earl Hooker died in Chicago in April 1970.

Hooker, John Lee: Guitarist and vocalist John Lee Hooker left his home outside of Clarksdale, Mississippi, to play on Memphis street corners. From there he moved further north, first to sing in gospel groups in Cincinnati, then to Detroit in 1943, where he played local clubs until the release of his trademark song "Boogie Chillen" in 1948. He has recorded prolifically since that time, with a number of hits reaching worldwide audiences. Born in August 1920, Hooker now lives near Los Angeles and continues to perform. Among the many recommended recordings is *The Legendary Modern Recordings: 1948–1954* on Virgin.

Hopkins, Lightnin': Guitarist Sam Hopkins, born March 1912 in Centerville, Texas, was inspired by the blues of his cousin Texas Alexander and those of Blind Lemon Jefferson. He played throughout Texas and did time at the Big Brazos Penitentiary before starting a recording career that reached well into the seventies. His first numbers were with piano player Thunder Smith. He had a number of very successful songs, but he reached his widest audience during the blues revival of the sixties, when he played colleges and festivals across the country. Hopkins's distinctive sound and style influenced many musicians. He died in Houston in January 1982. *Lightnin'* on Arhoolie, *Sittin' in with Lightnin' Hopkins* on Mainstream, and *The Gold Start Sessions* volumes 1 and 2 on Arhoolie are some of many great Hopkins recordings.

Horton, Big Walter: Also known as Shakey Walter or Mumbles, Big Walter Horton was one of the greatest harmonica players in blues history. He was born in April 1917 in Horn Lake, Mississippi, and played harp from a very early age. As a youngster, he played in W. C. Handy Park with Will Shade and Hammie Nixon. Horton came to Chicago in the early fifties and was in Muddy Waters's band for a short time. He recorded very little under his own name but was a favorite sideman, playing with Honeyboy, Johnny Shines, Jimmy Rogers, and many others. Listen to *Mouth Harp Maestro* on Flair and *Big Walter Horton and Carey Bell* on Alligator. Horton died in Chicago in December 1981.

House, Son: Born Eddie James House in March 1902 in Lyon, Mississippi, House was a preacher at the age of twenty and spent time in Parchman Penitentiary on a murder conviction at twenty-six. As a slide guitarist and singer he played with Willie Brown and Charlie Patton and influenced younger musicians Robert Johnson and Muddy Waters. After recording for Alan Lomax in 1941 and 1942, House left blues and moved to Rochester, New York. He enjoyed a career revival in the sixties, traveling to festivals around the country and in Europe. Representative recordings include *The Complete Library of Congress Sessions 1941–1942* and *Father of the Delta Blues: The Complete 1965 Recordings* on Columbia. House died October 1988 in Detroit.

Howlin' Wolf: Chester Burnett was a vocalist, harp player, and some-time guitarist born in June 1910 in Aberdeen, Mississippi. He played locally and farmed until the late forties, when he moved to West Memphis, Arkansas, to broadcast with his band on KWEM and record with Sun Records and the Bihari brothers. Howlin' Wolf moved to Chicago around 1952 and became one of the most popular blues artists of his time. Among his many hits were "Moaning at Midnight," "Smokestack Lightning," "Red Rooster," and "I Ain't Superstitious." Howlin' Wolf died in January 1976. You can hear him best on *Ain't Gonna Be Your Dog* on MCA-Chess.

Hunter, Ivory Joe: From Weirgate, Texas, Ivory Joe Hunter was born in October 1914. A musician from age sixteen, he got his start playing with traveling shows and circuses. In 1933 he recorded for the Library of Congress as Ivory Joe White. He moved to California in the forties and had a successful career with such hits as "Blues at Sunrise" and "Since I Met You Baby." Hunter moved to Nashville in the sixties and played country music. He died there in November 1974. Recommended Hunter recordings are found on *Sixteen of His Greatest Hits* on King.

Hutto, J. B.: Joseph Benjamin Hutto was born in Blackville, South Carolina, in April 1926 and raised in Georgia. He came to Chicago in 1949 and played drums for a short time before he led his own band, The Hawks, with a bottleneck guitar style influenced by Elmore James. He recorded and played in clubs and at festivals around the country up until his death in Chicago in June 1983. The Delmark recording *Hawk Squat* (with Sunnyland Slim) is recommended.

Jacobs, Little Walter: Blues harmonica has come to be defined by the sound of Little Walter Jacobs. Marion Walter Jacobs was born in Alexandria, Louisiana. Jacobs's birthdate, given commonly as May 1930, seems unlikely given Honeyboy's account. As a boy he played the streets of New Orleans and Helena, Arkansas. After he came to Chicago with Honeyboy he began playing with Muddy Waters's band. His career soared after the release of "Juke," and he began touring heavily afterward with his own bands, The Aces and The Jukes. He had numerous hits, including "My Babe," "Blues with a Feeling," and "Last Night." Jacobs died in Chicago in February 1968. *The Essential Little Walter* on MCA-Chess is recommended.

James, Elmore: James's trademark song, "Dust My Broom," was recorded in 1952 and has been covered by musicians countless times since. Born near Canton, Mississippi, in January 1918, as Elmore Brooks, James performed with Sonny Boy Williamson 2 on KFFA in Helena, Arkansas, and in local clubs. In the early fifties he moved to Chicago but made frequent trips back to the Delta. This innovator of amplified acoustic slide guitar died at an early age in Chicago in May 1963, but his influence is still felt in blues and rock music. For a sample of his sound, try *The Sky Is Crying* on Rhino and Capricorn's *King of the Slide Guitar*.

James, Skip: Nehemiah James was born in June 1902. He created a haunting vocal and guitar style that became known as the Bentonia style of blues, after his Mississippi hometown. He learned guitar from Henry Stuckey and the two often played for local parties and dances. He recorded in 1930 for H. C. Speir; several of these recordings featured his work on piano. For a time James performed gospel, and he was ordained as a preacher. He had been working outside of music for many years when he came to the attention of an international audience in the sixties. He died in October 1969. *The Complete 1931 Sessions* on Yazoo is highly recommended listening, as is the Vanguard recording *Devil Got My Woman*.

Jefferson, Blind Lemon: Jefferson was the most popular male blues recording artist of the twenties. Born in Couchman, Texas, in July 1897 and blind from childhood, Jefferson sang and played guitar in the Deep Ellum neighborhood of Dallas before his extensive travels in other southern states. He recorded more than eighty songs between 1926 and 1929 including "Matchbox Blues" and "See That My Grave Is Kept Clean." He died of exposure in December 1929 in Chicago. Recommended listening is *Blind Lemon Jefferson: King of the Country Blues* on Yazoo.

Jenkins, Piano Bo: Blues pianist Gus Jenkins, also known as Jaarone Pharoah, was born in Birmingham, Alabama, in March 1931. He toured with a number of R & B bands and made his way to Chicago in the forties. He moved to California in 1953, where he played with various musicians, including Johnny Otis's band. Jenkins performed locally around Los Angeles up to his death in December 1985. He is the pianist on Honeyboy's Chess recording *Drop Down Mama*, and can be heard on *Cold Love* on Diving Duck.

Johnson, Lonnie: A guitar player's guitarist, Lonnie Johnson recorded hundreds of songs during his long career. Born in New Orleans as Alonzo Johnson in February 1894, Johnson influenced many of the blues and jazz musicians who followed him. In addition to guitar, he played piano, violin, banjo, and mandolin. He traveled to London and New York; played on the steamboats plying the Mississippi; recorded with Louis Armstrong, Duke Ellington, Victoria Spivey, and

Texas Alexander; and lived long enough to have his career renewed during the sixties' folk revival before his death in Toronto in June 1970. His recordings can be heard on *Lonnie Johnson* volumes 1–7 on Document and Prestige-Bluesville's *Another Night to Cry*.

Johnson, Robert: The most influential and celebrated guitarist in blues history, Robert Johnson was born in Hazelhurst, Mississippi, in May 1911. He studied the performances of Son House and Willie Brown, and he watched Charlie Patton play. He spent his short life as an itinerant musician, dying in his twenties in Greenwood, Mississippi, in August 1938. Robert Johnson's 1936 and 1937 recordings have been listened to and copied by countless blues and rock musicians. Some of these songs include "Sweet Home Chicago," "Crossroads Blues," and "Come on in My Kitchen." These and more can be heard on the boxed set *Robert Johnson: The Complete Recordings* from Columbia. Johnson's unique guitar style changed the course of blues music.

Johnson's extraordinary talent and tragic early death combined with his enigmatic personality have made him as much myth as he was a man. As a young man, he followed Son House and Willie Brown to their performances and, when they would occasionally let him play, was not considered a great or perhaps even good musician. It was at this time that his young wife died in childbirth; his child died as well. Soon after, he left the Delta for a time and returned with a mastery of the guitar so profound that he astonished House and Brown. He became known as one who had sold his soul to the devil for his talent. This seemed confirmed by the lyrics of his songs and his actions. For the rest of his brief life he wandered incessantly, never able to settle down, in a town or with a woman. It is said, as Honeyboy mentions, that near death Johnson crawled like a dog, barking.

Johnson, Tommy: Tommy Johnson had considerable impact and influence on Delta blues and blues musicians. Though the number of recordings he made is small, they include some of the most outstanding songs in blues: "Big Fat Mama," "Canned Heat Blues," and "Maggie Campbell." Recommended listening is *Tommy Johnson* on

Document. Born in 1896 in Terry, Mississippi, Johnson played in various towns in the Delta before settling in Jackson, Mississippi, where he died in November 1956.

Johnson, Willie: Willie Johnson was born in Senatobia, Mississippi, in March 1923 and played guitar locally until he hooked up with Howlin' Wolf. He played with Wolf's band in Memphis and the surrounding area and came to Chicago in the fifties, where he continued to work with Wolf. Willie also recorded and played with Little Junior Parker, Roscoe Gordon, Elmore James, and others. He died in Chicago in February 1995. His highly regarded guitar work can be heard on Howlin' Wolf's recordings of 1947 to 1957 on MCA-Chess's *The Chess Box*.

Joiner (Joyner), Albert: Memphis piano player Albert Joiner Williams recorded with Joe Willie Wilkins in 1952 and can be heard on several recordings made at the Sun studios.

Jones, Floyd: Guitarist Floyd Jones roamed the South until the mid-forties, when he came to Chicago to play in the clubs and on Maxwell Street. He recorded, among others, "Stockyard Blues," "Schooldays," and "On the Road Again." An innovator of the Chicago blues sound, he can be heard on Chess's *Drop Down Mama* and Testament's *Masters of Modern Blues*. He was born in Marianna, Arkansas, in July 1917 and died in Chicago in December 1989.

Kansas City Red: This blues drummer played throughout the South with many important musicians including Robert Nighthawk, Elmore James, and Earl Hooker. Kansas City Red moved to Chicago in the fifties, where he performed regularly in the clubs. He can be heard on *Old Friends* on Earwig, with Big Walter Horton, Sunnyland Slim, Floyd Jones, and Honeyboy. He was born in May 1926 in Drew, Mississippi, as Arthur Lee Stevenson. He died in Chicago in May 1991.

Kelly, Jack: A popular performer in Memphis in the thirties, Jack Kelly was a singer and guitar player who was born between 1900 and 1910 and died around 1960. He played often in W. C. Handy Park, sometimes with Furry Lewis and Big-Eyed Willie Borum. *Jack Kelly and His South Memphis Jug Band 1933–1939* is available on Document.

King, B. B.: The Ambassador of the Blues was born in Indianola, Mississippi, in September 1925 as Riley B. King. The name B.B. is derived from Beale Street Blues Boy, a name given to him when his career began its ascent in Memphis. That ascent started in 1947 when he performed on KWEM in West Memphis, Arkansas, and then on WDIA in Memphis on a show sponsored by Pepticon tonic. King recorded for Sun Records in 1951, and "Three O'Clock Blues" became a number one R & B hit. "Every Day I Have the Blues," from 1955 and "The Thrill Is Gone" from 1970 kept his name prominent over the decades. King has played his guitar in venues the world over and has influenced many guitar players in blues and rock. He enjoys continued and well-deserved success and wide audience appeal. Try *King of the Blues* from MCA, *My Sweet Little Angel* on Flair/Virgin, or the MCA recording *Indianola Mississippi Seeds*.

King, Freddie: Guitarist Freddie King was from Gilmer, Texas, where he was born Freddie Christian in September 1934. He moved to Chicago in 1950, and from then until his death in December 1976, he contributed greatly to the modern blues sound. He had a hit with his 1961 song "Hide Away" and developed a following in both blues and rock audiences. *Freddy King Sings* on Modern showcases his talent.

Kirkland, Eddie: This vocalist and guitar player was born in Kingston, Jamaica, in August 1928 and was raised in Alabama. He came north in the early forties after playing on New Orleans street corners for tips, moving to Detroit where he began performing with John Lee Hooker. He recorded with John Lee Hooker, with King Curtis, and with Otis Redding in addition to recording his own titles. Kirkland lives in Macon, Georgia, and still occasionally performs and records. His *Where You Get Your Sugar* on Deluge is recommended.

Lacy, Rube: Rubin Lacy, born January 1901 in Pelahatchie, Mississippi, recorded "Mississippi Jail House Groan" and "Ham Hound Crave"(on Yazoo's *Mississippi Moaners, 1927–1942*). Around 1932 Lacy quit the blues and became a Baptist minister. He later moved to Bakersfield, California, and died around 1972.

Lewis, Noah: A harmonica and jug player from Henning, Tennessee, where he was born in September 1895, Lewis played with Sleepy John Estes and Gus Cannon's Jug Stompers in addition to playing for tips in Beale Street Park. Lewis left Memphis for Ripley, Tennessee, and died in February 1961. He can be heard on *Gus Cannon and Noah Lewis* volumes 1 and 2 on Document.

Lilly: No information is available on this violin player.

Linkchain, Hip: Spelled Linkchain, or Lankchan, this singer and guitarist's real name was Willie Richard. He was born in November 1936 in Canton, Mississippi, and came to Chicago in 1956. He played frequently with Little Walter Jacobs and Jimmy Rogers. His 1976 recording *I Am on My Way* is available on Storyville. He passed away in February 1989.

Little Milton: Born James Milton Campbell in Inverness, Mississippi, in September 1934, this soul and blues singer and guitarist started his career in Memphis with piano player Willie Love. He recorded for Chess during the sixties and has continued to perform and record with various labels since. *Annie Mae's Café* on Malaco and *The Sun Masters* on Rounder are recommended.

Lockwood, Robert Junior: Lockwood's birthplace in Marvell, Arkansas, was close to that mecca for blues, Helena. It was there that he played with Sonny Boy Williamson 2 on KFFA and became the first electric guitarist heard over the radio in the Delta. An even more important relationship of his was with Robert Johnson, who lived with Lockwood's mother for a time, and in whose honor Robert took the name Junior. Lockwood learned guitar from Johnson but went on to develop his own distinct sound. Lockwood moved to Chicago in 1950 and settled in Cleveland in 1961. Born in March 1915, he is still performing. *Steady Rollin' Man* on Delmark and *Robert Lockwood Does Twelve* on Trix are recommended.

Love, Willie: Born in November 1906 in Duncan, Mississippi, piano player Willie Love was an itinerant musician until he landed in Helena, Arkansas, in 1942 and began playing regularly with Sonny Boy Williamson 2 on the "King Biscuit Time" radio show. It was there also that he had the good fortune to date Honeyboy's future wife, Bessie. Love and Sonny Boy Williamson 2, along with Willie Nix and Joe Willie Wilkins, played throughout the Delta in the forties as The Four Aces. Pick up *Shout, Brother, Shout!* on Alligator to hear Willie Love. Willie died in August 1953 in Jackson, Mississippi.

Magic Sam: An originator of the soulful guitar style known in Chicago as the West Side Sound, Magic Sam was born Samuel Maghett in Grenada, Mississippi, in February 1937. He came to Chicago as a teen and played the clubs, including a stint in Homesick James's band, making his recording debut at the age of twenty. He maintained an enthusiastic local audience and recorded some outstanding work in the sixties. He was just beginning to receive well-deserved national attention when he died of a heart attack in December 1969. Two highly recommended recordings are *West Side Soul* and *Magic Sam Live*, both on Delmark.

McClennan, Tommy: Born in April 1908 in Yazoo City, Mississippi, Tommy's rough guitar style was popular in the juke joints of Greenwood, Mississippi, where he frequently played with his partner, Robert Petway, and with Honeyboy. McClennan attracted the attention of Bluebird's Lester Melrose in the late thirties, and he recorded "Bottle It Up and Go" for that label. He eventually moved to Chicago, where he died in 1962. Among the forty other titles McClennan recorded was "Deep Blue Sea Blues," which Honeyboy refers to as "The Bullfrog Blues." Try *Travelin' Highway Man* on Travelin' Man.

The Memphis Jug Band: Jug bands had been known as early as 1915 in Louisville, Kentucky, and Cincinnati, Ohio. Will Shade (Son Brimmer), who played instruments including harmonica, guitar, and jug, started The Memphis Jug Band in the mid-twenties, and the popularity of this group led to the formation of many others including The Beale Street Jug Band and Cannon's Jug Stompers. These bands, which featured a combination of guitar, fiddle, harmonica, kazoo, washtub bass, washboard, and jug, were enjoyed by blacks and whites and often played at the Peabody, Memphis' largest hotel. They also made annual trips to Mardi Gras, playing in towns from

Memphis to New Orleans. Many musicians drifted in and out of The Memphis Jug Band, which recorded approximately eighty songs ranging from blues to ragtime to waltzes, some of which can be heard on Yazoo's *The Memphis Jug Band*.

Memphis Minnie: Memphis Minnie was a tremendously popular artist for decades and one of very few female country blues musicians. Born Lizzie Douglas in June 1897 in Algiers, Louisiana, her family moved to Wall, Mississippi, while she was a young child. Her family nickname was Kid, and she was known as Kid Douglas when she was a young performer. In her early teens she played guitar and banjo on Memphis street corners and joined the Ringling Brothers' Circus. Memphis Minnie's "Bumble Bee Blues," recorded in 1930, was a hugely popular number. She recorded almost two hundred titles and spent many productive years in Chicago before returning to Memphis, where she died in August 1973. For Memphis Minnie's recordings look for Travelin' Man's *In My Girlish Days* and Indigo's *Bumble Bee*.

Memphis Slim: Born Peter Chatman in Memphis in September 1915, at age sixteen he was playing piano in the clubs of that town. Memphis Slim left for Chicago in the late thirties and recorded often in the next two decades as a soloist, with his own band, and as a sideman, often with Big Bill Broonzy. Memphis Slim went on a European tour in 1960 and in 1962 returned to Paris to stay. He became a very popular artist in Europe, and before his death in February 1988 the U.S. Senate named him Ambassador at Large of Good Will. *Memphis Slim: The Real Folk-Blues* on Chess is recommended.

Milburn, Amos: This Houston singer and piano player was born in April 1927 and played piano from age ten. He served in the armed forces during World War II, returning to Houston to play at the local clubs. By the end of the forties, he had three hits, including "Roomin' House Boogie," and had been named *Billboard*'s number one artist of the year. He continued to perform in the fifties and sixties before his health began to fail. He died in Houston in January 1980. Hear him on *The Best of Amos Milburn: Down the Road a Piece* on EMI and *The Complete Aladdin Recordings* on Mosaic.

Montgomery, Little Brother: This barrelhouse piano player started his career at age eleven when he began playing piano at levee and saw-mill camps. He played in New Orleans with several Dixieland bands and performed in Chicago clubs for many years. He played Carnegie Hall with Kid Ory's band and recorded with Sippie Wallace. He was born in Kentwood, Louisiana, in September 1906 and passed away in Chicago in September 1985. *Little Brother Montgomery at Home* from Earwig is recommended.

Moody, Bit: A harp player from Brownsville or Ripley, Tennessee.

Moore, Andrew and Tom: Honeyboy says "the Moores were the best guitar players you ever seen in your life." No other information is available on these unrecorded musicians.

Morris, Joe: No information is available on this harmonica player.

Murphy, Matt: Sunflower, Mississippi, native Matt Guitar Murphy was born in December 1929 and moved to Memphis as a child. There he came to play guitar in Howlin' Wolf's band and with Junior Parker's Blue Flames. He became one of Memphis Slim's House Rockers and recorded with them and others during the fifties and sixties. He also was in the Chess studios in the sixties with Sonny Boy Williamson 2. His talents were displayed to a wider audience in the 1980 movie *The Blues Brothers*. Murphy is still playing and recording. He can be heard on *The Blues Don't Bother Me* on Roesch.

Myers, Louis and Dave: The Myers brothers were born in Byhalia, Mississippi; Dave in October 1926, Louis in September 1929. They moved to Chicago in 1941 and were original members of The Aces, which came to be Little Walter Jacobs's band after Junior Wells's departure. Louis was a guitarist and harmonica player. In addition to his stint with Little Walter Jacobs, he worked with Otis Spann, Otis Rush, and others, both as a sideman and as a session musician. Louis died in September 1994. Earwig's *Tell My Story Movin'* is recommended listening. Dave is still a working musician, playing both bass and guitar. He can be heard on *Kings of Chicago Blues* volume 1 on Vogue. The Myers brothers' unique and masterful work with Little Walter Jacobs is available on *Blues with a Feeling* on MCA-Chess.

Nighthawk, Robert: Known by various names but born Robert Lee McCollum, Nighthawk's slide guitar could be heard in the forties on a KFFA show sponsored by Bright Star flour. He had already recorded and played throughout the Delta for years before then, having learned guitar from his cousin, Houston Stackhouse. He spent time in St. Louis and Chicago in the thirties, when he recorded with John Lee "Sonny Boy" Williamson and Big Joe Williams. He had a hit with "Black Angel Blues" in 1949 and recorded other titles for Chess. This small success didn't keep him in Chicago, though. Nighthawk continued to roam the South, playing in juke joints and again on KFFA. Born in Helena, Arkansas, in November 1909, he died there in November 1967. Two great Nighthawk songs are on the Chess recording *Drop Down Mama*; *Live on Maxwell Street* on Rounder and *Bricks in My Pillow* on Pearl are also recommended.

Nix, Willie: Blues drummer and vocalist born Willie Nicks in Memphis in August 1922, Nix as a boy was a tap dancer in medicine shows. He played with a number of musicians in Memphis including Big Walter Horton and Sonny Boy Williamson 2 and recorded at the Sun studios before leaving for Chicago in 1953. He eventually returned to Memphis and died in Leland, Mississippi, in July 1991. His work can be heard on *Sun Records: The Blues Years* on Charly.

Norwood, Sam: Guitar and mandolin player One-Leg, or Peg-Leg, Sam Norwood hailed from Crystal Springs, Mississippi, where he was born around 1900. He moved to Jackson, Mississippi, and Honeyboy tells us that One-Leg Sam used to play there with Tommy Johnson. He came to Chicago sometime in the forties and was frequently seen on Maxwell Street into the sixties, before his death in 1967. He recorded with Jaybird Coleman in the twenties, and can be heard on *Jaybird Coleman and Birmingham Jug Band 1927–1930* on Document; his gospel songs with Slim Duckett are on the same label's *Alabama: Black Secular and Religious Music 1927–1934*.

Parker, Junior: Harmonica player and singer Herman Parker Jr. played in Memphis with Sonny Boy Williamson 2, Howlin' Wolf, and The Beale Streeters before he started his own band, The Blue Flames. He recorded with Sun in 1953, "Feelin' Good," which was an R & B hit, and "Mystery Train," made famous by Elvis Presley. He moved to Houston to work with producer Don Robey and enjoyed a successful recording and touring career. His sweet voice and understated harp style can be heard on *The Best of Little Junior Parker* on MCA. Parker, who was born in West Memphis, Arkansas, in March 1932, died in November 1971 in Chicago.

Patton, Charlie: This early Delta blues guitarist was the most popular performer in the region and influenced nearly every other blues musician to follow. Born in Edwards, Mississippi, in April 1891, his family moved to the Dockery Plantation in the Delta when he was a boy. There he learned to play guitar, eventually performing throughout the Delta, picking up no fewer than eight wives along the way. His first recording, "Pony Blues," was made in 1929, and over the next five years he recorded approximately seventy titles. He died in April 1934. *Charlie Patton: Founder of the Delta Blues 1929–1934* on Yazoo is an excellent collection of his recordings.

Payne, Raymond: Guitarist Raymond Payne was a never-recorded musician who taught Fred McDowell.

Pejoe, Morris: Guitarist and vocalist Pejoe was born Morris Pejas in Palmetto, Louisiana, sometime in 1924. He started his musical career on the violin and spent time in Beaumont, Texas, where he came under the influence of Clarence Gatemouth Brown. Later, in Chicago, Pejoe gained local popularity and made a few recordings for Chess and others. He moved to Detroit in the seventies where he played locally until his death in July 1982. He can be heard on *Wrapped in My Baby* on the Pearl label.

Perkins, Pinetop: Barrelhouse piano player Pinetop Perkins was born in Belzoni, Mississippi, in July 1913 as Joe Willie Perkins. By 1943 he was playing with Robert Nighthawk, and then with Sonny Boy Williamson 2 on the "King Biscuit Time" radio show. Perkins went on to Memphis to record "Pinetop's Boogie" for Sun Records. He joined Muddy Waters's band in 1969 and stayed with him for twelve years. Perkins lives in Chicago and is still performing at age eighty-four. Two recommended recordings are Deluge's *On Top* and Earwig's *Pinetop Perkins with the Blue Ice Band*.

Petway, Robert: Not much information is available on this vocalist and guitarist who was Tommy McClennan's friend. Born approximately 1908, he disappears from sight sometime after a recording session in the early forties. He made the first and definitive version of "Catfish Blues" along with thirteen other recordings for the Bluebird label. "Catfish" can be heard on *Mississippi Blues: The Complete Works of Robert Petway* on Wolf.

Pork Chop: In the thirties, percussionist Eddie Hines played in medicine shows in Tennessee. In Chicago he often accompanied musicians such as Baby Face Leroy, Snooky Pryor, Floyd Jones, and Stovepipe, and he recorded with J. B. Hutto. He was a frequent sight on Maxwell Street in the sixties.

Prosperity: No other information is available about this lively washboard player.

Pryor, Snooky: Harp player James Pryor was born in September 1921 in Lambert, Mississippi, and lived a life similar to Honeyboy's, hoboing throughout the South and playing the streets and juke joints. Unlike Honeyboy, Pryor was in the army during World War II. He settled in Chicago after the war, playing on Maxwell Street and in the South Side clubs and recording for a number of labels. He dropped out of music for a time but now can occasionally be seen on the festival circuit. *Back to the Country* on Blind Pig is recommended as is *In This Mess Up to My Chest* on Antone's.

Rachell, Yank: Blues mandolin player Yank Rachell was born in March 1910 in Brownsville, Tennessee, where he played locally with Sleepy John Estes. In addition to their work with Hammie Nixon, the two of them joined Jab Jones to form The Three J's Jug Band, a popular trio in Memphis in the twenties. In the thirties, he performed and recorded with John Lee "Sonny Boy" Williamson. Yank's career surged during the sixties' folk revival, when he played frequently with his old partner, Estes. From 1958 on, Rachell lived in Indianapolis and performed right up to his death in April 1997. *Yank Rachell Mandolin Blues* on Delmark is recommended.

Robinson, J. C.: An unrecorded musician from the Delta, Robinson was about five years younger than Honeyboy and stayed in Scott and

Greenwood, Mississippi, eventually moving to Florida. Honeyboy also refers to him as Popcorn.

Rogers, Jimmy: Born in Atlanta in June 1924 as James Lane, guitarist Rogers went to Helena and West Memphis, Arkansas, as a teenager. He played with a number of musicians, including Robert Junior Lockwood and Robert Nighthawk, before heading north to Chicago. There he joined Muddy Waters's band, and his rhythm guitar became an essential element of Waters's sound. Rogers had his own hit with "Walking by Myself," recorded with Big Walter Horton. Rogers dropped out of the music scene for a time but, fortunately for all, is now an active, touring musician. *Chicago Bound* on MCA features Rogers; also listen for his sound on *Muddy Waters: The Chess Box* from MCA-Chess.

Satchmo: Trumpeter and vocalist Louis Armstrong was born in 1901 in New Orleans and came to be the greatest single figure in jazz history. During a stay at the Waifs' Home in New Orleans as a child, he learned cornet, and he spent the early years of his career playing with such greats as Kid Ory, Fate Marable, and King Oliver. The latter brought him to Chicago in 1922, and by 1926 Armstrong was dubbed the World's Greatest Trumpet Player. Of his many recordings, some of the greatest and most popular include "West End Blues," "Struttin' with Some Barbecue," "Ain't Misbehavin'," and "Hello, Dolly." He performed until his death in 1971. He was loved and admired the world over. For some of Armstrong's most exciting music, look for *The Hot Fives and Hot Sevens* volumes 1, 2, and 3 on JSP.

Shade, Will: Born in February 1894 in Memphis, this guitarist was the founder and manager of The Memphis Jug Band. He was also known as Son Brimmer (he was raised by his grandmother, Annie Brimmer). Will Shade died in September 1966. See The Memphis Jug Band above.

Shaw, Allen and son Willie Tango: Born in 1890 in Henning, Tennesee, Allen Shaw was an itinerant guitarist who spent much of his time in Memphis. He played with Noah Lewis and Howlin' Wolf and was best known for his songs, "I Beat My Woman with a Single-Tree" and "Chickasaw Special." Shaw died in 1940. His son, a guitarist named Willie, became known as Willie Tango on Beale Street. Willie Tango often played with Big Walter Horton, and Memphis Minnie even wrote a song about him, "Mr. Tango Blues." Allen Shaw is on the recording *Memphis Blues 1927–1937* from HK Records.

Shines, Johnny: This guitarist and powerful singer was born in Frayser, Tennessee, in April 1915 and raised in Arkansas. Johnny Shines hooked up with Robert Johnson in the mid-thirties and traveled with him. He also spent time in Memphis, playing frequently in Beale Street Park. He moved to Chicago in 1941 and recorded for OKeh and Chess but had no commercial success. He left the blues scene for a few years, but we are fortunate that his career revived in the late sixties. He died in Tuscaloosa, Alabama, in April 1992. Two of his songs are on Chess's *Drop Down Mama*, or try *Traditional Delta Blues* on Biograph, or *Johnny Shines and Robert Lockwood* on Paula (Shines is accompanied on these recordings by Big Walter Horton at some of his best).

Ship, Man: A regretfully unrecorded musician. Honeyboy has told us Man Ship was from Berclairs, Mississippi, and that he had a brother called Son Ship, a sister called Cora Ship, and another sister simply known as Monkey.

Short, J. D.: Honeyboy's cousin J.D., also referred to as Jaydee or Jelly Jaw, was born in December 1902 in Port Gibson, Mississippi. He moved with his family to the Delta and then settled in St. Louis in 1923. In addition to guitar, he played piano and harmonica. He played the clubs and streets of St. Louis alone and with Big Joe Williams for years, making a few recordings before his death in October 1962. *Piney Woods Blues* and *Stavin' Chain Blues* on Delmark showcase Short and Williams.

Shorty: No information is available about this drummer.

Smith, Funny Papa: Born John T. Smith around 1885 in Texas and known variously as J. T. Smith, Funny Papa, and Funny Paper Smith. Smith recorded nearly twenty songs in the early thirties, among them "Howling Wolf Blues," which can be heard on *Funny Papa Smith:*

The Original Howling Wolf on Yazoo Records. He was imprisoned for murder in the thirties and died around 1940.

Smith, Thunder: There are few mentions of Houston piano player Wilson Smith who recorded with Lightnin' Hopkins in the mid-forties. He can be heard on *Texas Blues: The Gold Star Sessions* on Arhoolie. He died in Houston in 1965 in an altercation with his drummer.

Son Joe: Memphis Minnie's third husband, guitar player Ernest Lawlar, was known as Little Son Joe. Born in Hughes, Arkansas, in May 1900, he married Memphis Minnie in the late thirties and lived, recorded, and performed with her through some very successful years in Chicago. They returned to Memphis in the fifties, where he died in 1961. Son Joe can be heard on some of Memphis Minnie's greatest numbers, including "In My Girlish Days" and "I'm So Glad." (See Memphis Minnie, above.)

Spann, Otis: Born in Jackson, Mississippi, in March 1930, Spann came to Chicago in 1951 after his discharge from the army. There he played the South Side clubs, eventually coming to the attention of Muddy Waters. He joined Waters's band in 1953, and his piano contributed greatly to that band's success for many years. He recorded often with them and also with other musicians at the Chess studio, including Howlin' Wolf and Little Walter Jacobs. In the sixties he branched out on his own, recording a number of albums. Spann died in April 1970. *Otis Spann's Chicago Blues* on Testament and *Muddy Waters: The Chess Box* on MCA are among his legacies.

Speckled Red: Rufus Perryman was a boogie-woogie piano player who was born in Monroe, Louisiana, in October 1892, moved with his family to Georgia, and eventually made his way to Detroit. He came south again and in 1929 recorded a hit song in Memphis, "The Dirty Dozens." He settled in St. Louis where he was a popular local musician until the mid-fifties, when he was brought onto the national stage. He died in January 1973 in St. Louis. *The Dirty Dozens* on Delmark is recommended. Honeyboy mentions that Speckled Red was part of the Chicago music scene early on, perhaps before he moved back to the South in 1929.

St. Louis Jimmy: Singer and pianist James Burke Oden was known for his song, "Going Down Slow." He was born in June 1903 in Nashville and moved to St. Louis in 1917, where he played at clubs and parties for years. In the early thirties he moved to Chicago and recorded and performed with Roosevelt Sykes. Try *St. Louis Jimmy Oden, 1932–1948* on Document. Poor health caused him to retire from performing by 1970, and he passed away in Chicago in December 1977.

Stokes, Frank and son Little Frank: Frank Stokes, born in 1887, was a very popular and influential guitarist in Memphis in the twenties and thirties. He and guitarist Dan Sane formed The Beale Street Sheiks and recorded "Mr. Crump Don't Like It," "Nobody's Business If I Do," and other classics (listen to Yazoo's *Creator of the Memphis Blues*). Stokes died in September 1955. Honeyboy calls Frank Stokes's son Little Frank, but his given name was Roosevelt Stokes. Little Frank occasionally played in Beale Street Park in Memphis.

Stovepipe: Also known as Daddy Stovepipe, Reverend Alfred Pitts, and Sunny Jim, this guitar, harmonica, jug, and kazoo player's real name was Johnny Watson. He was born in Mobile, Alabama, in April 1867 and was ninety-six years old when he died in Chicago in November 1963. As a young man he toured with minstrel shows in the South; played as a one-man band in Memphis; traveled to Texas and Mexico, working the streets; and moved to Chicago in 1948, where he was frequently seen on Maxwell Street. He is among the various artists on *Harmonicas Unlimited: 1924–1949* from Document.

Stuckey, Son: Henry Stuckey is best known as the guitarist who influenced the more famous musician Skip James. He was born in Bentonia, Mississippi, in April 1897 and died in Jackson, Mississippi, in March 1966. Throughout most of his life he played locally, and in the twenties and thirties he played with Skip James and ran a juke joint near Bentonia. He never recorded.

Sunnyland Slim: Born Albert Luandrew in Vance, Mississippi, in 1908, Sunnyland Slim left home at a very young age to work and play piano. As Honeyboy describes, he worked the levees, barrelhouses, and gambling joints in the Delta and beyond. He went to Chicago in 1942 and was a central figure in its thriving blues community. He recorded more than twenty albums with many musicians, including Muddy Waters, Little Walter Jacobs, Big Bill Broonzy, and Lonnie Johnson, and over the years performed in countries all around the world. He was the recipient of a National Heritage Fellowship and the gratitude of the many musicians he helped throughout the years. He died in March 1995 in Chicago, playing to the end of his life. He is featured on two Earwig recordings with Honeyboy, *Delta Bluesman* and *Old Friends*; other recommended recordings are Earwig's *Be Careful How You Vote*, the Airway recording *Live in Europe 1975*, and *The Original J.O.B./Cobra Recordings* from P-Vine.

Sykes, Roosevelt: Also known as the Honeydripper, Theodore Roosevelt Sykes was born in January 1906 in Elmark, Arkansas. The title song of his first record, 1929's *44 Blues*, became his trademark. Sykes played in Helena, Arkansas, barrelhouses and worked sawmill and levee camps throughout the South. He was an important and influential piano player in St. Louis in the thirties and continued to hold sway in Chicago in the forties. He moved to New Orleans in 1954, where he died thirty years later in July. Sykes's blues are on *The Honeydripper: 1929–1941* on Document.

Tampa Red: Tampa Red was the enormously popular singer and guitarist whose music dominated the thirties and beyond. Born Hudson Woodbridge around 1904, he assumed his grandmother's name, Whittaker, on the death of his parents. He came from Smithville, Georgia, but was raised in Tampa. Tampa Red's bottleneck style was unsurpassed. His first hit, recorded with Georgia Tom Dorsey, was "Tight Like That." It was followed by hundreds of recordings. He retired from music many years before his death in March 1981 in Chicago. Yazoo's *Bottleneck Guitar* and the Prestige label's *Don't Tampa with the Blues* are recommended. The Tampa Red Honeyboy saw playing on Maxwell Street must have been trying to take advantage of the genuine article's reputation.

Temple, Johnny: A very popular guitarist and vocalist in the thirties, Johnny Temple was born in October 1906 in Canton, Mississippi.

He played guitar and mandolin locally and then moved to Chicago in the thirties, when he recorded his biggest hit, "Louise Louise Blues." Temple performed for many years in the clubs of Chicago with bands including Big Walter Horton, Elmore James, and Honeyboy before he returned to the South. He died in Jackson, Mississippi, in November 1968. Look for *Johnnie Temple: Complete Recorded Works* on Document.

Thornton, Big Mama: Vocalist and harp player Willie Mae Thornton, born in December 1926, left her home in Montgomery, Alabama, as a young girl to join the traveling Hot Harlem Revue. After a number of years touring the South she settled in Houston where she recorded the hit "Hound Dog," later covered by Elvis Presley. She played locally and toured with Junior Parker before moving to San Francisco, where her career was revived in the sixties. She recorded and toured until she died in July 1984 in Los Angeles. For some of her best, try *Hound Dog: The Duke-Peacock Recordings* on MCA-Duke-Peacock.

Toy, Tom: Guitarist Tom Toy hailed from Leland, Mississippi, and was locally known for his version of "Catfish Blues."

Ukelele Kid: No information is available about Ukelele Kid.

Walker, Jimmy: Boogie-woogie piano player Jimmy Walker was born in March 1905 in Memphis. He has been in Chicago since the thirties, playing in clubs with a number of musicians including Big Joe Williams, Elmore James, and Homesick James. He recorded for the first time in the sixties with the Chicago piano player Erwin Helfer and made his first solo recording at the age of seventy-eight. He still lives on the South Side of Chicago and performed at clubs and festivals until recently. Try his *Original South Side Blues Piano* on Wolf.

Walker, Spence: No information is available about Spence Walker.

Walker, T-Bone: An early adopter of electric guitar and a highly influential guitarist and singer, Aaron Thibeaux Walker was born in May 1910 in Linden, Texas. He tap-danced and played guitar for medicine shows throughout Texas before gaining experience playing with Cab Calloway's band and other big bands in the thirties. In Los Angeles he began playing electric guitar, and at the end of the decade made his successful recording "T-Bone Blues." A few years later he recorded the classic song, "Call It Stormy Monday." He enjoyed a successful career during the blues revival era before he passed away in March 1975 in Los Angeles. *The Complete Imperial Recordings: 1950–1954* on EMI is the best of Walker.

Waters, Muddy: Muddy was born McKinley Morganfield in April 1915 in Rolling Fork, Mississippi, and raised by his grandmother on the Stovall Plantation in the Delta. He learned guitar and played locally, was recorded by Alan Lomax in the early forties, and moved to Chicago in 1943. There he found enormous success with Chess Records and went on to achieve international renown, becoming one of the most important figures in the blues. Waters died in Chicago in April 1983. Among his many hits are "Long Distance Call," "Got My Mojo Working," and "I Just Want to Make Love to You." For a sample of his work from his early years to late, listen to *The Complete Plantation Recordings* on MCA-Chess and *Muddy Waters: The Chess Box* from MCA-Chess.

Wells, Junior: Amos Blakemore, better known as harp player Junior Wells, was born in Memphis in December 1934 and moved to Chicago at the age of twelve. From a very young age he played parties and clubs with the Myers brothers and with them and drummer Freddy Below formed The Aces. When Little Walter Jacobs left Muddy Waters, Junior Wells took his place—and Little Walter Jacobs took over The Aces. Wells spent a few years with Waters's band before teaming up with Buddy Guy. Junior Wells continues to perform and record. A recommended recording is *Hoodoo Man Blues* on Delmark.

Wheatstraw, Peetie: Also known as the Devil's Son-in-Law and the High Sheriff from Hell, blues pianist Wheatstraw was born William Bunch in December 1902 in Ripley, Tennessee. He went to St. Louis in 1929 and enjoyed great popularity in the thirties, recording more than 160 titles. A sample of these can be heard on *The Devil's Son-in-Law, 1937–1941* on Blues Document. Wheatstraw died in St. Louis in December 1941.

White, Bukka: This guitarist was born in Aberdeen, Mississippi, as Booker T. Washington White in November 1909. At one time a secondhand furniture dealer, a ballplayer in the Negro Leagues, and a professional fighter, White spent his younger years playing the juke joints of the Delta. While incarcerated at Parchman Penitentiary on a murder charge, he recorded for Alan Lomax of the Library of Congress. The folk revival of the sixties gave new life to his musical career, and he toured and recorded widely. He died in February 1977 in Memphis. His work can be heard on *The Complete Sessions* on Travelin' Man and *Sky Songs* on Arhoolie.

Wilkins, Joe Willie: Sonny Boy Williamson 2's guitarist during the forties and fifties, Joe Willie influenced many listeners of the "King Biscuit Time" radio show. Born in January 1923 in Davenport, Mississippi, he played on the streets under the name Joe Willie, the Walking Seeburg. He recorded and performed as a sideman for many musicians before he died in Memphis in March 1979. Try *Joe Willie Wilkins and His King Biscuit Boys* on Adamo.

Williams, Big Joe: Joe Williams was born in October 1903 in Crawford, Mississippi, the oldest of sixteen children. He left home at an early age and wandered throughout the South, working the levee and sawmill camps and playing for minstrel shows. Joe was known for his nine-string guitar, an innovation Honeyboy mentions in the text. Joe spent a great deal of time in St. Louis when he wasn't roaming the South, and during the folk revival of the sixties his travels expanded to Europe. He had an extensive recording career, and throughout his life he worked with many noted blues musicians including Robert Nighthawk, John Lee "Sonny Boy" Williamson, and Walter Davis. He acted as a mentor to the young Charlie Musselwhite and Mike Bloomfield. Williams died in December 1982. Honeyboy was greatly influenced by him, both musically and in his adoption of Williams's wandering ways. Recommended listening includes *Nine-String Guitar Blues* on Delmark, *Big Joe Williams* volumes 1–2 (1935–1949) on Document, *Back to the Country* on Testament, *Big Joe Williams* volume 2 (1945–1949) on RST, and *Throw a Boogie Woogie* on RCA.

Williamson 2, Sonny Boy: Throughout the text, Honeyboy refers to Alex Rice Miller, who gave himself the name Sonny Boy after the original Sonny Boy, John Lee Williamson. In these appendices John

Lee Williamson is referred to as John Lee "Sonny Boy" Williamson; Alex Rice Miller is referred to as Sonny Boy Williamson 2. John Lee was an influential and popular harmonica player born in March 1914 in Jackson, Tennessee. His successful recording career was cut short by his murder in Chicago in June 1948, but his sound continues to influence musicians today. Sonny Boy Williamson 2 was known for his performances in the forties on the "King Biscuit Time" radio show on KFFA, a station broadcasting from Helena, Arkansas. He had an extensive recording career with Chess. Every title on *The Essential Sonny Boy Williamson* from MCA-Chess is excellent. Also recommended is *Keep It to Ourselves* on Alligator. He played with artists including Robert Jr. Lockwood, Robert Nighthawk, Elmore James, and Otis Spann and even with the Yardbirds in the sixties. His birthdate is variously listed, falling somewhere between 1894 and 1910; his birthplace Glendora, Mississippi. Honeyboy met him in 1929 and thought he was around thirty at that time. Sonny Boy Williamson 2 died in May 1965 in Helena, Arkansas.

Winter, Johnny: A guitarist from Beaumont, Texas, Winter entered the national blues and rock scene in 1968 with a successful recording and a performance at Woodstock. He had played locally in Texas in his early years, accompanied by his brother Edgar on piano. Winter's early love for blues showed through in his rock recordings; his later career has seen him turn back to the blues. He recorded in the seventies with Muddy Waters's band and acted as Waters's producer on four albums. *Johnny Winter* on Columbia will give you a good sampling of his blues sound. Winter was born in February 1944, currently lives in New York, and still performs.

Young, Johnny: Singer and mandolin player Johnny Young was born in 1918 in Vicksburg, Mississippi. He went to Chicago in the forties, where he performed regularly on Maxwell Street. He died in April 1974 after having enjoyed some popularity during the blues revival of the sixties. His recording with Big Walter Horton and Otis Spann for Arhoolie, *Chicago Blues*, is recommended, as is *Johnny Young and His Friends* on Testament.

Songs

The purpose of this appendix is to provide some background information such as recording dates, songwriters, and subsequent recordings on all the songs Honeyboy mentions in the text. Honeyboy often refers to songs by their first lines rather than their titles. They are listed here alphabetically as he refers to them.

"The Army Blues": Honeyboy's own song about World War II. He recorded it originally for Alan Lomax in 1942. It can be heard on *Delta Bluesman* from Earwig.

"Baby, Please Don't Go": Recorded by Big Joe Williams in 1935, this old folk song dates back to slavery times. Muddy Waters's version, recorded at the 1960 Newport Folk Festival, became a blues standard.

"Big Kate Adams": There were three boats named *Kate Adams*. The first of these gained fame for its record ninety-mile run in 1883 from Helena to Memphis in five hours and eighteen minutes. Five years later, the cotton-laden steamboat burned in a fire that killed thirty-three people. Honeyboy recorded this song as "Big Kate Allen" on *Delta Bluesman* from Earwig and attributed it to Alvin Moore.

"Blues come from Texas": Honeyboy refers to "Blues come from Texas," a line from "Got the Blues" originally recorded by Blind Lemon Jefferson in 1926.

"Bottle It Up and Go": This traditional song was also known as "Shake It Up and Go" and was The Memphis Jug Band's popular number, recorded in 1934. Tommy McClennan recorded it in 1939.

"Bo Weevil": The song "Bo Weevil Blues" was from a 1934 recording session with Charlie Patton and his wife, Bertha Lee. It dealt with the damage inflicted on cotton crops by the boll weavil.

"Bring it on down to my house, baby": This is a line from the song "Ain't Nobody Here but Me." This song was recorded by Little Brother Montgomery.

"Brother James": A traditional piece recorded by Big Joe Williams in the thirties for the RCA Bluebird label.

"Build Myself a Cave": Honeyboy recorded this song in 1951, along with "Who May Your Regular Be," the unissued song "Early in the Morning," and "Who Could Be Loving You Tonight" for the Artist Recording Company in Houston. A later version of "Build Myself a Cave" can be heard on his recording White Windows on Blue Suit.

"The Bullfrog Blues": Honeyboy refers to Tommy McClennan's 1941 recording, "Deep Blue Sea Blues."

"Bumble Bee": "Bumble Bee Blues" was recorded by Memphis Minnie in 1930.

"Call Me the Fat Man": "The Fat Man" by Fats Domino was recorded in 1949 on the Imperial label and sold more than one million copies.

"Canned heat mama, canned heat is killin' me": Is a line from the famous number "Canned Heat Blues" recorded by Tommy Johnson in 1928.

"Careless Love": Possibly originally an Irish folk tune, this song was popular with both jazz and blues artists including Lonnie Johnson, Homesick James, George Lewis, and Kid Ory.

"The Catfish Blues": Robert Petway made the first and definitive version of "Catfish Blues" in 1941.

"Cherry Ball": This tune of Son Stuckey's was recorded by Skip James in 1931.

"Cold Water Blues": The song "Cool Drink of Water Blues" was recorded by Tommy Johnson in 1928 and later interpreted by Howlin' Wolf in "I Asked for Water."

"Coming 'Round the Mountain": "She'll Be Coming 'Round the Mountain" is a traditional piece with a melody dating back to before the 1890s.

"Corinna": A Blind Lemon Jefferson number from 1926, this song became very popular. Bo Carter recorded a version "Corinna Blues" in 1928, and in 1971 Taj Mahal recorded another version.

"Cotton Patch Blues": Tommy McClennan recorded this song in 1939.

"Cross Cut Saw": A 1941 recording by Tommy McClennan.

"Drop Down Mama": A Sleepy John Estes recording from 1935. Honeyboy's version, with Gus Jenkins on piano, is on MCA-Chess's *Drop Down Mama*.

"Elevate me, mama": Honeyboy refers to John Lee "Sonny Boy" Williamson's "Elevator Mama," from 1945.

"The 44 Blues": A piano piece originally recorded by Roosevelt Sykes in 1927. The song was associated with a number of piano players before Sykes's recording, including Little Brother Montgomery and Sykes's mentor, Lee Green. The number most likely refers to train number 44, which ran though Vicksburg, Mississippi. Green's version of the song includes the line, "I heard the 44 whistle blow." Sykes's version refers to the train, the .44 caliber revolver, and a prison cell with that number. Forty-four is also half of the eighty-eight keys on a piano.

"Goin' down to Fannie Mae's": Honeyboy refers to the Sonny Boy Williamson 2's song "Don't Start Me Talking" from 1955.

"Hambone and Gravy Blues": The title of this song is actually, "Ham Hound Crave," recorded in 1928 by Rube Lacy and now on Yazoo's *Mississippi Moaners, 1927–1942*.

"Hey, baby, don't you want a man like me?": This line is from Little Walter's appealing song, which was recorded by him in 1958 for the Checker label, called "Confessin' the Blues." It was originally by Walter Brown and Jay McShann, recorded in 1941 on Decca.

"Highway 49": Recorded by Big Joe Williams in 1935.

"Hound Dog": Big Mama Thorton recorded this song in 1952. It was later covered by Elvis Presley, who had a huge hit with it.

"Howling Wolf Blues": From 1930, this song can be heard on Yazoo's *Funny Papa Smith: The Original Howling Wolf.*

"I'd give a thousand dollars just to have a big name": A line from an unrecorded song by Son Brimmer.

"If I catch you in my house again": Honeyboy is referring to a line from a song by Hacksaw Harney. "Tear It Down Rag" is Honeyboy's version recorded in 1942 with Alan Lomax. It can be heard on *Delta Bluesman* from Earwig.

"Isle of Capri": This song was written by Jimmy Kennedy and Will Grosz and recorded by Duke Ellington, Frank Sinatra, and a thirties combo known as The Wingie Manon Combo.

"I've had my fun if I don't get well no more": This song by St. Louis Jimmy Oden was recorded as "Goin' Down Slow" in November 1941 on the Bluebird label. It was recorded by Little Walter, Lightnin' Hopkins, and Howlin' Wolf as well.

"Joe Turner Blues": The fabled Joe Turner has been described both as a lawman who transported prisoners to the penitentiary and as a local philanthropist who left gifts of food and wood for people who were suffering hard times. Considered by some to be one of the earliest blues songs, this traditional song has been recorded by Mississippi John Hurt, Muddy Waters, and Big Bill Broonzy.

"John Henry": John Henry was a heroic figure of story and song who pitted his strength against a steam drill. Versions of the traditional song were recorded by Leadbelly, Furry Lewis, Henry Thomas, Sonny Terry, Memphis Slim, and many others.

"Juke": Little Walter Jacobs's number one instrumental R & B hit from 1952 and the beginning of his solo career.

"Killin' floor": Honeyboy refers to Skip James's song, "Hard Times Killing Floor Blues," recorded in 1931.

"Kind-Hearted Woman Blues": This Robert Johnson song was recorded by him in November 1936.

"Lay me down a pallet on the floor": More commonly, "Make me a pallet on the floor," a line from a folk standard which found its way into recordings by Mississippi John Hurt, Henry Thomas, Buddy Bolden, and others.

"Lemon Squeezer": Old-time lemon squeezers looked like large wooden nutcrackers and bore a vague resemblance to a woman's hips and legs—yet another example of a creative sexual reference in the blues. There are many blues songs that make reference to lemon squeezers, including John Lee "Sonny Boy" Williamson's "Until My Love Come Down" and Charlie Pickett's "Let Me Squeeze Your Lemon."

"Milkcow Blues": A 1934 recording by Kokomo Arnold, later made famous by Elvis Presley.

"Miss Martha King": Recorded by B. B. King in Memphis in 1949.

"Nickel's a nickel": This line is from an unknown artist's song called "Giving It Away" from 1930. It is also a line that was used in various other songs including Bill Wilbur's 1935 "Greyhound Blues," King Solomon Hill's "Tell Me Baby" from 1932, and Buddy Boy Hawkin's "How Come Mama Blues" from 1929.

"Number 13 Highway": Honeyboy refers to the song "13 Highway," recorded by Walter Davis and Big Joe Williams in 1938.

"Out in the Cold Again": Written by Ted Koehler and Rube Bloom and recorded by Dinah Washington, Gene Ammons, Sam Cooke, and others.

"Par-a-lee": Or "Pearlee," a folk tune of unknown origin, popular with the generation of musicians previous to Honeyboy's.

"Pea Vine": This song was Charlie Patton's tribute to a railroad line of the same name running from Rosedale through Dockery's farm to Cleveland. This song was recorded in 1929. Big Joe Williams recorded a version of it in the forties.

"Pony Blues": Charlie Patton's first recording and his trademark song, made in 1929. Honeyboy recorded it for the Trix and Folkways labels in the seventies.

"Poor Boy, Long Way from Home": The origin of this song is unknown. It is possibly an English folk song revised by Appalachian musicians. Gus Cannon recorded a version in 1927. Other versions were recorded by Barbecue Bob, Big Joe Williams, and Howlin' Wolf.

"Pot Likker Train": Harp player El Watson's song "Pot Likker Blues" from 1927–1928 can be heard on Document's *The Great Harp Players, 1927–1936.*

"Red Cross Blues": There are versions of "Red Cross Blues" by Lucille Bogan, Leadbelly, Walter Davis, and Fred McDowell, but it was originally recorded by Alabama Sam (Walter Roland) in 1933.

"Rocks in My Pillow": This song was recorded originally in 1935 as "Bricks in My Pillow" by Amos Easton, better known as Bumble Bee Slim. A 1991 version by Honeyboy is on Earwig's *Delta Bluesman.*

"Rollin' and Tumblin'": First recorded by Tennessee singer Hambone Willie Newbern in 1929, this song became a blues standard.

"Rooster crow before day": Honeyboy refers to a line from Charlie Patton's 1929 recording "Banty Rooster Blues."

"Shine on, Harvest Moon": By Jack Norworth and Nora Bayes, this song has been recorded by Count Basie, Jimmy Dorsey, The Four Aces, The Ink Spots, Artie Shaw, and others.

"Sitting on Top of the World": A popular recording by The Mississippi Sheiks in 1930, this song was a hit again in 1957 for Howlin' Wolf.

"Sophisticated Lady": A Duke Ellington number first recorded in 1932.

"Spoonful": Honeyboy's song "Spoonful" is based on Charlie Patton's 1929 recording, "A Spoonful Blues," a traditional ragtime number. Honeyboy's recording from 1942 of "Just a Spoonful" can be heard on *Delta Bluesman* from Earwig.

"Spread My Raincoat Down": Honeyboy refers to his version of an old plantation song. His 1942 recording of this song for the Library of Congress is on *Delta Bluesman* from Earwig.

"Stack O'Dollars": A traditional piece recorded by Big Joe Williams in 1935 for the RCA Bluebird label.

"Stag-O-Lee": An old folk ballad also known as "Stackolee," "Stack-O-Lee," or "Stack O'Lee." Stacker Lee was a Confederate cavalryman and was son of the founder of the Lee Line of riverboats and had a steamboat named after him. He had a son Stack Lee with a black woman. According to legend, Stack Lee was a bad man and a killer. Long Cleve Reed and Papa Harvey Hull recorded the original "Stack O'Lee Blues" in 1927; Furry Lewis recorded a famous version, "Billy Lyons and Stack O'Lee," in the same year. Mississippi John Hurt, Champion Jack Dupree, and others followed with their renditions. Honeyboy's version, recorded in 1942, is available on Earwig's *Delta Bluesman*.

"St. Louis Blues": Made famous by W. C. Handy, the definitive version of this song was recorded by Bessie Smith in 1929.

"Stop and Listen": Recorded by The Mississippi Sheiks in 1930 and on Yazoo's *Jackson Blues 1928–1938*. Sam Chatmon recorded it again in 1960.

"The Sunnyland Blues": "Sunnyland Train" was written by Sunnyland Slim (Albert Luandrew) in 1928.

"Sweet Home Chicago": The often-heard Robert Johnson song recorded in 1936 and based on Kokomo Arnold's "Kokomo Blues." Honeyboy recorded it for Sun Records in 1952 with Albert Joiner (or Joyner) Williams on piano, Joe Willie Wilkins on guitar, James Walker on washboard, and Dickie Houston on drums. A Charly reissue of this recording mistakenly credited Albert Williams instead of Honeyboy. It can be heard on *Memphis Aggressive Guitars* volume 2 and on *Sun Records: The Blues Years 1950–1958*.

"Sweet Home Kokomo": Kokomo Arnold's 1934 recording "Old Original Kokomo Blues" which gave him his nickname.

"Terraplane Blues": Recorded in November 1936 by Robert Johnson. The Terraplane was an automobile produced by the Hudson Motor Company, and "Terraplane Blues" one of Robert Johnson's most popular songs.

"Tight Like That": A very popular number from a 1928 Vocalion recording session with Tampa Red and Georgia Tom.

"Tom Rushen": Charlie Patton's paeon to a deputy sheriff in the Delta town of Merigold, Mississippi, recorded in 1929.

"Water Coast Blues": "Water Coast Blues" borrows lyrics from a number of songs, including "West Coast Blues," Walter Davis's 1937 song. Alan Lomax mistakenly noted it as "Watercourse Blues" on the Library of Congress recordings. You can hear it on *Delta Bluesman* from Earwig.

"West Helena Blues": Honeyboy's version of Roosevelt Sykes's "West Helena Blues" can be heard on *White Windows* from Blue Suit.

"When I Lost My Baby": An Ivory Joe Hunter number, "I Almost Lost My Mind," recorded in 1949.

"Who May Your Regular Be": This is Honeyboy's number, recorded in 1951 with Thunder Smith, and can be heard on the anthology *Water Coast Blues* on the British label Krazy Kat.

"Worried Life Blues": A Sleepy John Estes number from 1935 ("Someday Baby"), which Honeyboy recorded for Alan Lomax in 1942. This version is on Earwig's *Delta Bluesman*. Another version with different lyrics by pianist Big Maceo Merriweather became very popular with electric blues bands in the fifties and sixties.

"The Yellow Bee Blues": In 1934, Charlie Patton's wife, Bertha, accompanied him to a recording session and sang "Yellow Bee," a version of Memphis Minnie's "Bumble Bee Blues." At this session they recorded four blues duets and eight religious duets.

"You may look good, but you don't mean a thing to me": This is a line from Howlin' Wolf's 1961 recording "Shake for Me," written by Willie Dixon.

Discography

The following is a complete list of recordings including labels and catalog reference numbers that feature Honeyboy Edwards as a solo artist or as part of an anthology. Some of these recordings may be out of print or difficult to find. They are listed here chronologically by the date of the recording sessions.

1942 Field Recordings, Library of Congress L59

Folk Music in America Vol. 10, *Songs of War and History*, Library of Congress LBC10 (various artists)

Walking Blues, Flyright 541 (various artists)

Water Coast Blues, Krazy Kat 7445 (various artists)

Juke Joint Blues, Blues Classics 23 (various artists)

Sun Records: The Blues Years 1950–1958, Sun Box 100, 105 (various artists)

Memphis Aggressive Guitars Vol. 2, Sun Record Company 341 (various artists)

Drop Down Mama, MCA-Chess 93002 (various artists)

Fleetwood Mac in Chicago, Sire/Warner Brothers/Blue Horizon 452832 (various artists)

I've Been Around, Trix 3319 (with Big Walter Horton and Eddie El)

Bottleneck Blues, Testament 5021 (various artists)

Blues, Blues, Blues, Roots 518

Old Friends, Earwig 4902 (with Sunnyland Slim, Big Walter Horton, Floyd Jones, and Kansas City Red)

Mississippi Delta Bluesman, Smithsonian Folkways 3539

Blues Anthology Vol. 3, *Real Chicago Blues*, Echo/Adelphi 803 (various artists)

Blues Anthology Vol. 4, *More from Chicago*, Echo/Adelphi 804 (various artists)

King Biscuit Blues, Blue Sun Records 2000 (various artists)

The Chicago Blues Sessions Vol. 8, From West Helena to Chicago, Wolf 120.854 (various artists)

The Best of Slide Guitar, Wolf 120.103 (various artists)

White Windows, Blue Suit/Evidence 26039-2

Evidence Blues Sampler: The Third, Evidence 26048-2 (various artists)

Delta Bluesman, Earwig 4922

Roots of Rhythm and Blues: A Tribute to the Robert Johnson Era, Columbia 48584 (various artists)

The Best of Mountain Stage Live: Vol. 4, Blue Plate Music 004 (various artists)

African Portraits, Teldec Classics 6019 (with the Chicago Symphony Orchestra)

Earwig Music Company Sixteenth Anniversary Sampler, Earwig 4933 (various artists)

The World Don't Owe Me Nothing, Earwig 4942 (in production)

Bibliography

The following books were used for background information in preparing for interviews with Honeyboy and in compiling the appendices.

Barlow, William. *Looking Up at Down: The Emergence of Blues Culture*. Temple University Press, 1989.

Berkow, Ira. *Maxwell Street*. Doubleday, 1977.

Calt, Stephen and Gayle Wardlow. *King of the Delta Blues: The Life and Music of Charlie Patton*. Rock Chapel Press, 1988.

Charters, Samuel. *The Bluesmakers*. Da Capo Press, 1991.

Charters, Samuel. *The Country Blues*. Da Capo Press, 1975.

Charters, Samuel. *The Legacy of the Blues: Art and Lives of Twelve Great Bluesmen*. Da Capo Press, 1977.

Chatan, W. D. *History of Bolivar County, Mississippi*. Hederman Brothers, 1948.

Cobb, James C. *The Most Southern Place on Earth: The Mississippi Delta and the Roots of Regional Identity*. Oxford University Press, 1992.

Cohn, David L. *Where I Was Born and Raised.* University of Notre Dame Press, 1967.

Courlander, Harold. *Negro Folk Music USA.* Columbia University Press, 1963.

Daniels, Pete. *Deep'n As It Come: The 1927 Mississippi River Flood.* The University of Arkansas Press, 1996.

Dixon, R. M. W. and J. Godrich. *Blues and Gospel Records, 1902–1943.* Storyville Publications, 1982.

Donovan, Frank. *River Boats of America.* Thomas Y. Crowell Publishers, 1966.

Duncan, Oliver and Beverly Duncan. *The Negro Population of Chicago: A Study of Residential Succession.* The University of Chicago Press, 1957.

Evans, David. *Big Road Blues.* Da Capo Press, 1982.

Feather, Leonard. *Encyclopedia of Jazz.* Da Capo Press, 1960.

Federal Writer's Project of the Works Progress Administration. *Mississippi: A Guide to the Magnolia State.* Hastings House, 1938.

Federal Writer's Project of the Works Progress Administration. *Tennessee: A Guide to the State.* Hastings House, 1939.

Ferris, William. *Blues from the Delta.* Da Capo Press, 1978.

Garon, Paul. *The Devil's Son-in-Law: The Story of Peetie Wheatstraw and His Songs.* Studio Vita Ltd., 1971.

Garon, Paul and Beth Garon. *Woman with Guitar: Memphis Minnie's Blues.* Da Capo Press, 1992.

Gerzhaft, Gerard. *Encyclopedia of the Blues.* The University of Arkansas Press, 1992.

Glennon, Lorraine, ed. *Our Times: The Illustrated History of the Twentieth Century.* Turner Publishing, 1995.

Guralnick, Peter. *Feel Like Going Home: Portraits in Blues and Rock and Roll.* Harper & Row, 1971.

Guralnick, Peter. *Last Train to Memphis: The Rise of Elvis Presley.* Little, Brown & Company, 1994.

Guralnick, Peter. *Lost Highway: Journeys and Arrivals of American Musicians*. Harper & Row, 1989.

Hall, B. C. and C. T. Wood. *Big Muddy: Down the Mississippi through America's Heartland*. Dutton, 1992.

Harris, Sheldon. *Blues Who's Who*. Da Capo Press, 1979.

Harrison, Max, Charles Fox, and Eric Thacker. *The Essential Jazz Records* vol. 1. *Ragtime to Swing*. Da Capo Press, 1988.

Hart, Mary L., Brenda Eagles, and Lisa N. Howorth. *The Blues: A Bibliographic Guide*. Garland Publishing Inc., 1989.

Hoh, LaVahn G. and William H. Rough. *Step Right Up: The Adventures of Circus in America*. Betterway Publications, 1990.

Hubbard, Freeman. *Encyclopedia of North American Railroading*. McGraw-Hill Publishers, 1981.

Johnson, Charles A. *The Frontier Camp Meeting: Religious Harvest Time*. Southern Methodist University Press, 1985.

Leadbitter, Mike. *Nothing but the Blues*. Hanover Books, 1971.

Leadbitter, Mike and Neil Slaven. *Blues Records 1943 to 1970: A Selective Discography*, vol. 1 and 2. Record Information Services, 1987.

Lomax, Alan. *The Land Where the Blues Began*. Pantheon Press, 1993.

Malone, Jacqui. *Steppin' on the Blues: The Visible Rhythms of African-American Dance*. The University of Illinois Press, 1996.

Manchester, William. *The Glory and the Dream: A Narrative History of America, 1932–1972*. Bantam Books, 1974.

Marcus, Greil. *Mystery Train: Images of America in Rock and Roll Music*. Plume Books, 1990.

McKee, Margaret and Fred Chisenhall. *Beale Black and Blue: Life and Music on Black America's Main Street*. Louisiana State University Press, 1993.

Oliver, Paul, ed. *The Blackwell Guide to Blues Records*. Basil Blackwell Ltd., 1989.

Oliver, Paul. *Blues Fell This Morning: Meaning in the Blues*. Cambridge University Press, 1990.

Oliver, Paul. *Blues Off the Record: Thirty Years of Blues Commentary*. Da Capo Press, 1984.

Oliver, Paul. *Screening the Blues: Aspects of the Blues Tradition*. Da Capo Press, 1968.

Oliver, Paul. *Songsters and Saints: Vocal Traditions on Race Records*. Cambridge University Press, 1984.

Oliver, Paul, Max Harrison, and William Bolcom. *The New Grove Gospel, Blues, and Jazz*. W. W. Norton & Company, 1980.

Olsson, Bengt. *Memphis Blues*. Studio Vista Ltd., 1970.

Oshinsky, David. *Worse than Slavery: Parchman Farm and the Ordeal of Jim Crow Justice*. The Free Press, 1996.

Palmer, Robert. *Deep Blues*. Penguin Books, 1981.

Percy, William Alexander. *Lanterns on the Levee: Recollections of a Planter's Son*. Louisiana State University Press, 1973.

Rowe, Mike. *Chicago Blues: The City and the Music*. Da Capo Press, 1988.

Sandberg, Larry and Dick Weissman. *The Folk Music Sourcebook*. Da Capo Press, 1989.

Santelli, Robert. *The Big Book of Blues: A Biographical Encyclopedia*. Penguin Books, 1993.

Scarne, John. *Encyclopedia of Games*. Harper & Row, 1973.

Scarne, John. *Scarne on Cards*. Crown, 1963.

Shaw, Arnold. *Honkers and Shouters: The Golden Years of Rhythm and Blues*. Collier Books, 1978.

Smith, Frank E. *The Yazoo River*. University Press of Mississippi, 1954.

Sobel, Mechal. *Trabelin' On: The Slave Journey to an Afro-Baptist Faith*. Princeton Paperbacks, 1977.

Titon, Jeff Todd. *Early Downhome Blues: A Musical and Cultural Analysis*. The University of Illinois Press, 1979.

Index